Nancy Beagley

THE HEALING PRESENCE

THE HEALING PRESENCE

How God's Grace Can Work in You
to Bring Healing
in Your Broken Places
and the Joy of Living in His Love

Leanne Payne

CROSSWAY BOOKS • WESTCHESTER, ILLINOIS
A DIVISION OF GOOD NEWS PUBLISHERS

To Lynne, Connie, Patsy, and Lucy

Table of Contents

And he [Moses] called the place Massah [testing] and Meribah [quarreling] because the Israelites quarreled and because they tested the Lord saying, "Is the Lord among us or not?"

(Exodus 17:7)

Man is not genuinely human without the Spirit of God. This is the testimony of the Scripture and tradition of God's people. This is the witness of those made competent to disclose the meaning of things because of their living union with God. This is the doctrine of the prophets, apostles, and saints. This is the gospel of the Lord Jesus Christ.

(Thomas Hopko, *The Spirit of God*, p.ii)

Acknowledgments

*T**he Healing Presence* is born out of many years of ministry to others through healing prayer. I have not the words to fully express my gratitude and love for those who, drawn to a like ministry, have stood with me in this. The discoveries we have made together—about our own souls and the souls of others, and about God's willingness to restore even the most wounded of us—is awesome.

A group that has to be one of the greatest blessings God could bestow upon one of His ministers is made up of four remarkable women: Lynne Berendsen, Connie Boerner, Patsy Casey, and Lucy Smith. We've been meeting regularly for prayer now for about ten years, and have been ministering together in the work of healing prayer for almost that length of time. To these women, all such gifted leaders in their own right, go my special thanks. They give the term *sisters in Christ* its full meaning. To them this book is dedicated.

God hears His praying women, and early on He quickly answered our prayer for strong men not only to stand with us in the ministry of prayer and healing, but to lend the masculine strength, giftedness, and direction that only they can give. Their strength, together with ours, has allowed us all, men and women alike, to fully and creatively collaborate with God to do the work at hand. To the women, then, God added Paul Berendsen, Ted Smith, Mario Bergner, Clay McLean, and Bob Boerner. All are Christian leaders involved in other ministries, but they have a vision for and are called to the work of this ministry. God has sovereignly set each one in place, and their input never ceases to bless and amaze me. These, then, make up what is known as the Pastoral Care Ministries team, and for these faithful ones I shall always be grateful.

Besides these, my thanks go to other Christian leaders who have in very special (and constant) ways come alongside us and lent their full support and giftedness to this ministry: Pastors Larry Evans, Jerry Soviar, and Jean Holt of Grace Community Church in Toledo, Ohio; John Fawcett of Wheaton, Illinois; and Fr. William Beasley and his wife, Anne, of the Episcopal Church of the Resurrection in West Chicago,

Illinois; David Blackledge in England; Dr. and Mrs. Daniel Trobisch in Austria and Germany; and Denis Ducatel and Arianne Du Chambrier of Switzerland, these latter giving invaluable help in the matter of translations of lectures and books into the French and the German languages.

Together with these are so many others through the years; I can't begin to list them all: Professor Carol Kraft who has always (it seems), like the Rock of Gibraltar, been there in prayer and in a myriad of ways; Ivy Belle Upton who saw a great need and rushed in to meet it in a phenomenal way, one that enabled me to recuperate after a period of great physical exhaustion; John and Mary Stocking who have helped in ways no one else ever could. . . . To all these dear ones, I simply say again, Thanks.

All of us are profoundly aware that to God alone goes all the credit. I think most every one of us feels, from personal experience, that if God could seek out and heal even me, He could find and save anyone. For me, Johann Sebastian Bach said it best, as he placed a *J.J.* at the top of every musical composition and an *S.D.G.* at the bottom. Those Latin initials stood for, "Jesus, help me" at the beginning of the work, and "*Soli Deo Gloria*" ("To God alone be the glory") at its finish. To God alone be all the glory, for He alone is the Healer of mankind. He alone prepares and then gifts us with such delightful comrades for the Journey into Him and eternal life.

Finally, I want to thank Dr. Thomas Howard for permission to quote from an unforgettable lecture he gave years ago at Wheaton College, and Martha Kilby for her more than gracious permission to quote from her late husband's unpublished work. At age eighty-seven she is still leaping for joy at the hearing of truth, and in this she is exactly like her husband, Clyde Kilby, who until his death at age eighty-four, did the same.

Preface

One thing have I asked of the Lord, that will I seek after, inquire for
and (insistently) require, that I may dwell in the house of the Lord (in
His presence) all the days of my life, to behold and gaze upon the
beauty (the sweet attractiveness and the delightful loveliness) of the
Lord, and to meditate, consider and inquire in His temple.

(Psalm 27:4, *Amplified*)

Let us fix our eyes on Jesus. . . .

(Hebrews 12:2)

When I began this book, now six or seven years ago (other writings crowded in, demanding to be attended first), I had what seems in retrospect an unusual "seeing" or vision. I had been praying about how to begin such a book, one about the Lord's Presence with us, and was keenly feeling the weight of the task and my own inadequacy. At the time I lived in a little third-floor attic, one with few windows and therefore not much light, especially in the long, dark winters. There was one window, however, that made the little eyrie livable both summer and winter. Its mullioned face peered through the graceful, widespread boughs of a magnificent mountain ash, and directly onto the beautiful shoreline and ever-changing surface of Lake Michigan. There in front of that window, as the sunshine bounced off the blue-green waters and tumbled into my little attic space through the topmost branches of that red-berried, green-leaved tree, I did my most earnest work of praying, studying, and writing.

God loves all His creatures: myself, the lake, the tree, the sun. On this day, as I prayed, His other "creatures" seemed almost to dance before Him. Sparkling and seeming to rejoice in their own creation, they poured themselves in through my window in their fullest array of light and warmth and color to bless me too. It was then that I had the vision, one not easily explainable.

The vision was of a painting, yet not a painting, for Christ's living face glowed through it. While it was the Divine Face, yet it was aglow with and framed by the richest of earth's sun-baked hues. It was a vision of Incarnation, the Uncreated shining through the created. Deeply quieted, I experienced a heightened sense of well-being and of His Presence filling and completing all things: surely a small foretaste of the fullness of being all creation will one day experience. In the gentle joy of that moment, I began this book with these words:

> I see a smiling face, many times larger than life, and it glows in sun-drenched, earthly colors. Strongly through earth's rosy hues streams the Uncreated Light, and I, a creature, bask in the face of Jesus, the God-Man who died and rose again. The "Word of God our flesh that fashioned" ("Jesu Joy of Man's Desiring") smiles through the incarnate Son of Man, still dusty with earth's radiance, and the two are one. And He is behind me, overlooking my work; in front of me, blessing me as I look up to Him. He is all around me; He is even within me.

Now as I return to the book, I find that this vision, yet vivid in my memory, still best expresses what this book is all about. How is it that God (the eternal) shines through us (the finite)? The Uncreated through His creatures? How do we minister in His name and power? How do we move in the healing gifts of the Spirit? How is it that we *become persons*, that we find our true selves and are completed in Him? The answer has always to do with His sovereign Presence over us, with us, within us: Incarnational Reality. That is what this book is about.

In Him we become fully human. In Him we begin to do His works. This involves *incarnation*, a descent of the Spirit into our deepest being and lives. In Him, the will, intellect, imagination, feeling, and sensory being are hallowed and enlivened. We begin to fully live, to participate in the eternal, the immutable, the indestructible.

We live in a day, however, when few—even among those who call themselves Christian—believe in Christ's Real Presence with us. Pope John Paul II made the sobering statement that for modern man, the sense of God is vanishing from the earth.

I am personally grateful that the circumstances of my early adult life, though extremely painful at the time, brought me to the place of seeking the face of the Lord with all my heart. In the midst of great personal need, I found the Healing Presence of Christ. I found all the treasure Christ's gospel promises to the poor, the brokenhearted, those bound by their own and others' sinfulness and pride. The ship in which I moved through life had foundered on the jagged, sharp shoals of divorce, and I was left with no doubt whatsoever of my need for a Savior, One who would *remain with me*, uniting His eternal life and *fullness of being* to my creaturely finiteness, immaturity, and incompleteness. "Never will I leave you; never will I forsake you" (Hebrews 13:4) and other Scriptural promises were never far from my lips. So their truth and vitality sank as pure light into all the darkened and lonely spaces of my soul.

Also, though by nature optimistic, I knew beyond all shadow of doubt that my Savior must be my guide. I no longer cherished naive illusions about the benignancy of the world, or about my own natural capacity to make my way through it. Mary's great affirmation became mine: "Be it unto me according to thy word." I sought His will, not my own, and found my way in such Scriptures as these:

> Whether you turn to the right or to the left, your ears will hear a voice behind you, saying, "This is the way: walk in it." (Isaiah 30:21)

> . . . guide me in your truth and teach me, for you are God my Savior, and my hope is in you all day long. (Psalm 25:5)

> "But when he, the Spirit of truth, comes, he will guide you into all truth. He will not speak on his own; he will speak only what he hears, and he will tell you what is yet to come." (John 16:13)

I was learning to see the invisible with the eyes of my heart, to hear the inaudible with the ears of my heart. In other words, I had come to rely on God's Healing Presence with His people. The pain of having arrived at the utter end of any confidence in myself had brought me into the haven of God's love and care. There, in His Presence, as one would spread an extremely valuable but shattered vase before a master craftsman, I could dare to lay out the broken pieces of my mind and heart. There, in fullest confidence in His healing love, my eyes fixed on Him in obedience, I watched as He not only mended my broken heart, but united it with His.

This is what the healing ministry is all about. To preach the Good News *in the power of the Spirit* is, at the same time, to heal. It is to bring lost and foundering souls into wholeness in Christ. It is to see the wrecked and splintered pieces of their foundered ship not only repaired, but made for the first time truly seaworthy, with Another at the helm.

He it is who come and heals. It is He who befriends the sinner, releases the captive, and heals the lame in mind and body. It is His

Presence I want to point to in this book on healing. From the vantage point of His Presence, I lay the theological foundations for ministering in the healing gifts of the Spirit. In this we imitate Christ, who turned His face to the Father and resolutely did only what He saw the Father doing:

> 'In truth, in very truth I tell you, the Son can do nothing by himself; he does only what he sees the Father doing: what the Father does, the Son does. For the Father loves the Son and shows him all his works.' (John 5:19, 20, NEB)

Jesus' words were directed to the religious leaders of His day who were angry over His having healed on the Sabbath day a man crippled for thirty-eight years. Jesus amazed them with the truth that the Father's love is always streaming forth: "'My Father has never yet ceased his work, and I am working too'" (John 5:17, NEB).

We learn to practice the Presence of Jesus within (our bodies are temples of His Holy Spirit), without (He walks alongside us as Companion and Brother), and all around (He is high and lifted up, and we exalt Him as Sovereign God). And we ask Him to love the world through us. We learn to collaborate with Him. We do what we see Him doing. We begin to move in the "spirituals," the gifts of the Holy Spirit, which work through us because He is really with us. Our believing on Him is no longer purely intellectual, but is taken into every facet of our lives. Jesus was once asked what we must do "'if we are to work as God would have us work,'" and He replied to His disciples of that day: "'This is the work that God requires: to believe in the one whom he has sent'" (John 6:28, 29, NEB).

This one work is ours, and no longer relying on our own cleverness at presenting the gospel, we simply trust in His Presence with us.

PART I

THE POWER OF THE PRESENCE

CHAPTER 1

Celebrating Our Smallness

"We do not know what to do, but our eyes are upon you."

(2 Chronicles 20:12b)

Your inadequacy is your first qualification.

(John Gaynor Banks, *The Master and the Disciple*)

I well remember one radiant April morning, the sunlight streaming down upon the work cluttering my desk, when a young man burst through my office door. Shy, but driven by his need, he quickly introduced himself as Charles and cried out, "Can you help me?" Just as quickly I nodded assent, for I could see in his eyes that bands of fear and depression were gripping his mind in a deadly embrace.

This was not the time for a rational analysis of what had brought him to this point. After a few preliminary words, I got him comfortably kneeling, so I could pray for him with the laying on of hands. First I applied holy water to his forehead and began the prayer by invoking the Presence of the Lord. In Christ's name, I then broke and put to flight the demonic force that had been banding, ever more tightly, this young man's mind. Next, anointing his forehead with the healing oil (making the sign of the Cross as the symbol of present and future protection of his mind), I prayed for God's healing light and love to enter in and fill his mind and heart, to dispel all fear and torment, and to grant peace and quiet. Going on to gently press his temples, I sensed this cleansing and healing taking place, and continued thus to pray until I could give thanks to God that it was done.

Charles, a psychology major in college, later wrote a paper describing what his mental condition had been:

Sheets of blackness and fear gnawed at my dying mind. Pressure like fingertips tormented my eyes and brain. Sweat poured profusely from my veins as my body struggled to move in a thousand conflicting directions. My stomach burned as my lungs and heart pumped uncontrollably. Every day the hell I lived in grew blacker than the day before. Fear that I'd never come out of this condition haunted my thoughts moment by moment. The words "some things are worse than death" made me wish I'd never seen the earth or the so-called life I'd come to know. Time struggled with my mind, and seconds passed like hours—hours that I cursed. As I crawled through life my one concern was to find the way out of the worst hell I ever imagined.

Charles then described our time of prayer, and its immediate effects upon him. "That night," he said, "I watched the blackness roll out of my mind. I slept for the first time in months, quietly and in peace."

This was the beginning step in his recovery, for there were circumstances and patterns in his life that had to change in order for him to mature psychologically and spiritually. There was, in other words, *the true tale of his existence* (inner and outer), and it must now be unrolled and spread out before the Lord. In Christ's light, the dark seeds and bitter roots underlying his passivity, self-hatred, fear, and guilt would be revealed and yielded up to God. Until this was done, Charles would be subject to a return of the darkness, for he must understand, renounce, and be healed of that which was an opening for the oppression. But the healing was begun in this first prayer session, and it is very safe to say that had he not received the ministry offered in Christ's name, he would soon have been hospitalized, perhaps never to return to an active life and wholeness. He is today a minister of the gospel.

The prayer with Charles happened many years ago when I was first beginning to pray for people with serious problems, and if I had looked into myself to find an adequacy to meet his need, I would never have prayed for him. I have begun with the story of this healing rather than a recent one in order to stress the fact that after many years in the ministry, I still do the same simple thing: invoke the Presence of Jesus and trust in Him. I am still as inadequate in the face of any one of the needs I see today as I was in the face of Charles's need so long ago. I now have more experience and more knowledge of the faithfulness of God. But I could celebrate my inadequacy, my smallness then, and I can now. To stop celebrating it would gravely threaten the ministry of prayer for healing. "When I am weak (in human strength), then am I (truly) strong—able, powerful in divine strength" (2 Corinthians 12:10b, *Amplified*).

There is a perfectly wonderful incident in *Perelandra*, C.S. Lewis's book about an unfallen planet, that illustrates the point I am here making. In this mythic novel, God saves a world from falling through an ordinary, very human Christian named Ransom. It is a book about Incarnational Reality, God in and with us, flesh and bone though we be. Near the end of the story, the Adam and Eve of that world, who did not fall as our first parents did, ascend their rightful thrones in great glory and splendor. Ransom, gazing in awe upon them and realizing the part he had played in helping the royal pair overcome the Tempter, is overwhelmed and begins to fall to the ground. At this point he hears the angel, Malacandra, speak to him and say:

> Be comforted. . . . It is no doing of yours. . . . Be comforted, small one, in your smallness. He [God] lays no merit on you. Receive and be glad. Have no fear, lest your shoulders be bearing this world. Look! it is beneath your head and carries you.[1]

To celebrate our smallness does not mean we do not prepare ourselves by learning all we can about the spirits, souls, and bodies of men and women, and the laws of health and wholeness concerning them. The more true knowledge we have of the intense internal conflicts (whether spiritual, psychological, or physical in nature) going on within or around the human person, and the provision made by God for resolving these conflicts, the better counselors and pray-ers we can be. Our prayers can be more specific, our counsel better able to open the eyes of the person to the true nature of his difficulty. But we can never substitute our learning and counseling "skills" for the simplicity of opening the eyes and ears of our hearts to God. There, in that stance of *listening prayer*, we discover His mind on the matter, and we can then pray the prayer of faith that begins to free the person from his infirmity and bondage. No matter how qualified the Christian minister, physician, psychologist, or counselor, he is still one who is inadequate, apart from God, in the face of his own and others' needs. And this is where faith in the Unseen Real comes in.

> Scripture says, 'Everyone who has faith in him will be saved from shame'—everyone: there is no distinction between Jew and Greek, because the same Lord is Lord of all, and is rich enough for the need of all who *invoke* him. For everyone, as it says again—'everyone who *invokes* the name of the Lord will be saved.' (Romans 10:11-13, NEB)

Truly, there is Another who is with us, and He does the work—if we are careful to do (and keep on doing) the one work the Father has given us to do: that of believing "in the one whom he has sent." We can go right on celebrating our smallness while leaning joyfully and heavily on the Son's greatness and love. We learn to practice His Presence. We trust Him to be, always, our adequacy.

CHAPTER 2

Practicing the Presence

"And surely I will be with you always, to the very end of the age."

(Jesus, in Matthew 28:20)

S ome folk, thinking they are being honest, suffer from the notion that to practice the Presence is an exercise not in faith, but in mere credulity. But to acknowledge the Presence of *the God who is really there* is actually a form of prayer, a way of praying always as the Scriptures exhort us to do. When we do this, the eyes and ears of our hearts are opened to receive the word He is always speaking. We enter into a path of obedience perhaps unknown to us before where we joyfully acknowledge, "Jesus is Lord."

But the acknowledgement that God is always with us—even when in our sensory being we are least aware of it—is not always easy. It requires discipline.

Acknowledging the Unseen

To acknowledge the Unseen Real requires a concerted effort of the will at first. We might think of it as actually *practicing the Presence*. It is all too easy for us moderns to regard the supernatural world (e.g., the Holy Spirit, angels, demons) and activities (e.g., spiritual warfare) as somehow less real than the world we behold with our senses. As twentieth-century Christians, we live in a materialistic age, one in which our systems of learning have long based their conclusions on scientific truth alone. The presuppositions of such systems have misled many generations of students, blinding them to the truths of God and the Unseen Real, whether moral or spiritual. Because of these intellectual blocks, we moderns have more difficulty with invisible realities and perhaps a much greater need for the discipline of *practicing* the Presence than did our forefathers in the faith. In the very beginning of the Christian

Era, however, St. Paul spoke of the practice by saying: "We fix our eyes not on what is seen, but on what is unseen. For what is seen is temporary, but what is unseen is eternal" (2 Corinthians 4:18). The practice of the Presence, then, is simply the discipline of calling to mind the truth that God is with us. When we consistently do this, the miracle of seeing by faith is given. We begin to see with the eyes of our hearts.

The Presence of God in Contrast to a Sense of the Presence

[T]he presence of God is not the same as the *sense* of the presence of God. The latter may be due to imagination; the former may be attended with no "sensible consolation." The act which engenders a child ought to be, and usually is, attended by pleasure. But it is not the pleasure that produces the child. Where there is pleasure there may be sterility: where there is no pleasure the act may be fertile. And in the spiritual marriage of God and the soul it is the same. It is the actual presence, not the *sensation* of the presence, of the Holy Ghost which begets Christ in us. The *sense* of the presence is a super-added gift for which we give thanks when it comes.[1]

This simple lesson, expressed here by C.S. Lewis, must be learned by all the saints of the Church, small and great.

Often the persons with the most dramatic conversions or healings will be the very souls who have the most difficult time figuring out that the Presence of God differs from *sensations* they had in their experience of Him. Such persons, caught in the subjective trap of attempting to "realize" God in sensory experience, will find themselves looking inward. This introspection, if persisted in, turns into what may be called "the practice of the presence of self," or "the disease of introspection." I was just such a person in my youth, and through frustration born of this misunderstanding I finally left off trying to be a Christian. It was later, after hard circumstances, that I received the grace to pray, "Lord, if I never again know [meaning *sense*] Your Presence, I will yet obey You." These were the words the Lord was waiting to hear. This understanding of the "practice of the Presence" will always be an integral part of any writing or ministering I do.

My failure to understand this cost me the precious years between adolescence and age twenty-six, years when I could not hear and obey God.

Abiding in Christ: Andrew Murray and Oswald Chambers

Some of the great devotional writers such as Andrew Murray and Oswald Chambers refer to the practice of the Presence as *abiding* in Christ. This term is taken from Christ's own invitation and promise to us:

"Abide in me, and I will abide in you." Referring to this Scripture, Oswald Chambers writes:

> In the initial stages it is a continual effort until it becomes so much the law of life that you abide in Him unconsciously.[2]
>
> Notion your mind with the idea that God is there. If once the mind is notioned along that line, then when you are in difficulties, it is as easy as breathing to remember—Why, my Father knows all about it! It is not an effort, it comes naturally when perplexities press.[3]

Frank C. Laubach

I first understood the simplicity and greatness of the practice of the Presence through the life and writings of Frank C. Laubach, a man through whom God blessed so many. (Among his many accomplishments was teaching illiterate people throughout the world to read.) He writes movingly of his beginning discipline, one that began in early 1930:

> Perhaps a man who has been an ordained minister since 1914 ought to be ashamed to confess that he never before felt the joy of complete hourly, minute by minute—now what shall I call it?—more than surrender. I had that before. More than listening to God. I tried that before. I cannot find the word that will mean to you or to me what I am now experiencing. It is a *will* act. I compel my mind to open straight out toward God. I wait and listen with determined sensitiveness. I fix my attention there, and sometimes it requires a long time early in the morning. I determine not to get out of bed until that mind set upon the Lord is settled. After a while, perhaps, it will become a habit, and the sense of effort will grow less. . . .
>
> As for me, I never lived, I was half dead . . . until I reached the place where I wholly, with utter honesty, resolved and then re-resolved that I would find God's will and I would do that will though every fibre in me said no, and I would win the battle *in my thoughts*. It was as though some deep artesian well had been struck in my soul of souls and strength came forth. I do not claim success even for a day yet, not complete success all day, but some days are close to success, and every day is tingling with the joy of a glorious discovery.[4]

By September of 1931, he wrote:

> It is very simple, so simple that any child could practice it. This simple practice requires only a gentle pressure of the will, not

more than a person can exert easily. It grows easier as the habit becomes fixed. Yet it transforms life into heaven.[5]

Mother Theresa of Calcutta

It is thrilling, as well as fascinating, to see the "practice of the Presence" in Mother Theresa's life. Having taken the following words of Christ's parable to heart, she ministers to the poorest of the poor as if she were ministering to Christ:

> "I tell you the truth, whatever you did for one of the least of these brothers of mine, you did for me." (Matthew 25:40)

In answer to a question from Malcolm Muggeridge (*Something Beautiful for God*), Mother Theresa draws a contrast between her vocation and that of a social worker. When ministering to the needy, she and her nuns "do it *to a Person*." Her love and devotion to Christ, her ministry to her present but unseen Lord as she labors among the poor of India, is a witness to the entire world. She, in this way, in the body of one humble little lover of Christ, has done what social organizations and nations could not do.

"We do it to a Person."

C. S. Lewis

> What is concrete but immaterial can be kept in view only by painful effort.[6]

Few, in my opinion, write more compellingly about the Presence of God than does C. S. Lewis. But the practice of the Presence of the Unseen Real was not easy for him. He suffered in himself all the intellectual blocks of the highly developed philosophical mind, one that was thoroughly steeped in several centuries of intellectual skepticism and unbelief. Even more than that, he knew the old sin nature in each one of us, that which would disregard the Real Presence and deeply desire to remain separate from it. He knew, therefore, that to fix one's mind on God was not only to torment the old sin nature, but to kill it—a thing that God requires and fallen man resists. "Christ says, 'Give me all. I don't want so much of your time and so much of your money and so much of your work: I want you.'"[7]

> That is why the real problem of the Christian life comes where people do not usually look for it. It comes the very moment you wake up each morning. All your wishes and hopes for the day rush at you like wild animals. And the first job each morning

consists in shoving them all back; in listening to that other voice, taking that other point of view, letting that other larger, stronger, quieter life come flowing in. And so on, all day. . . .

We can do it only for moments at first. But from those moments the new sort of life will be spreading through our systems because now we are letting Him work at the right part of us.[8]

Because Lewis dared to put this practice into his own life, he perhaps speaks more effectively and powerfully than any other soul to the dilemma of modern man—that of the schism between head and heart, spirit and matter, the intellect and the imagination. In doing this, he has become one of the truly great defenders of Scriptural orthodoxy, for he has enabled us to once again be "at home" with *miracle*, the native air of the Scriptures and of the Spirit-enabled life. Thus the souls of many, having the full dimensions of truth and Scriptural reality restored to them, as well as the language with which to speak of it, are healed through reading his works.

Brother Lawrence

For Brother Lawrence, the practice of the Presence was an easier matter. "I always considered that His presence was with me, even *in* me!"[9] But he too spoke of the discipline of the will and taught others the same:

> In order to first form the habit of conversing with God continually and of referring all that we do to Him, we must first apply ourselves to Him with diligence. After a little such care, we shall find His love inwardly excites us to His presence without any difficulty.[10]

Because he dared to love Christ in this way, this humble little footman turned monk left a few letters and an example in his own life that has influenced the Christian world since the seventeenth century. *The Practice of the Presence of God* by Brother Lawrence was first printed in French in 1692.

> I decided, instead of continuing as a footman, to be received into a monastery. I thought that perhaps there I would be made, in some way, to suffer for my awkwardness and for all my faults I had committed. I decided to sacrifice my life with all its pleasures to God. But He greatly disappointed me in this idea, for I have met with nothing but satisfaction in giving my life over to Him.[11]

Brother Lawrence, writing to a friend who is in great pain and suffering, tells her what it means to see "the sovereign Physician, who is the healer of both body and soul," with the eyes of the heart:

In a little time, I will go to God. What comforts me in this life is that I now see my Lord by faith. In seeing Him by faith I actually see so well I sometimes say, "I believe no more! I see!"

I can *feel* that which faith teaches; I can sense what faith sees. This, of course, works great assurance in me. . . . So continue always with God. To be with Him is really your only support and your only comfort during affliction.[12]

In another letter to her, he writes again of the senses and faith:

God seems to have endless ways of drawing us to Himself. Perhaps his most unusual way is to hide Himself from you. What can we do when we can no longer find the Lord? The key is found in the word *faith*. Faith is the one thing, perhaps the only thing, which will not fail you in such a time. Let faith be your support. The very foundation of your confidence must be your faith. . . .

I would willingly ask God for a part of your suffering, yet I know that I am so weak that if the Lord left me one moment to myself I would be the most wretched man alive. But, I cannot even consider that He could ever leave me alone. You see, faith gives me just as strong a conviction as the *senses* ever could that He never forsakes us.

Yes, I sense His presence continually, but if I should lose that sense, my faith that He is with me would be as strong as the sense had been.

Have but one fear: fear to leave Him. Be always with Him. Let us live in His Presence. Let us die in His presence.[13]

Others See God in Us

I was invited to hold a mission in a large church, one that was influential on account of its wealthy political- and civic-minded parishioners. The church's rector had invited me, and I quickly saw that he was one who had suffered a great deal for his faith and for his faithful promulgation of it among the liberal and unbelieving. He had invited me in hopes that there could be renewal in his parish, even though he was finally leaving it to go to another parish where faith accompanied the Scriptures and Sacraments. He hoped that another minister could do for this congregation what he felt he had failed to do. As we began our meetings on a Sunday morning, with the sunlight dancing in great streams through exquisitely colored cut-glass windows, he celebrated the Eucharist before a crowded church congregation. During the prayer over the elements, I looked up to where he was officiating, and I saw not only him but Christ Himself filling him. My spiritual eyes were opened as in a vision, and I saw his "Spiritual Man," his spirit in union with Christ, as a little larger than his natural, physical body.

Christ Himself was gloriously present in and with this man, and was ministering to us. This of course I know apart from any special "seeing," but for some reason I was allowed to—for the briefest moment—see Him in this dear brother. I saw *Incarnational Reality,* a thing I would shortly be teaching these same folk about, in hopes that the eyes of their hearts and minds would be more fully opened to believe.

I am convinced that when we begin to faithfully acknowledge God's Presence with us, we find that others around us begin to "see" Him as well. Throughout the years of my ministry, I've emphasized *Incarnational Reality,* the acknowledgment of God's Presence with and within us, and perhaps because of this I see such things happen more often than usual. The word preached is confirmed with this particular sign following. One thing I know for sure: there is nothing needy souls need more than *enablement to believe the Scriptural revelation that God is indeed with them and loves them.* And, as in the Scriptures, He sometimes shows Himself in unusual ways.

A while after my experience of seeing our Lord so vividly in the life of one of His faithful servants, I was ministering in a place that had a very great need for understanding how to bring souls into the Presence of God for healing. This huge church was located in the midst of a teeming population immersed in the worst excesses of secularism and pleasure-seeking, and received on its hot-line ten thousand calls per month. In this church hundreds of lay ministers led by a few ordained clergy were attempting to meet such overwhelming needs.

In ministry to the ministers in this place, as well as to the multitude of needy ones they brought into the meetings, I became totally exhausted. My weariness was such that I could not concentrate; I could not prepare a coherent lecture, or plan a healing service to follow it. Sitting in that great auditorium, therefore, and waiting for my last time to speak and minister, I could only "practice the Presence." I prayed, "Jesus, I'm so tired I'm not sure I could tell anyone my full name today, and I do not know how I'm going to speak and minister one more time. But I love You, Lord, and I have come to do Your bidding. I have no strength left. Please love these people through me, Lord; You will have to do it all today." As I was called up to speak, I consciously and deliberately reached out my hand and took His as we, my invisible Lord and I, walked up to the podium. No sooner had I situated myself and my Bible at the podium and begun to speak than people all over that great auditorium began to weep. It had nothing to do with what I was saying, this I well knew. So I simply thanked Him for blessing His people, prayed a general healing prayer over them, and then closed the meeting. No sooner had I stopped speaking than people rushed up, saying, "Do you know that the whole time you were speaking Christ was standing next to you? He was like a cylinder of Light, standing beside you."

Christ stood with me and ministered to the people that day, just as He always does when His messengers go in His name and at His bidding. But in my extreme weakness, He showed Himself strong. He revealed Himself to the people in a very special way.

On Being Present to God
Henri Nouwen writes:

> Over the years we have developed the idea that being present to people in all their needs is our greatest and primary vocation. The Bible does not seem to support this. Jesus' primary concern was to be obedient to his Father, to live constantly in his presence. Only then did it become clear to him what his task was in his relationships with people.[14]

Saints of all ages have made it their business to be present to God, and out of this has sprung their truest vocation. They become, therefore, the ones who blaze spiritual trails for others. Every generation of Christians must courageously face dark wildernesses, peculiar to the time in which they live. These "perilous woods" through which a path must be hewn are made up of the choking undergrowth and dark flowering of the sins and blindnesses of generations past, and they always stand as formidable roadblocks to the next generation of Christians. The saints who make it their full intention, therefore, to practice the Presence (however they term this) become the courageous pathfinders, whether for the many or the few. And in the doing of this, no matter how much they suffer, they are to be accounted doubly blessed, for they have discovered what they were born to do.

CHAPTER 3

Spiritual Power and Authority

Great is the Lord and mighty in power.

(Psalm 147:5)

. . . how tremendous is the power available to us who believe in God. The power is the same divine energy *which was demonstrated in Christ when he raised him from the dead.*

(Ephesians 1:19, 20, *Phillips,* emphasis mine)

*T*he power to heal and to be healed is available because God Himself is in our midst. His Presence and His power are mysteriously one, and we who live and move and have our being in God are called to preach, teach, and heal in that spiritual power and authority. Oswald Chambers expresses it this way: "'Ye shall receive the power of the Holy Ghost'—not power as a gift from the Holy Ghost; the power *is* the Holy Ghost, not something which He imparts."[1]

We become ministers of God's healing love and power, therefore, as we learn to invoke the mighty Presence of our Lord, and as we learn to become the vessels through which He ministers in our midst. He can then begin to love the world through us, for we have made ourselves available to Him. His "divine energy," moving through us who believe (most often when we are the least aware of it), brings life where before unbelief and death have been at work. "To this end I labor," said St. Paul, "struggling with all his energy, which so powerfully works in me" (Colossians 1:29). To know the spiritual power that St. Paul speaks of is to know the Presence of God among and within us, bringing us into relationship with Himself and that which is *other* than the self-in-isolation.

Jesus Is Our Model

Jesus, "full of the Holy Spirit," collaborating with "the power of the Lord," is always our model: "And the power of the Lord was present for him to heal the sick" (Luke 5:17b). "Jesus, full of the Holy Spirit, returned from the Jordan and was led by the Spirit . . ." (Luke 4:1). Luke, the beloved physician, wrote about Jesus "giving instructions through the Holy Spirit to the apostles he had chosen" (Acts 1:2). We preach, teach, and heal the way Jesus did, the way He taught us to.

> Jesus went through all the towns and villages, teaching in their synagogues, preaching the good news of the kingdom and healing every disease and sickness. When he saw the crowds, he had compassion on them, because they were harassed and helpless, like sheep without a shepherd. Then he said to his disciples, "The harvest is plentiful but the workers are few. Ask the Lord of the harvest, therefore, to send out workers into his harvest field." He called his twelve disciples to him and gave them authority to drive out evil spirits and to cure every kind of disease and sickness. (Matthew (9:35—10:1)

The gifts of healings, part of God's "energy" entrusted to God's people, are a ministry of the Spirit's Presence in our midst, and are never, as someone has aptly said, the precocious effort of some individual. When Jesus died in our place on the Cross, He not only freed us from the dark spiritual powers in our fallen world, but made it possible for us to take our place in Him, our risen Lord, and to become channels of His power and authority.

Healing Has to Do with Mended Relationships

Christ empowered and commanded His followers to heal because He knew that all men, in their exterior relationships and within themselves, are broken and separated. In order to gain wholeness and the opportunity to mature as *persons,* we must acknowledge and deeply repent of the *separations* in our lives. The primary separation is between the self and God, out of which issue the separations between the self and other selves, the self and nature, and the self and one's "deep heart." The healing of this latter separation brings into harmony the intellect and the heart—that is, the cognitive and intuitive capacities and ways of knowing, and these "two minds" are thereby enabled to balance and complete each other. The will, the emotions, the intuitive and imaginative faculties are cleansed and receive the very life of God. With this healing, the self is freed to come into the Presence of the Unseen Real—the Presence of God Himself—where we "become partakers of the divine nature" (2

Peter 1:4). It is in this way that we become persons. True personality is rooted in relationship: first of all in God, the Uncreated, then with everything He has created.

Although not all our relationships with other people can be healed in this life, we can forgive and release everyone who is unable to love or accept us, or unable to relate to us in a manner pleasing to God. We can, by the grace of God, forgive those who have so deeply wounded us. As we forgive them, we find that not only do our own wounds begin to heal, but our experience becomes the source of healing knowledge and power for others.

The key to forgiving even the "unforgivable" and to the healing of relationships comes through being filled with God's Spirit. We receive this fullness as we seek to dwell in His Presence. This means choosing union and communion with God rather than one's own separateness, which is in effect the "practice of the presence" of the old Adamic fallen self. To be filled with the Spirit is to choose the heaven of the integrated and emancipated self rather than the hell of the disintegrated self in separation. It is to choose the same love that has bound together the Father and the Son throughout all eternity. It is to enter the Great Dance of healthy relationships with the self, others, God, and His creation. (For a splendid imaginative treatment of the Great Dance, see C. S. Lewis's *Perelandra*, the entire book, but especially Chapter 17. It is the dance of all creation as it participates in Incarnational Reality. It is Christian orthodoxy.)

Once we have entered the Great Dance of mended, wholesome relationships, we are authorized to bring others into it, saying: "The Kingdom (the Presence of God to save—i.e., regenerate and make you whole) is come nigh unto you."

"As you go, preach this message: 'The kingdom of heaven is near.' Heal the sick, raise the dead, cleanse those who have leprosy, drive out demons. Freely you have received, freely give." (Matthew 10:7)

Joyful are the Christians who faithfully proclaim the Word of the Kingdom and move in its power to free and heal. But such a ministry is never, to my knowledge, without personal suffering. Those I've known who are effective in the healing ministry—that is, in helping others heal their relationships—incur the severest wrath of the Evil One. They may find every close personal relationship under an utterly demonic and irrational attack. This, of course, is because Christians who come into spiritual and psychological wholeness are thereby freed to go out and take the world for Christ. "Do not be bewildered," the Apostle Peter enjoins us, "by the fiery trial that is upon you," but know that "It gives you a share in Christ's sufferings, and that is cause for joy" (1 Peter 4:12, 13, NEB). Christ taught His disciples and the listening crowds (Matthew 5) that those persons were *blessed* and therefore should rejoice and be glad when they suffered persecution for doing right.

When undergoing authentic Christian suffering (see Chapter 13 of this book), it helps to take Christ's admonition as a command to be obeyed—to rejoice in spite of dismay over the injustice. Christ can then free us from unhealthy (and sinful) subjective reactions, and we can enter into a holy objectivity filled with God's grace. We then possess a mastery over circumstances that can turn dark situations into ongoing occasions for God's love to spotlight. "How blest you are, when you suffer insults and persecution and every kind of calumny [slander and reproach] for my sake. Accept it with gladness and exultation, for you have a rich reward in heaven."

A Christian author, well-known in the healing ministry, once told me that she had learned to pray God's protection around her family, especially at times when God had given her a particular work to do. She had discovered that when the Evil One could not get at her directly, he would try to strike at her through those she loved. I too have found this to be the case. Any Christian who is truly *effective* in his calling will discover he has an enemy, one who would thwart the work. To begin to practice the Presence of Christ is to find oneself facing formidable "principalities and powers," evil presences and forces. These powers of darkness hate those who walk in the light, and they will do anything they can to thwart them. But in the Victor, no matter how fierce the battle, there will be the joy and peace of His Presence, as well as the power to stand.

The Cross and Spiritual Power

> . . . we preach Christ crucified: a stumbling block to Jews and foolishness to Gentiles, but to those whom God has called, both Jews and Greeks, Christ the power of God and the wisdom of God. (1 Corinthians 1:23, 24)

While the wisdom of this world ignores the Incarnation and the Cross, we Christians are foolish enough to proclaim a virgin-born Christ nailed to a cross. And in doing that we see the floodgates opened and God's wisdom and saving, healing power released into the lives of all who look to Him.

I never cease to be awed at the simplicity and the extent of the spiritual and psychological healings that take place when we ask a person to look and see, with the eyes of his heart, Jesus on the Cross. As he looks to the One who took into "his own body on the tree" the sin, the darkness, the pain that is killing him, he is then enabled to yield up to the dying Christ the "death" that is in his own members. This is why Oswald Chambers could say:

> Re-state to yourself what you believe; then do away with as much of it as possible, and get back to the bedrock of the Cross of Christ. In external history the Cross is an infinitesimal thing; from the Bible point of view it is of more importance than all the empires of the world. If we get away from brooding on the tragedy of God upon the Cross in our preaching, it produces nothing. It does not convey the energy of God to man; it may be interesting, but it has no power. *But preach the Cross, and the energy of God is let loose.*[2] (italics mine)

All of man's wisdom, good works, and searching out are incapable of finding God. Instead, God and His way of redemption found man. This is why the Cross and its way of saving man stands at the heart of the Christian faith, for it is here that the Life that came into the world in the Incarnation is poured out for us. At the Cross we who believe take, as it were, our place in Christ's death. There we die with Him to our own sins and the sins of the world. Dying with Him, we also rise with Him. Dying to our old sinful natures, we are made righteous by His sinlessness. That is why God's way of saving us is faith in Christ crucified .

Some too quickly reject the crucifix as a valid symbol for today, forgetting that we must daily take our place in His death as well as in His resurrection. In the work of the Cross there is an ongoing reality, one to be proclaimed in the present moment. When we do so, God's energy is indeed "let loose." People repent and are forgiven; people forgive others and are healed.

God's message to His people has ever been the same: "I have loved you with an everlasting love; I have drawn you with loving-kindness" (Jeremiah 31:3). Christ lived by every word that issued from the mouth of the Father. In obedience to the Father's will and word—that is, to His love for us—Christ "accepted even death—death on a cross." Therefore all power was given unto Him. True spiritual power and authority have their roots in the Cross of Christ, in the redemption wrought through its way of finding man. And the way it finds us is always and only by our listening-obedience to the love of the Father, the way that channels His love to a dying world.

The Nature of This Power

> The Holy Spirit is sheer, unadulterated power, a flow of compassionate energy. When the power grows dim in us, it is because

we have not kept open channels for the power to flow in. (Agnes Sanford)

The prophet Isaiah spoke beforehand of the power that would rest upon Christ, and of the way in which He would move in it:

The Spirit of the Lord will rest on him—the Spirit of wisdom and of understanding, the Spirit of counsel and of power, the Spirit of knowledge and of the fear of the Lord. *He will not judge by what he sees with his eyes, or decide by what he hears with his ears*, but with righteousness he will judge the needy, with justice he will give decisions for the poor of the earth. (11:2-4, italics mine)

With Christ as our supreme example, we learn to stop speaking our own unaided wisdom and instead seek and find the mind of God. The servant of the Lord who successfully moves under the Spirit's anointing, and who effectively collaborates with the Spirit to heal God's people, has a secure grasp of Scriptural truths which never change. He has learned to listen to (i.e., obey) God. He too will not "judge by what he sees, or decide by what he hears."

Zechariah the prophet and Zerubbabel, a man with a great gift of organizing and building, are good examples of effective listening to God. As the Jews were returning from their long captivity in Babylon, Zerubbabel was given the awesome task of rebuilding the Temple in Jerusalem. The magnitude of the work and the difficulties surrounding it (not the least of which was the murderous and unrelenting opposition of powerful enemies) made completion of the Temple seem impossible. Zerubbabel must have been feeling his own smallness and inadequacy when God sent him this healing, encouraging word through the prophet Zechariah:

"This is the word of the Lord to Zerubbabel: 'Not by might nor by power, but by my Spirit,' says the Lord Almighty." . . . "The hands of Zerubbabel have laid the foundation of this temple; his hands will also complete it." (Zechariah 4:6, 9)

And the work that was impossible, humanly speaking, was by the power of the Spirit completed.

In the Presence there is spiritual power, and under the anointing of the Holy Spirit, we are to do the works of God. Whether our task, like Zerubbabel's, is one of building a place where a nation can once again find its true identity in the worship of God, or if, like Zechariah's, it is one of proclaiming truth and healing, we are *authorized* and *under a mandate* to move in the power the Spirit gives. We can then celebrate our smallness and our inadequacy, knowing that it is by His Spirit that we are to transcend our limitations. We do not run ahead, nor do we lag behind, but we moment by moment obey God. When we wait upon the Lord for His mind on the task or the difficulty, then we are spared from substituting our own limited vision and unaided wisdom for the mighty work He would do.

Futhermore, when we are not hearing God speak a word, we can be quick to say so. Some of the most remarkable healings happen when we say to a person, "God's not showing me a single thing about your situation." Then we continue to pray. I'll never forget a very anxious man who had traveled from another country to get to a healing seminar. After sitting through the sessions and having his faith piqued to the limits, he felt that all but him were being helped. It looked as if he would have to leave, still with his terrible problem, and that no one would have time to pray with him.

It was after the conference had ended and everyone else was rejoicing and packing to leave that we finally sat down to pray. Tears in his eyes and a tremor in his voice revealed the frustration and disappointment he had been feeling. My heart went out to him as he began to pour out his concerns. He had had a problem with uncontrollable anger all his adult life. It was unpredictable. He never knew why he'd have a strong reaction at one time and not at another. To make matters worse, this anger would be directed at the very ones he loved the most. It was ruining his life and his career.

In listening to his story, I would ordinarily have had some insight into his difficulties, but there was no discernment whatsoever. Knowing how desperate this man was for help and how far he had come to get it, I could have been tempted to come up with some answer on my own. But God always has the answer, and I have far too much experience of God's faithfulness to replace His answer with mine. So I told the dear man truthfully, "The Lord is not showing me a thing. I have not the least insight into your problem, and I usually would, just from hearing your story. But I will lay hands on you and pray." Had I tried to come up with something to appease his fear or lack of faith, my own "wisdom" would have gotten in the way of the healing God had in mind for him.

"The effect of prayer is union with God, and if someone is with God, he is separated from the enemy." So said Gregory of Nyssa many centuries ago, and it is still true. No sooner had I in prayer touched his forehead with holy water than a demonic spirit came out, tearing him as it came, causing him to froth at the mouth. I grabbed a towel and then got a washcloth for him. I next anointed him with healing oil and prayed that the Light of Christ would come in and fill the space where that alien, dark thing had been. It was not in his spirit, for he was a Christian, but it came up from deep in his abdomen where it had been lodged since he was a small child. It had affected his entire life. He was set free and knew it. He literally leaped in jubilation. I hate to think of the despair that man would have known had I tried to substitute some unaided wisdom of my own for the healing God had for him. When God is not saying a word, we should not insert our own or weakly fall back on some method or Scripture verse we vaguely hope will apply. Rather, we pray in faith, knowing that God will do with the person that for which he is ready.

We must never allow some preconceived idea of what is wrong or of what is the usual remedy to get in the way of what God wants to do. A wonderful example of this principle is found in the story of Elisha, his servant Gehazi, and the Shunammite woman. Elisha saw the woman coming in great haste to meet him. Realizing that something was urgently amiss with her, he sent his servant Gehazi to meet her. But the nature of this woman's need was so great that she would not tell Gehazi nor slacken her speed. She knew she had to get to Elisha, the man of God who had prophesied that she, a barren woman, would have a son. When she reached Elisha, though Gehazi tried to prevent her, she took hold of the prophet's feet and clung to him. Elisha, reproving Gehazi, said:

"Leave her alone! She is in bitter distress, *but the Lord has hidden it from me and has not told me why*" (2 Kings 4:27, italics mine).

Had Elisha depended upon some method or system, he would not have been listening for a word from the Lord. He would have been casting about for a way to understand and categorize her need, and then for a way to help her "cope" with it. This, of course, is not entirely unlike what any of us would do, whether or not we have studied some particular system for helping others. But had we been content with our own system for understanding the matter, and had we failed to trust God for the next step, we would have missed the mind and the will of God. And so would have Elisha.

As it so happened, the woman's young son, born to her through Elisha's intercession, had died. Elisha, listening closely to what she said, and then to what God led him to do, one step at a time, saw the woman's son raised from the dead and given back to his mother.

The concept of listening to God and moving in the power and authority He gives to heal is strangely alien to many modern Christians. They have become dependent upon medical science for their healing needs, and upon the secular (both rational and occult) psychologies and therapies devised for gaining personal wholeness. Wherever true scholarship informs the study of man, the resulting insight and procedural skills are to be received by the Christian with thankfulness. To his own peril will he ignore such wisdom and experience. Much of the wisdom, in fact, the Church has had at one time, but has since forgotten or ignored it.

The greater peril today, however, lies in the Christian's loss of his own superior truth system, both intellectual and symbolic. With this truth he is to evaluate the systems and therapies of the day. If he is to move in God's power and authority, the servant of the Lord must know that even the best wisdom of the day is insufficient. It cannot fully grasp the mystery of the human spirit, soul, and body. Looking to God and listening to Him is essential.

There are a number of reasons for our failure to pray. Many of us are simply guilty of spiritual sloth. To learn to pray effectively requires discipline. Others, faithful in intercessory prayer, simply have never been taught the more direct kind of ministry we are to have with others. Christ has modeled this prayer for us, but we haven't seen our elders in the faith praying effectively in this fashion.

Still others, inexperienced in this kind of prayer and psychologically trained, feel uneasy about introducing prayer into the counseling process. It seems to conflict with either the principles or the method they are trained in, and they complain of confusion. (Indeed, even though "baptized" for use by Christians, secular wisdom often *does* conflict with the life of faith.) They feel it is easier and less "risky" to rely on prevailing educational and psychological theories, those that help them maintain a "professional distance" in contrast to the personal involvement prayer entails.

The feeling here is that the "system" or "method" approved and taught through the educational systems can then absorb the blame for "not working" should no help come to the sufferer. The therapist would then not feel as though he or his prayers had failed. This person needs to overcome fear of failure, learn to trust God, and develop a more comprehensive psychology and theology.

A related error is even more grievous because it affects so many Christian leaders. It amounts to a "psychologizing" of the gospel message, a serious reductionism of the faith. Thinking only of the person's emotional needs and the current wisdom for meeting them, the modern minister forgets to invoke the Presence of God and call down upon the needy person the grace to repent. He has neglected the root healing, out of which all ongoing progress comes. The essential will in the needy person is left untouched, and he will be unable to stand.

Such Christian leaders, no matter how many divinity or doctoral degrees they possess, cannot act as true ministers. To be a Christian minister is to call the needy to a radical and full repentance, and then, in the power of the Spirit, to proclaim forgiveness in such a way that the repentant one can receive it. The Christian minister is a sacramental channel through which God's forgiveness flows.

Finally, much of the above is related to unbelief, which, along with pride, accounts for the greater part of all prayerlessness. The gravest problem underlying our prayerlessness is that we are idolatrous—we want to bring healing or help to people through our own cleverness, apart from dependence upon God.

The Gathered Church's Need to Recognize the Healing Presence

Besides our tendency to self-reliance, we need to recognize genuine blind spots, historically speaking, in the Church's practical (not her theological) teaching.

One of the first things I see each morning are these words, lovingly done by a friend in crimson, gold, and blue needlepoint and now mounted on my bedroom wall:

> *Christ has died.*
> *Christ is risen.*
> *Christ will come again.*

From the beginning of the Christian era, in liturgies ancient and new, the gathered Church has chanted these awesome words. Her people have understood what each line means and in their worship have joyously affirmed it as true. But in a way difficult to comprehend, the Church has generally failed to understand and teach Christ's Presence with us today, in the *now* of the present moment. Perhaps the fact that the Church found it harder to spell out this truth in a one-liner and thereby liturgically lead people in constant affirmation of it has had something to do with its neglect. More likely to blame, however, are later omissions from the liturgy and worship practices, omissions that have deprived us of the vital reminders.

Dom Gregory Dix, commenting on the effects of changing the eucharistic section of the liturgy, writes:

> Whenever and wherever the eucharistic action is changed, *i.e.*, whenever and wherever the standard structure of the rite has been broken up or notably altered, there it will be found that some part of the primitive fulness of the meaning of the eucharist has been lost. And—in the end—it will be found that this has had equally notable results upon the Christian *living* of those whose Christianity has been thus impoverished. It may sound exaggerated so to link comparatively small ritual changes with great social results. But it is a demonstrable historical fact that they are linked; and whichever we may like to regard as the

cause of the other, it is a fact that the ritual change can always be historically detected before the social one. To take two cardinal instances: There is an analysable relation between the *non-communicant* eucharistic piety which begins in the later fourth century and certain obvious weaknesses and special characteristics of the Christianity of the dark and middle ages, which first show themselves in the fifth century. There is again a clear relation between, on the one hand, certain special tendencies of Latin eucharistic piety in the later middle ages which come to full development in the sixteenth century all over the West, and on the other that post-renaissance individualism, first in religion and then in living, which has had such outstanding consequences upon the general situation of Western society in the eighteenth, nineteenth and twentieth centuries.[3]

I have no difficulty at all in understanding this, for I see the spiritual and psychological problems individuals have simply because of an *omission* in their congregational worship, one that left no opportunity to receive the needed healing. The Church's liturgy, whether high or low, formal or informal, must provide the *space* for the needed steps and opportunities of praise, worship, and thanksgiving, for repentance, for teaching of the Word, *experience* of the Word in the Eucharist, and last but not least, in the invocation of the Presence of Christ in such a way that the healing gifts are part of our worship.

It seems the lot of fallen man that, Christian though he be, he is exaggerating some truth of the gospel at the expense of another, or that he is falling away from some part of the truth altogether. In regard to the matter of spiritual power, the truth is that historically the people of God have seldom comprehended the "divine energy and power," as well as the authority with and in which they are to move. This is in spite of the fact that the truth is plainly spelled out in the Scriptures and in the history of the Early Church.

In the past several centuries, this difficulty in our understanding has been greatly exacerbated because the Western Church's teachings have become increasingly abstract. Conceptual knowledge *about* God has almost entirely replaced even the pious attempt to *walk with* God. Kierkegaard, in the last century, cried out a warning to the Church, one she has so far ignored: "We've forgotten how to *exist, to be.*" We can only *think about* being. In other words, we can think in terms of Christian dogma, but we cannot love and obey God.

The Early Church's Feast of the Presence
The Early Church had no such difficulty, no schism between mind and heart. Their worship was quite literally a celebration of the Presence. After our Lord's death and resurrection, the early Christians came

together knowing that He would meet with them in a special way once again. Rather than going *to* church (their minds were not clouded with the notion that buildings or organizational structures were the Church), they came together *as* the Church to fellowship in His Presence.

And we might say they "practiced the Presence" in a number of ways or modes. "Christ has died, Christ is risen," part of the earliest liturgy, was in some of their hearts an incredible *remembered* experience. Memories of lives shared together in the breaking of bread, in long journeys, and in the teaching of multitudes must have been vivid ones for many. Beyond memories of Christ's Presence, however, they knew by virtue of His Spirit descending on them at Pentecost that He was always present, indwelling them. In yet a third way, pertinent to what we are here considering, these early disciples knew that when they invoked Him, Christ would "come again" by His Spirit as they gathered to worship, hear the Word, and break bread (make Eucharist) together.

The Invocation of the Presence

The oldest liturgical prayer that we know about is a command prayer, or prayer of invocation (see 1 Corinthians 16:22; Revelation 22:20b; and the *Didache,* a Christian document dated 90-110 A.D.). It was joyously spoken at the end of the Communion Meal. The Word had been taught—now the Word was to be experienced, affirmed to them with "signs following." Only three words in length, it is, I think, the most wonderful and powerful prayer in all Christendom: "Come, Lord Jesus!" The early Christians must have shouted this prayer aloud with great fervor, knowing that He, their risen Lord, would by His Spirit be present to them in a most special way again.

The Church's liturgy, then, from ancient times was designed to lead us to the highest peak of worship, the joyous moment when Christ comes, in a special way, to His own. Traditionally, it was at this time that the gifts of the Holy Spirit (the *charismata* or *spirituals*) were in operation, the time when the people received the word and the healing the Lord was sending for that time, that place.

This joyous meeting at table with their Lord was understood to be a foretaste of the Great Day that is to come and of the Marriage Supper of the Lamb when all who are blood-bought will sit at table with Him in a reunion that has no ending. This part of the worship experience then harks back to the joyous affirmation made earlier in the liturgy: "Christ will come again!"

Where the Presence of the Lord is truly invoked, there is little difficulty in believing on Him or moving in the spiritual power and authority He brings.

To regain what we've forgotten or omitted requires not only illumination and a complete change of mind-set, but a deep and profound repentance. If few understand His Presence with us, fewer still understand how it is we are to collaborate with God to do His bidding. We have to learn again the lessons of how the life of God is expressed, sacramentally, with and through us as individuals and as the corporate Body of Christ. Repentance for our failure to love God and to love one another comes first.

Spiritual Power Lost by Disunity Among Christians

Renewal of God's Presence and power in a fellowship of Christians continues only so long as they are reaching out to others. Denominational groups are prone to become ingrown, often being led that way by leaders seeking to establish different kinds of controls. When this happens, fellowships lose the priceless *anointing* they have been given. The gifts of the Holy Spirit may remain, but they jangle as a "noisy gong" or a "clanging cymbal." These gifts, turned inward, become narcissistic and lack depth and content. Love is missing. The Kingdom of God then ceases to go forward in that particular group.

Disunity among themselves, an equally pernicious thing, usually begins the loss of vision. The Holy Spirit is seriously grieved by our disunity and *absents* Himself. We are no longer abiding in Christ.

In the Church, disunity is therefore one of the chief evils clogging the channels through which God's healing power is to flow. It is when people come together in love one for another and in one accord in the Spirit that we see the healing power of God flow so generously. Agnes Sanford, in her book *The Healing Gifts of the Spirit*, writes of how even a prayer group can become destructive instead of creative when its members set themselves apart from the rest of the congregation. Agnes felt that the greatest work of the prayer groups she taught was that of "extending the power of God into the church for the benefit of the entire congregation."[4] In the following quote, she shares the principles by which her prayer group brought the unity of the Spirit and the protection of God to an entire church:

This work for the congregation was never announced. Many never know why that church so increased in power that even to go into it lifted up the heart and strengthened the body. If we had made the work public, it would have lost power.

We went to church some ten minutes early in order to pray for the presence of Jesus Christ to fill that church with His healing and redeeming love. When the minister entered, we prayed for him; not that he should do what we wanted him to do or even believe what we wanted him to believe, but simply that God would pour out upon him His blessing and bring forth the highest potential of his being. Next we looked about the church to see whether there was anyone whose face made us feel uncomfortable—in other words, anyone whom we did not like, of whom we disapproved, who had hurt us or who disapproved of us—and we prayed for that one. We did not deny that person's faults. We redeemed them through prayer. We asked the love of Christ to come into us and go through us into this person, healing the memories and bringing forth all that was good and lovely in his nature. Then we gave thanks as one does in the prayer of faith, and with inspired imagination we made in the mind a picture of that person transformed into the image of his real Christ-self and we rejoiced that this was so.

Inevitably our feeling about this person changed. Through our prayer we gave birth to his spirit; therefore he became to us a spiritual child and we brooded over him as a parent over a child, striving in prayer until the picture that we saw in the mind was accomplished. Moreover this person's feeling also changed! . . .

After some years of this kind of prayer there was not so far as I know a quarrel of any kind in the church; not even a jealousy, not even a hate. Why should there have been? The prayers of the faithful in that church had healed the Body of Christ among them. Naturally!

Next we prayed for healing for certain individuals, often sharing our projects beforehand and sometimes making them our special intention for the Communion and receiving for them with prayer and fasting. *And all in secret*. (Matthew 6:6)

Finally we prayed for the healing power of the Lord to touch the mind and heart and body of any in that church who needed healing.

And it worked. The most wonderful healings that I have ever known took place through the silent prayers of that prayer group in and among and through the whole congregation.[5]

Unbelief

Even before the problem of disunity, however, or perhaps what issues out of it (see John 17:21), is the problem of unbelief. This proud unbelief sticks with the world's viewpoint even in the face of powerful testimony and God's renewing work in lives. Today the greater part of the Church is literally cursed with unbelief of one kind or another, and is thereby separated from God's protection. Man, in unbelief, steps out from under the mercy of God, and brings about his own destruction. The Psalmist (78:22, 32), writing about God's wrath on Israel, cries out the reason for it: "for they did not believe in God or trust in his deliverance . . . in spite of his wonders, they did not believe."

Recently an editor and publisher of Christian books, amazed at the unbelief on the part of Christian leaders he had been meeting with, sounded a great deal like the Psalmist. "I can't believe it," he cried out, "it is the Christian leaders themselves who are accepting the humanistic assessments of man and his *psyche*. Even those who claim to believe the Scriptures do not believe in incarnational truth, the fact that God is really with us! That He *can* transform us from within!"

And such is the state of unbelief in which much of the Church lies buried today. This unbelief often emanates the strongest through those persons who most vociferously claim God as their Father. But there are signs, whisperings in the tops of the mulberry trees, that the Church, while holding fast to the sovereignty of her God, will once again make room for Sacrament, for incarnation, for the holy in the midst of the earthly.

Separation from the Presence: The Fall from God-consciousness into Self-consciousness

For it is in Christ that the complete being of the Godhead dwells embodied, and in him you have been brought to completion.

(Colossians 2:9, 10, NEB)

S eparation from the Presence is, quite literally, what the Fall *is*. As a result of the Fall, mankind slipped from God-consciousness into the hell of self and self-consciousness.

Such a state is at once sinful and incomplete. This fallen self, turned inward and narcissistic, dwells in misconceived feelings and attitudes, those that arise from listening to the self-in-separation and to the voices of a fallen world. That self is to be "put off"—we are not to practice the presence of that self:

> You were taught, with regard to your former way of life, to put off your old self, which is being corrupted by its deceitful desires; to be made new in the attitude of your minds; and to put on the new self, created to be like God in true righteousness and holiness. (Ephesians 4:22-24)

Reckoning ourselves dead to that body of sin in our members (the old man) and alive to God through Jesus Christ our Lord, we "put on" our new man, the true self (see Romans 6:3-14). Practicing His Presence, we live decisively out of that new self. To practice His Presence, therefore, is also to practice the presence of the new man (self) rather than the old.

The soul, with its new center in Christ, radically changed and redirected, is to be *accepted*. There is the oddest thing about the history of Christian teaching. This new, real self is largely ignored, feared, or even denied. If one doubts this, he need simply run through the references in the best Bible helps. There the old or false self is catalogued and referenced in every possible way, which is absolutely good and necessary. But where is the real self acknowledged? It goes largely uncelebrated, unreferenced, and in effect unaccepted. For the "walk in the Spirit," the true self is required. Is this why we are so backward in teaching what the "walk in the Spirit" really is? It is no wonder that Christians have a hard time with self-acceptance, a moral as well as Christian virtue necessary to consistent living *in Christ*.

Until this redeemed self is acknowledged and accepted, we live out of the immature, unaffirmed self, and we cannot hear God aright. From that center, we also "mishear" our fellows, and they become the target of the diseased "matter" that yet resides within our souls—that is, our fears of rejection, our bitterness, envy, anger, and sense of inferiority. These invariably project themselves into the minds and hearts of those we love the most, piercing them like deadly arrows. Until we accept the new self, we are dangerous to ourselves and to others; even though we are Christians, we are still enthralled by the voices of this world and obey them. We fail to abide in Christ and instead remain self-conscious.

A right understanding of the true self and our acceptance of it is necessary to a sound and balanced theology. Christ who is my everything is also my righteousness. In accepting myself in Him, I am no longer trapped in the mode of trying to win my own righteousness or God's love, or in trying to keep the law, the very thing that Christ fulfilled.

The true self finds "fullness of being." It knows completion, for it is in the Perfect One. When our Lord told us we must be perfect, even as our Heavenly Father is perfect, He was saying we must be completed. The word *perfect*, as translated in the Scriptures, can mean "without flaw," but it also means "completed, finished, made whole." We are here dealing with a number of profound things, one of which is personhood. We are *becoming persons*. We *become* as we remain in Christ, a state of God-consciousness. Focused on the word the Father is always sending, obedient to it, the new self is not in bondage to the voices the old self listened to, those that pull the soul toward death and non-being.

The Movement from Separation to Union and Identity

There is great beauty in the movement of the soul as it forsakes its alienation and its inability to hear and know God, and comes into a position of listening, illumination, and union with Him. There is a splendid simplicity to it.

On entering the Presence, no matter how twisted and bent the soul has been toward its idols, it receives the grace to renounce them. As one's *will* is thoroughly converted and made one with God's, one has a new backbone, upright and strong, with which to stand erect in the vertical, receiving position with the Father. The soul sees, it *hears*, it comes into holy converse. It finds that:

> [T]he word of God is living and active. Sharper than any double-edged sword, it penetrates even to dividing soul and spirit, joints and marrow; it judges the thoughts and attitudes of the heart. Nothing in all creation is hidden from God's sight. Everything is uncovered and laid bare before the eyes of him to whom we must give account. (Hebrews 4:12)

It finds that God's love is truly "something more stern and splendid than mere kindness,"[1] that it is the kind of Love that divides the darkness from the light, the old self from the new self. It finds that "everything, when once the light has shown it up, is illumined, and everything thus illumined is all light" (Ephesians 5:13, NEB).

A new self, with one face, turned up to God, seeing and hearing with singleness of heart, is born. Christ, the Word, comes to birth and is formed within that soul, and there is therefore the capacity to communicate with the Father.

In this way, we find a new self (or new nature, or new man). We have been brought into Christ, and Christ into us. *Completion*. There is a profound beauty and simplicity in this way of *getting a self*, of finding healing and wholeness.

In contrast, modern psychology tends to make the process of finding the self, of becoming a whole person, into a very complex process. Or, even worse, many systems of humanistic psychology have no clear picture of what the true self even looks like. This is understandable because they do not take into account either the Healing Presence or the Sacred Writings.

The healing of the soul *is* a very complex matter—in fact, there is no end to its unmet need—when we bypass the Incarnation and the Cross, God's way, through His Son, of bringing us back into *communication* with Himself.

Language as Mystery

Our capacity to speak, hear, comprehend—our use, that is, of language—is a most profound mystery. Only man, of all God's creation, talks—that is, *symbolizes*—continually. In this we are in the image of God, for God speaks.

So it is that God and man *talk*. Christ, the Word, who spoke the world into existence and created man, breathed into Adam the spark of life and called him into communication with Himself. And he gave him the task of *naming* all that is created.

Walker Percy, in *The Message in the Bottle*, reminds us that the greatest philosophers, linguists, and scholars cannot tell us *what* language *is*. They can tell us something about its structure, grammar, phonemes, morphemes, the relation of one language to another, its historical changes, and so on, but how it is that man knows, symbolizes, talks—that in which we differ from all other created organisms—even our greatest minds do not know.

> Why is it that scientists, who know a great deal about the world,
> know less about language than about the backside of the moon,
> even though language is the one observable behavior which most
> clearly sets man apart from the beasts and the one activity in which
> all men, scientists included, engage in more than any other?[2]

Why, Percy wonders, are scientists anxious to convince man how much he is like other creatures rather than face this incredible difference—man, an animal who talks?

Language is primordial; its roots are safely hidden from us as scientific man. *Language has to do with the very nature of man, man made in the image of God. God and man are called into conversation.*

I had a very interesting discussion with a young linguist-philosopher who had studied language in post-graduate studies at one of our finest universities, and who was at that particular time an unbeliever studying theology. He had read my book *The Broken Image* and was asking the kind of questions about healing prayer that the skeptical, scientifically trained mind would ask. Knowing he had done special work in linguistics, I queried him about the matter of speaking in tongues, especially as it related to the *mystery* of language. He quite genially said to me, "There is no category to even talk about this." As naturalists and materialists, we have lost a vital category, that of comprehending the Unseen Real, that of dealing with paradox and mystery.

This, of course, is what lies behind the awful fact that for most moderns the sense of God has vanished from the earth. Just as the young scientist could not think in terms of supernatural speech, so the modern has no "categories" with which to think, much less speak, of God's Presence. Naturalism or materialism, as modern philosophies, simply reflect the fallen condition, as well as the subject of this chapter: that to be fallen is to be separated from the Presence.

To be without this "category" is to continue in a state of primal loneliness.

The Loneliness of Man

> We are born helpless. As soon as we are fully conscious, we dis-
> cover loneliness.[3]

> Our Lord can never be defined in terms of individuality and
> independence, but only in terms of personality, "I and My
> Father are one." Personality merges, and you only reach your
> real identity when you are merged with another person. When
> love, or the Spirit of God strikes a man, he is transformed, he no
> longer insists upon his separate individuality. Our Lord never
> spoke in terms of individuality, of a man's . . . isolated position,
> but in terms of personality—"that they may be one, even as We
> are one."[4]

To speak of the true self, of personality at all—that is, of man as
fully human—is to speak of man's fellowship with God and with others.
Even before the Fall, with its catastrophic disruption of all relationships,
God said: "It is not good for the man to be alone . . ." (Genesis 2:18). The
poet Milton, commenting on this word, said: "Loneliness is the first thing
which God's eye nam'd not good." We know ourselves only in relation
to God and others.

Philosophers and theologians, with notable and wonderful excep-
tions in my own experience, are usually quite rational and seldom reveal
more than the powers of cognition and abstraction in their lecturing.
Perhaps it is for this reason that I still recall with what pathos and feeling
Dr. Paul T. Holmer of Yale University said, "If we know ourselves at all,
it is with the greatest of difficulty." (This capacity for pathos and feeling,
together with his very great intellectual capacities, made him a lecturer
far beyond the ordinary, especially when it came to understanding the
intellects and emotional capacities of other great scholars such as
Kierkegaard, Wittgenstein, and C. S. Lewis.) The full truth of his lone
statement, with all its many facets and dimensions, seemed to stand out
starkly for a moment. To know ourselves at all is to begin to be healed of
the effects of the Fall.

Evil, theologically speaking, is separation from God—and in that
condition, separation from our fellows, the good earth, and all creation as
well. Evil, psychologically speaking, is separation within ourselves. In
truth, the fallen self cannot know itself.

Before the Fall, of course, man experienced God's Presence continually.

In *Perelandra*, C.S. Lewis's novel about an unfallen world, he
depicts an unfallen Eve (the Green Lady) who, basking in pure goodness,
listens always to Maleldil (God). She is blissfully unaware that she is

"separate" from Him. Unlike the Green Lady, however, our first parents fell, and the first thing they did was to hide themselves from the Presence. They knew themselves to be separate. The Bible records the history of man's guilty flight from the Presence of God, and of the ways in which lost souls are sought and wooed back to the One who completes them. It is a record of the way in which God mediates His presence to a fallen world and His word to hearts that have long been in bondage to other voices.

We are lonely, then, because we are separate. As I wrote in an earlier book:

> Born lonely, we try hard to fit in, to *be* the kind of person that will cause others to like us. Craving and needing very much the affirmation of others, we compromise, put on any face, or many faces; we do even those things we do not like to do in order to fit in. We are bent . . . toward the creature, attempting to find our identity in him. Slowly and compulsively the false self closes its hard, brittle shell around us, and our loneliness remains.[5]

Spiritually and psychologically, to use C. S. Lewis's telling image of fallen man, man is "bent." The *unfallen* position was, as it were, a *vertical* one, one of standing erect, face turned upward to God in a listening-speaking relationship. It was a position of receiving continually one's true identity from God. But fallen man is bent toward the creature and trapped in the continual attempt to find his identity in the created rather than in the Uncreated.

The Lonely, Bent Position

When I pray with someone who is seeking wholeness, one of the first things I do after invoking the Presence of the Lord is look to see *in whom* or *in what* this person is attempting to gain his or her identity. From what person or thing (money, status, professional degree, accomplishment, sexual prowess, etc.) is he or she demanding, "Tell me who I am"? We then know what the person's idol is, what "loves" need either renouncing or setting in perspective and right order.

In the absence of finding our identity in God, we fallen ones love selfishly. The drive to dominate, possess, or manipulate persons and things in order to meet our own needs taints (or replaces altogether) the healthy, satisfying relationships we are designed to have and by which we are to be nurtured.

The key to healing these bent ones is simple but profound, and the same for all: It consists in renouncing and utterly forsaking the "bent" posture toward the creature, and "straightening up" into Christ.

There, standing upright in the vertical position, fully focused on God, our bonds from the old bent position fall off. With ears alert to catch His every word, we are brought into the place of *becoming*. It is the free state of listening-obedience where we find healing, completion, and our true identity. In this posture, our arms are stretched straight up to the Father, our palms are opened wide to receive all that is good—all, in other words, that really *is* and therefore *completes* us spiritually, psychologically, and physically.

> "If you, then, though you are evil, know how to give good gifts
> to your children, how much more will your Father in heaven
> give good gifts to those who ask him!" (Jesus, in Matthew 7:11)

Personhood, identity, *being itself* come from Him as our hands and hearts are open (through merely asking!) to receive. Focused on Him, we climb up and out of the hell of self and self-consciousness. Listening to the words He speaks, we are freed from the words that emanate from our unhealed hearts, from the unhealed hearts of our fellow creatures, or from the powers of darkness: those that accuse and tempt us toward separation and death. In listening to the words that come from God, we *become* all we were created to be.

This, in a nutshell, is what the ministry of prayer for spiritual and psychological wholeness is all about. It consists simply of learning to invoke the Presence of the Lord, of coming into that Presence with the needy one, and there listening for the healing word that God is always sending to the wounded and alienated. We listen with the needy person until such time as we can teach him to listen for himself. The bondages of the "bent position" fall from him, and all idols he would still cling to are shown up for what they really are.

Bentness versus Being

In God's Presence, we've come before the One who speaks worlds into being, who delights in speaking new worlds of *being* into our very souls, affirming, as He does so, those very parts of ourselves that have (for whatever reason) not been called forth and blessed in our families and earthly relationships.

In the human family, it is the father who affirms us as male and female and as persons. It is the masculine voice we are listening for at puberty and thereafter, that time when we are separating our sexual and personal identities from that of our mothers. But when we've failed to gain the needed affirmation, we can rest assured that there is available to us the healing needed to clear up any gender and personal identity confusion and inferiority feelings. This is sure and absolute, for in the

Presence of God the Father, when we learn to listen to and obey Him, we are affirmed as real men, real women, real persons. Solidity of being is imparted.

> No human father, but God alone, is properly, truly and primarily Father. No human father is the creator of his child, the controller of its destiny, or its savior from sin, guilt, and death. No human father is by his word the source of its temporal and eternal life. In this proper, true and primary sense God—and He alone—is Father.[6]

God the Father, who has the Power of Being, heals and affirms us. By fiat He spoke the worlds into existence; by fiat He can and does create in us a new and solid sense of being.

Through healing prayer, this process (God's fiat) is greatly quickened. Healing prayer, rightly understood and ministered, is the most creative work in the world, for through it a way is made for God's command to be uttered, and by it the soul is made ready to hear and receive it.

> Master: Eager souls may have their healing instantaneously, if they can quickly adjust to that perfection which I behold in them. The works that I do shall ye do also, and greater works. . .! And if I cured men of their disorders instantaneously, you should do the same. Your work is retarded and healing procrastinated because of unbelief; because you do not expect results! Or you expect results to manifest very gradually. See Me in each one for whom you pray. See the Divine Image rising obedient to your word of power. Encourage the timid ones with Apostolic hope. Bless each one with Apostolic love, and speak forth your prayer of faith in the Divine Present.[7]

This does not mean that we have ignored great insight (psychological and otherwise). All truth is God's. We need understanding into the false emotional and value structures in our minds, into the difficulties we may have had in the necessary identification process with our parents and within the family.

The more insight we have here, the better able we are to converse with God about it. Then, as we go into the Presence, we find that there is indeed the power to get our identities separated from that of our parents as well as from others.[8] There is the power to see and acknowledge bentness toward the creature: our emotional dependencies[9] and our co-dependencies[10] and to forsake them. There is the power to objectify the inner cluster of attitudes behind our compulsive neurotic behaviors.

There is insight into these and all our other difficulties, as well as instructions for freeing ourselves from them.

In the Presence there is the power to forgive others, even the "unforgivable." There is power to receive forgiveness from God and to stop identifying ourselves by the sin from which we have been delivered. For example, one who is delivered from lying is no longer to be called liar, and the same with every other sin. Our sins, whether of adultery, murder, sexual perversion, envy, drunkenness, and so on, once banished, no longer have the power to name us. In the Presence is the power to receive healing into the deepest deprivations, even that failure to gain in those first months of life, in a mother's arms, that most basic sense of *being* or of *well-being*.

In this way, healing prayer differs from counseling and spiritual direction per se. All of these, if truly Christian, have to do with insight and forgiveness of sin, and they need to be properly timed and wisely brought together. Healing prayer is not the "instant fix," nor the bypassing of slow and steady growth. It is that which clears the path and makes such progress possible. It is the appropriation of the power given us at Pentecost—power having to do with God's Presence with us, issuing forth through us quietly, unobtrusively, or, at times, dramatically, to the healing of persons.

John the Baptist said to those repenting of their sin, "I baptize with water, but he [the Christ] will baptize you with the Holy Spirit." Jesus baptizes with the Holy Spirit, and when He does, He imparts Himself to man. The Pentecostal Presence and power is vital in the healing of neuroses. It is the passing on of life to the soul lacking life, the passing on of being from the Source of all being to the one who has heretofore more nearly identified with non-being. The message of Pentecost is that God centers Himself in His people; we are a people of the Presence. Every soul coming out of the world's lifestyle needs to pray for a personal Pentecost—and receive it. He is then centered in God, and God is centered in Him. He can then hear God while standing and walking with Him in the vertical position.

Centeredness versus Bentness

When God is centered in us and we in Him, we have a *home* within, a true self or center out of which to live. We cannot live from that center and at the same time be bent idolatrously toward the creature. To fail to live from our center is to be in need of both spiritual and psychological healing. This "bentness" as over against "centeredness" is often described in terms of emotional dependency. But some of the "lesser" forms, those that aren't "pathological," but keep us back from wholeness, often go unnoticed, both by our counselors and ourselves.

Seeing our own individual forms of bentness is not always easy. The more blatant idolatries we can see. But the more subtle ones, in addition to having (as most problems do) much that is good and perfectly natural within them, often have to do with deeply entrenched cultural, social, and religious mores.

Even though they are injurious to us, resulting in, for example, emotionally dependent and painful relationships between man and wife, we are blind in regard to them.

From the standpoint of helping people come into freedom through the ministry of healing prayer, I find that often the more subtle, hard-to-recognize idolatries have to do with our unmet needs for affirmation in our gender identities. The gender drive, with its particular energy, is then off-track. It is misguided and causes trouble in our initimate relationships. For that reason, I give below brief examples of the "bentness" we as Christian men and women often fail to recognize or understand.

These also illustrate the fact that we either learn to listen to God with all our hearts or, remaining ignorant of what is amiss, we exploit and manipulate others. Also, we allow others to shape and manipulate us in futile attempts to get our identity and love needs met.

The Bentness Christian Women Often Do Not See

> As human beings, our primary identity is that of our sex. We are born male or female; we become men or women.[11]

At the beginning of my adult Christian life, in sorrow over the havoc and loss divorce had wrought in my life, I began to understand Genesis 3:16.

> To the woman he said, "I will greatly multiply your pain in childbearing; in pain you shall bring forth children, yet your desire shall be for your husband, and he shall rule over you." (RSV)

I saw very clearly that woman is bent toward man by reason of the Fall, and wants to find her identity in him. I saw also that while the secular world pushes woman toward finding her identity in herself as sex object, the popular teachings in the Church, equally mistaken, encourage woman to find her identity in her roles as wife and mother rather than in her status as a person in Christ, a daughter complete in Him.

As the Lord opened the Genesis passages and other Scriptures to my understanding, and as I earnestly sought to obey Him, I saw also that in woman's redemption there is healing of this bent position. There is the possibility of full identity in God, and with that the discovery of both true Christian submission and true Christian freedom.

Women are brought into freedom and into the walk in the Spirit in the same way men are: by listening to God and doing what they hear Him say. This is Scriptural truth, and most Christians would say, "Yes, I believe that." But in practice another way is often lived out. For example, as I pointed out in "Women in Crisis" (Chapter 6 of *Crisis in Masculinity*), women often have difficulty coming into the freedom of the vertical position in Christ because they've either been mistaught the Scriptures on submission of woman or have misunderstood them. The gender drive in woman, that of the strong natural need and desire to respond to the male, can lead her into the bondage of the "bent" position toward him. She may be expecting the man she loves to tell her who she is, to give to her a sense of wholeness and identity. This, of course, he cannot do.

This is not to say that he cannot be an affirming, healing agent in her life. Many a woman, unaffirmed and unaccepted by her own father, has found it much easier to accept herself as a woman through the wonderful gift of her husband's love and acceptance. But should he encourage or allow her to bend toward him in an idolatrous way, listening to and obeying him before or in exclusion to God, both he and she will suffer.

The Christian woman, unaffirmed as a woman or as a person, must find her truest identity in Christ, and in Christ alone. Listening to Him she, like her husband, becomes. It is only then that the great blessings that come out of the natural polarity and complementarity of the sexes can begin to operate in the marriage. Only then can she bring the fullness of her feminine gifts into the marriage. She, like him, must be free to obey God.

The problem of misunderstanding headship and authority and of being wrongly "bent" toward it is not restricted to women. The masculine and personal identities of some men are utterly repressed due to mistaken ideas about what constitutes Christian obedience to parents, bosses, and religious leaders. I have seen heads of families, as well as groups of men in certain religious orders and Christian communities, put the real self to death and call that obedience to God—all in the name of humility and Christian submission. The man who entertains false notions about Christian submission cannot listen to God and obey Him. He cannot effectively call to accountability those over him who, having either a mistaken, sinful, or immature "drive toward power," would exercise a wrong kind of spiritual leadership over him. Their communities, their children, their wives feel the loss of the masculine giftedness and cannot fill in the gap such a loss leaves.

The Bentness Christian Men Often Do Not See

As the essence of femininity is response, masculinity's is the power to initiate. The masculine principle is one of orientation, direction, order, and responsibility. After the Fall, man has had to earn his living by the sweat of his brow. His masculine powers of initiation are to be taxed to the fullest. Because Adam followed Eve in disobedience, God said to him, "Cursed is the ground because of you; through painful toil you will eat of it all the days of your life" (Genesis 3:17).

Just as woman's special giftedness often is perverted by the Fall, so is man's. His power to initiate can turn into a raw drive toward power. He uses his natural masculine giftedness then to try to find identity and meaning in how successfully he toils: his professional status, his income, his degrees, his sexual conquests, and so on. In prayer for the healing of men, I always look to see what is happening with this natural gender drive, and toward what it is bent.

Man needs to be able to express the feminine virtues within himself—response to God, to others, and to the creation over which he has been given dominion (and the wisdom that comes from understanding the interconnectedness of all things). When man is separated from these virtues and from a complementary relationship with true woman, his power to initiate can become a harmful drive toward dominance and power.

In recent times, due to the mass media, we've seen extreme examples of this problem. We've watched in dismay as one posturing male after another has attempted to found a religious kingdom in his own name and image, and made expert use of the mass media to do it. The masculine drive toward power is out of control in such a man, and he lacks the wisdom and gentleness, the authentic power and authority of Christ, and the Scriptural model of saints, apostles, and teachers. His whole body language will be that of chauvinistic power. He will rant and rave against sin and darkness, yet be unaware until it is too late of the dark striving toward dominance and power within himself. He may idealize woman, hold his wife in high esteem, while at the same time he is threatened by truly strong and wise women. He will be afflicted with (usually a deeply unconscious) other-sex ambivalence. Loving idealized woman (his own symbolic fantasy about who she is), he will yet be unable to commune with (in reality know and touch) the true, down-to-earth woman in his midst. He will be afflicted with what has been called the virgin-whore complex, and will see woman as either the idealized virgin (i.e., hold her at arm's length and adore her) or the enticing whore (one he would seduce or be seduced by). He will be, like an adolescent, sexually immature and exceedingly vulnerable to falls. His misdirected drive toward gender identity and power easily leads him into crass sexual sin.

Though recent examples are scandalous and horrifying, scaled for the public stage for all the world to see and suffer dismay, many a Christian home experiences this same "bent" drive toward power, with all its dread consequences. This same gender imbalance and inferiority in the father will be scaled down to the private anguish of family life. It will devastate the family, for true headship will be missing. There are many degrees of this difficulty, of course, but always matters of control and submission will be factors.

True Headship

When Christian man's giftedness is in the vertical position—that is, "unbent" toward his own ego needs and under the Lordship of Christ—then the Church and the home enjoys true headship.

So many, when dealing with these problems, ask, "What is true masculinity and headship? What is true Christian submission?"

It is very hard to sum up a great concept in one sentence, but it seems to me that the Apostle Peter has done it with this exhortation to the elders and the young men of the Church:

> Clothe yourselves with humility toward one another, because, "God opposes the proud but gives grace to the humble." (1 Peter 5:5)

Peter, with full apostolic authority, wrote this in the context of addressing his fellow elders and exhorting them to true headship:

> Be shepherds of God's flock that is under your care, serving as overseers . . . *eager to serve; not lording it over those entrusted to you,* but being examples to the flock. . . . (1 Peter 5:2, 3, italics mine)

He then addressed the young men, exhorting them, "in the same way, be submissive to those who are older" (1 Peter 5:5).

The Rev. David Mains addresses the confusion we have over headship in *Living, Loving, Leading.*

> Scriptural references to headship are found most in the writings of Paul. The apostle uses headship to mean supremacy when referring to Christ. For example, Ephesians 1:22 reads, "And God placed all things under his feet and appointed him [Christ] to be head over everything. . . ."
>
> The difficulty in interpreting related passages arises when the same word refers to a husband's relationship to his wife.[12]

David Mains then quotes from Ephesians 5:23, 24, and 1 Corinthians 11:3, where the husband is shown to be the head of the wife as Christ is the head of the Church, and writes most significantly that:

> This lends ego gratification to the male if he gives headship the supremacy meaning. Yet few of us, knowing even a little about the nature of Christ, would hold that our Lord viewed the male sex to be supreme.
>
> Lording it over others was not Jesus' style. In no way could you detect in his relationship with women an attitude of male supremacy. Jesus' supremacy stems from his divine nature, from his being the Christ, not from his sex.[13]

Headship for the husband turns out to resemble the headship the Apostle Peter described to the elders and the young men of the Church. It is light-years away from the definitions and content some would attribute to headship, definitions that derive from the differing cultures, prejudices, and even, sorry to say, the male pathologies (such as misogyny, hatred or fear of woman) that many men suffer. As David Mains writes:

> Male chauvinism and biblical headship are galaxies apart. The first is anti-Christ, the second is Christlike. . . .
>
> Unfortunately, many Christian men like the honor that goes along with headship but are [unenthusiastic] about the job description. Many have no concept of how to define spirituality or spiritual authority, and they have few models that demonstrate how to be the head of a family. . . .[14]

David Mains ends by advising Christian husbands to take the real job of headship, and reminds them that:

> The two most important ingredients to exercising spiritual headship are a functioning spiritual head and a functioning spiritual co-head.[15]

True headship is exciting indeed, and to find it is to find healing of the "bent" position one toward another; it is part of becoming all we were created to be.

The Bentness in Gender Confusion

We have just considered the kinds of bentness related to man's and woman's natural though unaffirmed heterosexual gender drives. The following story illustrates how the unmet need for bonding with the same-sex parent can result in a kind of "deprivation neurosis," an intense inner pain and sense of masculine gender inferiority that leads one to try to make up the deficit in other persons of the same sex.

A young pastor, married several years, came up and thanked me for writing *The Broken Image,* for he was healed of his homosexual compulsions and gender inferiority through reading it.

He told me his story, beginning with his wedding night when his deep sense of inferiority as a male crashed in on him. This tall, well-built, virile-looking young man realized, as his lovely bride turned to him, that "she expected me to put my arms around her, to protect and hold her."

"But I needed a hug; [at this point he threw his big arms around himself as if to illustrate] I needed a man's arms around me to protect me!" he cried. This young man had never experienced the love and protection of a father. His whole being still cried for that which was missing, and for that which was necessary to his development and acceptance of himself as a man.

The shock of this realization to his whole being, as well as his inability to love his wife in the way she was expecting, was so great that he turned to the homosexual lifestyle in an attempt to get his craving for a man's arms alleviated.

Here we see the bent condition sexualized between those of the same sex. This behavior, or course, did not ease his inner pain, and it was not until he learned to look to God the Father that he was healed of his inner deprivation.

These three brief examples, the first two quite general, are given to illustrate the fact that we are all healed the very same way: We renounce our idols—those persons or things in which we attempt to find ourselves—and we straighten up into the vertical, listening relationship to God.

What the Unfallen Would Not Know

Let us return for a moment to the Green Lady, the unfallen Eve of C. S. Lewis's novel, *Perelandra.* Because she is unfallen, there are a good many things she does not know—all the things that have to do with sin, loneliness, bentness. She does not know herself to be separate from God. Therefore, her spirit is radiantly alive, and she lives from that center—listening always to God and exercising a benevolent authority over all the animals, plants, and nature on that planet. She also, of course, exercises this same authority over her own soul and body; she is not enthralled to it, enslaved to it. Her soul (mind, will, emotions, intuitive faculty, feeling being) is entirely under the control of her center. Because she is completely filled by the Presence of her Maker, she is utterly alive.

The attempt by the Unman to bring about her fall is the chief drama in this novel. We experience this terrible ordeal through the eyes of Ransom, the "ordinary" Christian who has been sent from our fallen planet to speak the truth to her and thereby offset the lies of the tempter. The story is incredibly painful to read at some points—striking at the very heart of our own fallen experience and predicament.

What is her temptation? To see herself walking alongside herself. To abdicate her own center. To lose the sense of being at home within her own self, and therefore her authority. To abandon the true self and accept the false self.

The tempter holds up a mirror before the Green Lady, tempting her to see herself separate from herself, and lies:

"That is what it means to be a man or a woman—to walk alongside oneself as if one were a second person and to delight in one's own beauty. Mirrors were made to teach this art."[16]

He then attempts to instill in her a dramatic view of herself, a self separate from God. Ransom, anxiously watching her face, saw that:

The image of her beautiful body had been offered to her only as a means to awake the far more perilous image of her great soul. The external and, as it were, dramatic conception of the self was the enemy's true aim. He was making her mind a theatre in which that phantom self should hold the stage. He had already written the play.[17]

The Tempter of our souls even now says to us: "I want you to see yourself walking alongside yourself; I want you to gain a sentimental view of yourself as noble, or great, or tragic. I want you to gain a dramatic view of yourself as the center of all things, and then to pity yourself when you are not."

Self-pity, envy, covetousness, pride are all voices of temptation in a fallen world. When we begin listening to them, we don't listen to God. We obey the other voices.

The Green Lady is being tempted to create and live out of a cluster of diseased feelings and attitudes about herself and others. Earlier she had said to Ransom, "I have never done it before, stepping out of life into the Alongside, and looking at oneself living as if one were not alive."[18]

Here is the schism between thinking and being, between the two minds, the head's and the heart's—the very thing neuroses are made of.

The Green Lady's will is one with Maleldil's (God's); therefore she doesn't fall. "I am His beast, and all His biddings are joys."[19]

Acknowledging herself to be creaturely, she centers herself in Him who has created and fills all things. Centered in Him, she does not abandon the true self and can live securely from her own center. Listening patiently and always, she obeys His voice.

In contrast, the Adam and Eve of our world willed to know evil experientially. They listened to the voice of the Tempter, obeyed that voice, and fell from God-consciousness into self-consciousness. Their human spirits, then darkened, fell into the black labyrinths of their now unenlightened souls—there to listen (practice the presence) of all the other voices. Out of relationship to God, they were now disrelated.

As those who are fallen, this is where we find ourselves: *disrelated*—assailed by other voices. As those who heal in Christ's Name, this is where we find the needy ones—listening to all the other voices.

Adam and Eve hid. So we all do, all who've listened to and obeyed the other voices. Here is the self-in-separation: autonomous, denying the Presence, wanting to be God.

Worship of God is the ultimate denial of this old self in separation.

Jesus, the New Adam, came practicing always the Presence of the Father. ". . . the Son . . . can do only what he sees the Father doing, because whatever the Father does the Son also does" (John 5:19). After His baptism, He was led by the Spirit into the wilderness to be tempted—even as Adam and Eve were—by the Devil. Satan ended his temptation by showing Christ the kingdoms of this world: "All this I will give you, if you will bow down and worship me."

Worship is at the base of all Satan's temptations. He fell from the Presence, descended into the hell of his self. He desires worship. He says, in effect, "Practice my presence, I will make you great, I will make you a god."

If you and I do not practice the Presence of God, we will practice the presence of another. If we do not listen for the Word, we will be in subjection to the words of the world, the flesh, and the Devil.

Jesus said, "Away from me, Satan! For it is written, Worship the Lord your God, and serve him only."

Rather than taking shortcuts to power, Jesus chose to practice the Presence of the Father. His was never the way of manipulating others, but the way of love, the way of the Cross.

In obedience to what He heard the Father say, He redeemed a fallen world. He died that the true self in each one of us might be transformed, come fully alive, then eternally *become*.

After he was tempted, Jesus began to preach the Good News of the Kingdom, healing all diseases and torments. He collaborated with the Holy Spirit to do the works of His Father. He taught us to do the same. In the doing of this, we come to understand a little about *creative power*.

Prayer for Healing of the Will

When we make our will one with God's, we find that integration of personality begins to take place. This is because, as we make our will one with His, we free Him to gather up those valid parts of ourselves from which we are alienated, estranged. He then affirms and blesses them to us.

> *I pray, Lord, for the release and strengthening of my will, that creative, masculine part of me, that with which I initiate change, choose life, and with which I forsake the bent, idolatrous position of attempting to find my identity in the creature.*
>
> *Show me any way in which I am bent toward the creature; O Lord, reveal any idolatrous or neurotic dependency on persons or things, show me any way in which I demand from the created the identity I can gain only from You, my Creator.*

Visualize (see with your heart) any bentness the Lord is showing you, then see yourself deliberately straightening up from that idol as you pray:

> *I choose, Lord, to forsake this bentness, I confess it to you, just now, as the sin that it is, I renounce it in Your Name, and I thank You for Your forgiveness, I receive it.*

To those who truly repent, I proclaim you forgiven, in Christ's Name. Receive this forgiveness now.

Then pray:

> *Descend into me, divine, masculine, eternal Will, descend into me, radiate up through me. Lord, command what Thou wilt, then WILL what Thou commandest.*
>
> *I thank You, Lord, that my weak and insufficient will is now one with Yours. May I know more and more what it means to be in-willed, in-godded by you. Thank You, Lord, that Your completing, healing work is commenced in me, and will continue in this world and in the next.*

Write in your prayer journal the images of bentness you saw toward mother or father, husband or wife, son or daughter, someone of the same sex or other sex, any way in which you have made an idol of job, money, fame, self (narcissism); then converse with God about them. He will give you understanding of them, and enable you to begin to get at the roots of the idolatries or dependencies that have held you back from full freedom in Him.

CHAPTER 5

Creative Power

*M*an is a *maker*. This is part of what it means to be in the image of our Creator God. As we learn to collaborate with Him, He confirms and mightily blesses the work of our hands. The following prayer of Moses is one that blesses me, even as I pray it, whether for myself or another. It's as if our Heavenly Father eagerly awaits this prayer so He can pour forth His power to bless us in our making.

May the favor of the Lord our God rest upon us: establish the work of our hands. (Psalm 90:17)

When we allow God to bestow His favor and beauty and delightfulness (see the above verse in *Amplified Bible)* on the work of our hands, He makes artists of even the humblest (in terms of natural giftedness) among us.

Christian man is also a *blesser*. This is another part of what it means to be in the image of God, and also of what it means to be in the priesthood of all believers (see 1 Peter 2:4-9). As blessers, we in this priesthood not only reflect the light and life of a holy God to an unholy world, but we are to be sacramental channels of that inestimable blessing to the world. It is as we discover how to be the conduits of God's life and blessing to others that we discover both what the priesthood of all believers means, and our own priesthood. We discover and are awed by the creative power inherent in our role as priest. We learn to bless in the power of the Spirit, and to collaborate with the Spirit to do the works of Christ. (We imitate Christ in this. See Luke 4:1; 5:17; Acts 1:2.)

By and in the power of the Spirit, then, we both make and bless. Thus the artist and the priest are brought together in us. And we find that the ministry of true prayer, that which brings healing to a fallen world and is therefore vital to *soul-making,* is the most creative work in the world.

He who alone has the *Power of Being* said, "Let there be light," and there was light. Let there be worlds, archangels, crabs on the bottom of the ocean floor. *Ex nihilo*, out of nothing, God spoke *being*. He "thought" the world, imagined it, then spoke it into being. "God," said Nicholas Berdyaev, "created the world by imagination."

We as makers do not create in this way, out of nothing. Strictly speaking, only He can ever be called a Creator. But we, in His image, "make" according to the creative principle. (See *The Mind of the Maker* by Dorothy L. Sayers, the classic on this great subject.) An idea or a thought "comes" to us; then we see with our mind's eye (i.e., we imagine) the painting, the building, the book, the project—whether the work of a conference, the creative work of parenting, or prayer for healing, etc. We see it, if ever so vaguely, as the finished whole. Then, as *makers,* we work hard to uncover the work that now has form (if only in the imagination) and therefore an existence apart from ourselves. If we are Christians, there is an added dimension, for we know that we are collaborating with the Spirit of our Creator God to bring to light this work of art.

The prayer of faith illustrates this principle. We first of all get the mind of God on how to pray. Second, we make our request specifically and simply. Third, we see with the mind's eye God's will being done. And fourth, we thank Him most sincerely in advance for doing it.

Originality is, as Lewis has said, the property of God alone. He saw himself as a collaborator with the Spirit of God and knew that for himself, as for the true artist of any kind, the Spirit descended into him and did the work: "When we act from . . . God *in* ourselves—we are collaborators in, or live instruments of, creation."[1]

History records that early Christian martyrs, being carried to their deaths in the Roman arenas, would cry out, "Another will be in me who will suffer for me."[2] They understood and experienced, from the very threshold of their deaths, Paul's words, "yet not I, but Christ liveth in me" (Galatians 2:20, KJV). They understood Incarnational Reality.

Lewis, Dorothy Sayers, and other great Christian artists have understood this from the standpoint of being Christians, but they also understood fully this principle as it applies to art. Artists who are far from understanding the Christian reality have, from the Greeks up to our century, generally understood this principle. Most have realized and acknowledged that from sources outside and higher than themselves have come both the inspiration and the true breadth and depth of the finished work. And they've been humbled in the face of it. (In Greek thought this principle of inspiration coming from without was represented by nine goddesses, the Muses, who presided over literature, the arts, and sciences: Calliope, Clio, Euterpe, Melpomene, Terpsichore,

Erato, Polyhymnia, Urania, Thalia. They more or less personified the spirit that was thought to inspire poetic or scientific genius.)

Artists, like saints and martyrs, find they must die to the clamorings of the old self in order to discover and then serve the work that is already there. That work has an existence apart from themselves. "I am pregnant with book," said Lewis. An author, he said, does not necessarily understand his own work better than someone else. The artist learns that he must die to a myriad of other voices in order to faithfully "listen to the work" and thereby uncover it for others to see. Michelangelo said of his *Moses* and his *David* that they were in the stone clamoring to be freed. He chipped away the stone to uncover the masterpieces.

The artist, then, is not creator. He is merely discoverer and servant to the work that is already there. The work says: "Release me from chaos; give me my form, my shape, my being." And listening to the work, the artist frees it to become, to *be*.

The Spirit brings form out of chaos. In the beginning God gave perfect form and beauty to the earth. The angelic rebellion brought chaos: "And the earth was without form, and void; and darkness was upon the face of the deep. And the Spirit of God moved [hovered] upon the face of the waters" (Genesis 1:2, KJV). The Spirit gave form and beauty back to the earth.

So it is with the soul of man. Fallen, it is chaotic, like the earth after the angelic fall. Without form and void, it cries out to be delivered from chaos, to be given its form, its beauty.

Even as the work of art has an existence apart from the artist, so the soul of man has an existence apart from the priest who would bless and minister to it. The priest, while recognizing and revering the unique soul, listens intently to its cries for help. He listens also, with all his being, to God, the Creator of his soul, and collaborates with the Spirit of God to free it from chaos, to order, to give form and meaning to the soul that *is* there—whole, complete in the mind of God.

"Give to me my form, give to me my being," the soul in chaos cries out. "Separate me from the darkness, the stone. I'm here—*all* of me is here—free me!"

And the Spirit, when we invite Him, broods over us and the situation. He comes into us who are priests of Almighty God, and He does it!

This is healing prayer. This is true creativity.

PART II

INCARNATIONAL REALITY: THE PRESENCE OF GOD WITHIN US

We need a new center,
not a transformation but a transposition
We need the completion
not of the soul but of its radical change
A new order of life and love
A new ethic born of the spirit.[1]

(P.T. Forsythe)

CHAPTER 6

The Presence of God Within Us

*And I will put my Spirit in you and move you to follow my decrees
and be careful to keep my laws.*

(Ezekiel 36:27)

G od sends His Spirit into ours, and there His life abides. Christ is
formed within. St. Paul, in his prayer for the Ephesians, expresses
it this way:

> I pray that out of his [the Father's] glorious riches he may
> strengthen you with power through his Spirit in your inner
> being, so that Christ may dwell in your hearts through faith.
> (3:16, 17)

To experience this prayer fulfilled in our lives is to find our true center, the "home within" that is strong and solid, a place of rest and
strength. From that center we live. From that center we "abide" in Christ
and He in us. We are to practice His Presence. We no longer have to live
from the center of the lower self, the unspiritual or incomplete self which
is compelled and driven from its position of self-centeredness.

Fr. John Gaynor Banks writes of this true center:

> There is a Center in every man in which and through which God
> works. To that Center He speaks; through that Center He acts.
> When a man discovers his own divine Center, he stands at the
> gateway to powerful living.[1]

But we can be Christians and yet, when immature or unhealed psychologically, fail to live from our true center. Rather, we live out of a

complex of diseased feelings, attitudes, and, as we shall see, images or symbols that have nothing to do with our new selves in Christ.

There are three blocks to discovering one's true center. The first two have to do with the forgiveness of sin: either our failure to *forgive* others, or our failure to *receive forgiveness* from God. The third has to do with one's own inner vision of oneself and the failure to acquire the virtue of self-acceptance. However much a person lives out of diseased attitudes and feelings toward the self, to that extent he will fail to find and live from his true center where God dwells, speaks, and empowers him.

In the Presence the True Self Emerges

In two of my earlier books, *The Broken Image* and *Crisis in Masculinity*, I tell about one person after another who could not live from the center because of a diseased inner vision of themselves. And they were all healed the same way. They came into the Presence of God and *listened*. There illumination, forgiveness, cleansing, and healing took place. Fixing their eyes solely on Him, they climbed up and out of the old center of self and into their new center, which is His Presence living in them. (Note here the practice of the Presence of God in His sovereign otherness, His objective reality. To lose that is to lose His immanent dimension.) To remain in the true center is to gain not only release from diseased attitudinal patterns, but the great virtue of self-acceptance.

Only the real "I," shedding its illusory selves, can draw near to God. In His Presence, my masks fall off, my false selves are revealed. I stand stripped and naked before Him. To continually abide in His Presence is to have one face only—the true one. To draw near Him, therefore, is to find the real "I" as well as its true home, my true center. Prior to this, I am split; I walk alongside myself, I am egocentric, I am uncentered.

When a Man Walks Alongside Himself: The Split Condition

In *Crisis in Masculinity*, I tell about Richard, a man who was split off from his true self. He lived (most of the time) out of the immature, hurting little boy: the small lad who early in life, due to grievous reaction to trauma and to an ongoing inability to relate meaningfully to his father, began to live out of diseased, inferior feelings about himself. He was unaffirmed as a male (sexual identity) and as a man (full gender identity). He was unable to separate his personal and sexual identity from that of his mother's. He saw his father as manly and masculine, but he could not "touch" it in him. He could not bond with his father's masculinity in such a way as to find his own "ignited" and blessed. His own masculinity was all there, but his feeling about himself was such that he could never recognize it. These feelings took up such an autonomous life within him that affirming words from others simply went in one ear and out the other—he could not receive them.

He did not live from the center as an affirmed son would, that blessed stance which is a more or less unconscious position. Instead, he lived very self-consciously out of a cluster of diseased attitudes and feelings toward himself. He was split. There was a terrible chasm of non-being within him. He therefore had the disease of introspection. Richard stood, as it were, outside himself, analyzing, hating, rejecting, pitying, despairing over himself. If we think of this in terms of a complex of inferior, negative feelings about the self, we can see that he was living from the *locus* of an inferiority neurosis. That was his home, his center.

To live from that center is to live from that which is not real but illusory, an illusory person living in an illusory world. Richard, before his healing, was not living from the real self, the real Richard. As a Christian, he had a home within, a divine center from which to live, but he knew nothing of it. Unhealed, he was still bent toward the creature and living from the wrong center.

In the more serious cases, this illusory or insubstantial self spins whole paranoid and delusional worlds out of its diseased feelings and imaginings. It may weave around itself another personality entirely. Joseph, feeling sexually inferior and rejected, can become Josephine, an illusionary woman, a female impersonation. He can begin to live as a "woman," a thing that has no real existence. The thing that is not then takes to itself an autonomous, compulsive existence, replete with new sets of diseased feelings and lusts from which the real Joseph will have to be delivered. Until he is set free, *that which is not will have him in bondage*.

We are not here referring to multiple personality disorder or related psychological disorders. But this illustration exemplifies an imaginary life spun out of the abnormal and the crooked: all the diseased feelings arising out of the sins of self-pity, envy, fear, hate, and so on. This is in absolute contrast to an imaginary world which arises out of the normal and the straight, and from the appropriate desires and feelings arising out of the good, the true, and the beautiful. The character of Anne in L. M. Montomery's novel *Anne of Green Gables* is a wonderful example of a child with normal and appropriate feelings. Her imaginings are an extension of the real, not the illusory world. Although her circumstances are extremely difficult as an orphan, she is always looking for that which gives "scope for the imagination"—in other words, for that which broadens her horizons to see beyond herself and her present predicament. She has the imaginative capacity to see the silver lining in every rain cloud, to see the straight and the beautiful when faced with the crooked and the bleak. And she survives by imagining it until such time as she realizes it!

The wonderful thing about healing prayer is that we are given the power to recognize and hate the delusion—and to walk away from it. And we are given the power to accept the true center and walk into it.

An awful example of failure *to choose* to live from the center is given us in Charles Williams's novel *Descent into Hell*. In it he shockingly images one man's fall when he elects to love himself in exclusion to the more troublesome and time-consuming flesh-and-blood woman. In her place he takes to himself a succubus, an occult term for an imaginary woman. This is in actuality the practice of masturbation with an accompanying fantasy life. The reader watches in horror as the real personality of this man, Wentworth, deteriorates, as his grasp on a real woman loosens, and as the illusory world he step by step *chooses* becomes more important, compulsive, and even horrifyingly bleak to him. We then see Wentworth's deliberate and devastating descent into the hell of the false or narcissistic self. The real Wentworth is finally swallowed up by the illusionary self, a center or locus from which he is finally unable to choose the good. He is then utterly passive and unfeeling, even though he *realizes* he is falling into perdition.

Here the creative masculine will, that which can choose joy and initiate change, has been utterly abdicated; it is now helpless. "Hell," says Charles Williams, "is an image that bears no more becoming." In Dante's *Inferno*, Satan is set into a block of ice in the bottom rung of Hell. That is the image Charles Williams had in mind when he made this statement. Wentworth is now, like Satan, set in ice. For him there would be no more becoming.

Sin has to do, in a very real sense, with rebelliously demanding to experience *what is not*—what God did not create and can never look upon, much less bless. The facets of evil we call black magic, witchcraft, and sorcery illustrate this. The evil magician or sorcerer evokes the phantoms, the illusions that would *consume* the naive, the unwary, those who are not living from the center. The evil magicians call into "being" the illusory, that which hates reality.

Satan and his minions hate all that is created: all of Nature, the very *matter* that goes to make up our world, our minds and bodies. The Satanic aim is to twist, defile, and destroy us—spirit, soul, and body. To achieve his aim, he uses that which is spun from our illusory, bent selves and worlds. The pornographic images, including those of murderous hate and death, openly portrayed and hawked on such a great scale throughout the world, are demonic. They participate in witchcraft. Of this kind of evil, Charles Williams writes:

It is cold, it is hungry, it is violent, it is illusory. The warm blood of children and the intercourse at the Sabbath does not satisfy it. It wants something more and other; it wants "obedience," it wants "souls," and yet pines for matter. It never was, and yet it always is.[2]

Here and in his novels and poetry, Charles Williams is concerned with how that which *never was* takes form. In an unfinished poem, "The Figure of Arthur," he uses the myth of King Arthur to further explore this same unreality. Arthur, in his lust, unknowingly lies with his half-sister, the evil Queen Morgause, and she gives birth to their son, Mordred, who kills his father. C. S. Lewis, explicating this poem, explains that Williams's

concern is not with the psychological origins of evil but with its metaphysical 'procession,' its intrusion from nightmare into reality, the horrible stages whereby what ought not to be at all becomes an image, and what ought to be only an image becomes stone, and what ought to be only stone becomes a woman, and what ought to be only a woman becomes her son.[3]

Thus we have a clearer picture of how that which *never was* takes form.

All that is evil and untrue has an illusionary character to it, and can seriously bluff us when we are without God's wisdom and knowledge. While all that participates in the lie, in evil, can only fragment and destroy, all that participates in the Good is substantively real and creative.

Williams shows us evil as miscreation: Morgause gives birth to the misbegotten Mordred, who betrays and murders his father, the King. According to C.S. Lewis, it is "the bringing to be of what must not (and even in a sense cannot) be, yet now *it is,* as though monstrous members, horns, trunks, feelers, tusks, were sprouting out of the body."[4]

We must see the connection that evil as miscreation has with diseased attitudinal patterns and fantasy lives, things common not only to full-blown neuroses (sexual and otherwise), but to all who fail to find and live from their true center.

For Richard and for every one of us, it is dangerous to live out of the compulsive, illusory self—that center of pride, inferiority, fear, and pain, the hurting, unhealed childish attitudes within. We are often told to accept that self. *We are not to.* The "child within" is healed, accepted, and integrated into our being as a whole. But we must die to its misconceived attitudes and illusory self, for we cannot abide in Christ there. To abide there is to abide in misbegotten feeling; it is to abide in the lie, in the illusion which the Tempter would con us into accepting.

People who have long lived out such a diseased center find their way to our Pastoral Care Schools and healing meetings, where we simply lift up Christ and His Cross and invite Him to heal. After finding healing and learning to live from their true center, they return home, practicing the Presence of Jesus and listening for His every command. It is then not unusual to receive a letter from them describing the spiritual battle that took them by storm, of the intense pull of the powers of darkness, often during the night, to snatch them out of their true center and back into the old—that place where the Evil One steals our minds, our giftedness, our lives. That is when they begin to learn that the Evil One, though he can seriously bluff us, has only the power we give to him. That is when they learn about the spiritual authority available to all who are united to Christ and His people and who live from the center where He dwells and speaks.

Sometime after this battle is won, it is not unusual to get yet another letter. An interesting thing about us mortals is that we are often afraid of our true selves. We have to accept them, but we tend to run from them. Pauline Anstruther, the heroine of *Descent into Hell*, illustrates this condition we must face once we determine to live from our true center. She is in contrast to Wentworth, who chooses to live only for himself. But she too is immature. She lives out of, we might say, a complex of inner fears, one that culminates in abject terror when, as on occasion it happened, she sees herself coming toward herself. She runs from the vision of the real. Finally she decides not to run and to face the other Pauline, and the immature, fearful self vanishes.

The Green Lady, you will recall, said to Ransom:

"I have never done it before—stepping out of life into the
Alongside and looking at oneself living as if one were not alive.
Do they all do that in your world, Piebald?"[5]

The answer is, yes—we all do it in Piebald's world. And some of us keep on doing it for all our lifetime. And that is what spiritual and most psychological illness is. The Good News, the gospel message, is that we don't have to be split; we don't have to live out of "the Alongside." I hope by now it is perfectly clear that it is not at all difficult for God to heal us—if only we choose to die to the illusion. The process of recognition can be gradual or can be instant. Then we only need practice His Presence, make our will one with His, and draw near Him and our own center.

O Lord, send the warm, even blazing fires of Your Holy Spirit to melt any icy block that has frozen me into no more becoming in You. May I become throughout all eternity. Grant to me greater actuality of soul, of being, even now in this very moment, O Lord, as I emerge out of the icy hardness.

Teach me to pray the prayer of faith for others who are even now being hardened in such a hellish mold. Bless Your Church, Lord, that it might become more and more the Fellowship of the Holy Spirit, and thus be aflame with the healing Light that sends its rays instantly through the hearts of men, freeing them to become. Father, in Jesus' name I ask that You make any immaturity, any neurotic complex within me apparent, so that from this point on I will recognize it instantly and will know the very moment I am living from that center rather than from my true center in you.

I thank You, Lord, that You have heard my prayer, and that You are even now answering it.

(Quietly wait, allowing Him to show you your heart and speak His truth to you.)

CHAPTER 7

Incarnational Reality:
The Christian Union with God

"On that day you will realize that I am in my Father, and you are in me, and I am in you."

(John 14:20)

G od's great secret, and Christians' hope of glory, as St. Paul tells the Colossian believers, that secret kept from the generations and the centuries past, is this: "Christ in you" (Colossians 1:27).

The Christian union with God is Christ in us, uniting us to God the Father and all that is ultimate reality. This differs radically from all ideologies concerning union and communion with God. It differs even from many ideologies and theologies that purport to be Christian, but in fact are "other gospels." There is no way to synthesize or reconcile the reality of Christ in us with the various other modes men devise to get to God. We do not climb a ladder of knowledge, goodness, or good works to God. Any such mode bypasses the Incarnation and the Cross. Rather, Christ descends to us and into us. He incarnates us. We are indwelt, ingodded.

Keeping the Balance

It is theologically proper to assert that God is essentially and primarily transcendent and secondarily immanent. This is to say, he is above us before he is within us and beneath us.[1]

As a theologian, Dr. Donald Bloesch reminds us that God is first of all sovereign and transcendent. His immanence is based in His transcen-

dence and proceeds out of that. If we lose the objective dimension in the
practice of His Presence, we will soon lose the immanent (subjective)
dimension as well. The subjective real depends on maintaining the objective real. Oswald Chambers says it this way:

> Spiritual leakage begins when we cease to lift up our eyes unto
> Him. The leakage comes not so much through trouble on the
> outside as in the imagination.[2]

Recently I was startled to have a divinity student exclaim to me, "I
must go pray to the God within me." I immediately said, "No, you may
thank God that Christ's Spirit is within you, saving you, hallowing you,
linking you to Him. But when you pray, you look up to the God who is
other than you, sovereign over all." We do not pray to God *in* us, but look
up and out of ourselves to the Three in One. Otherwise we are leaky vessels. Otherwise our imaginations have lost the real pattern and full
dimension of Incarnational Reality: the fact that God comes down to us.

Therefore, even though we joyously affirm, "Another lives in me,"
there is a vital sense in which we are always needing to "draw near" to
Him in order that He might draw near to us (James 4:8; Hebrews 10:22).
If we lose God's otherness and our own balance in this matter, then He
will have to once again say: "Am I only a God nearby . . . and not a God
far away?" (Jeremiah 23:23). We must constantly cry out to Him to come;
we must invoke His Presence. But the whole meaning of the Incarnation
is that the Sovereign Lord has become present to us, through His Son and
by His Spirit. Jesus mediates the Presence of the Father to us. By the
Father's Spirit, Jesus lives in us. Therefore, "Be ye holy, because I am
holy" (1 Peter 1:15). And He is with us, enabling us so to be.

How We Lost the Incarnational Understanding

In the fourth century, immense changes occurred within Christendom,
among them a critical shift in perspective. From the understanding of
being an indwelt and therefore a holy people, we began to think in terms
of holy *things*. In an unholy fear of God, the individual Christian began
to lose God's immanent, comforting presence. (We see this phenomenon
over and over again in some Christians who come for healing prayer.
They can only think in terms of God's sovereignty and not of His immanence and their own unworthiness apart from His sanctifying Presence.
This is why historically revival and renewal are characterized by bap-
tisms in the Spirit, the restoration of the sense of God's holy Presence
filling the human temple.)

The Lord's Table then became a fearful, holy place, one where the
eucharistic Cup (like our Sovereign God) was to be held high above us

and adored (in effect, worshiped). The difference between this conception and the incarnational one the early Christians held is striking indeed. The early disciple raced to the Lord's Table to take once again his place "in the Cup." This was a symbolic action. But it was not merely a symbolic one, for in doing this he "died" once again with Christ to the sins of the world, his own included. He also rose with Christ once again in newness of life, forgiven and strengthened anew to do Christ's mighty works in the world. This is still what makes the Communion service the greatest healing service the Church has to offer, for when this action is rightly understood and experienced, forgiveness of sins, known and unknown, comes to us. The psychological as well as spiritual implications of such a change are enormous. From seeing the Lord's Table as an extension of the work of baptism, strengthening him once again to be a faithful witness and extension of Christ in the world, the individual Christian slipped to the dreadful position of cowering guilt, fear, and immaturity. He then cried out for someone or something between himself and God.

This shift is related to the Edict of Toleration proclaimed by Constantine in 313 A.D., when the world quite literally rushed into the Church. With the great masses of people coming for baptism, it was impossible to fully prepare them for it. Their sins were not properly dealt with. There was little or none of the basic healing prayer work that prepares the catechumen for baptism. Therefore, though baptized, these souls were filled with guilt and darkness and cried out for a mediator between themselves and God. It was here that we lost (for all practical purposes) the New Testament concept of the "priesthood of believers" and developed the notion of the "laity"—those who demand a priest or some other mediator between themselves and a holy, righteous God. From the willingness and capacity to be a witness and a powerful channel of God's Presence in the world, even in the face of martyrdom, the individual Christian became one fearful even to "take the Cup."

Charles Williams notes a later hardening of this critical shift in thought at the time of the Renaissance. In *Descent of the Dove: A Short History of the Holy Spirit in the Church*, he tells of Felicitas (an early Christian martyr who died in 205 A.D.), who "in a sentence defined the Faith." While in prison she gave birth to a child, and in her pain she cried out. Her jailers asked her

> . . . how, if she shrieked at that, she expected to endure death by the wild beasts. She said: "Now I suffer what I suffer; then another will be in me who will suffer for me, as I shall suffer for him." In that Felicitas took her place for ever among the great African doctors of the Universal Church.[3]

Writing then of the later historical period, and referring back to Felicitas's marvelous reply, Charles Williams wrote:

The cry of "Another is in Me" had faded, the Renascence glory was not attributed to the acts of that other.[4]

The final hardening, however, and one toward which this shift was steadily moving, occurred in the eighteenth century. It is one from which the Church and all of the Western world is presently reeling. We are indebted to C.S. Lewis for his insights here, as Calvin D. Linton writes:

One of Lewis's major contributions as a literary historian and scholar was to show that the great watershed in Western sensibility came not with the Renaissance, as is still often popularly preached but with the Romantic movement. . . . In showing that the basic alteration in man's view of himself in modern history (that is, since A.D. 500) is the eighteenth-century shift from a God-centered universe of order, hierarchy, purpose, and "dance and harmony" to a man-centered (that is, self-centered) cosmology of the psyche, Lewis has provided a frame within which we can better understand the Middle Ages and the Renaissance, and more fully accept the validity of the Scripture's warning that to worship the creature rather than the Creator is to bring disarray to all aspects of human existence.[5]

From the eighteenth-century on, we have the non-practice of the Presence of God increasing, whether within the human temple, the Sacraments, or even our planet home, the earth itself. The astronomers had discovered something of the astounding size of the universe, and no longer believed that the earth itself was the center of it. The people of God, having steadily lost even the power to conceive of Christ's Presence within—that is, God incarnationally centering Himself in His people—could only be overwhelmed at the size of the universe and themselves apparently adrift and unattached to God within it. The discoveries of the great astronomers seemed only to confirm the absence of God which people were already feeling. Having first shoved Him out of themselves and into holy things, they then shoved Him out into the earth itself as if it were somehow a geographical center of God's love and concern. From there they shoved Him out into the cosmos, where He became merely the Great Watchmaker, and finally, with Nietzsche, out of the universe altogether. No longer holding an incarnational view of man and reality, the Christian imagination failed. It was unable to integrate the new scientific findings into its diminished picture of religious truth. Its symbolic system held the picture of an aloof and (on the whole) terrifying God.[6]

This profound and deep dualism reached its ultimate philosophical expression in Rene Descartes's famous maxim, "I think, therefore I am." We can properly speak of a "Cartesian revolution" because Descartes's thought fueled not only the Enlightenment but also the Romantic Movement and such destructive Post-Romantic movements as Nihilism and Modernism. For a clear and concise understanding of Descartes, the issues of the time that impelled him, and his dualism that ended by separating mind from soul and body, see William Barrett's superb book *Death of the Soul: From Descartes to the Computer*. In response to a cosmos expanded beyond man's power to imagine it, Descartes, as a thinker, projected "human consciousness to the center of philosophy."[7] He then attempted to lift man out of his profound state of uncertainty about his place in the cosmos through the consideration of himself as a *conscious perceiver* of the universe. Descartes's solution was: Even if we doubt everything else (objective reality), there is no doubt of ourselves as conscious subject. I have a light within me, so to speak. The light is my consciousness. With that tiny light, I can look up into the cosmos and know myself as a conscious "I," a perceiver.

> Thus Descartes launches himself on his famous systematic doubt, through the course of which the ego remains as an unshakable point of departure and return. I may doubt the existence of objects in the external world, but I cannot doubt my own consciousness of them. If I doubt the existence of my own consciousness, the doubt itself is a conscious act. So the ego comes back upon itself in its own unshakable self-certainty, shining luminously against a dubitable world.
>
> But having thus extracted the mind from its world, Descartes is hard put to get it back into the world. For that purpose he must invoke the help of God. The laborious doubt has left him with a painful sense of his own finitude and imperfections, but he has also the idea of a Perfect Being, complete and self-grounding, embracing all reality. This idea cannot be from himself, imperfect as he is, and therefore must have been produced in him by this Perfect Being itself. Moreover, being perfect, God must exist, since non-existence would be an imperfection. . . .
>
> Armed, then, with the premise that there is a God, Descartes can now set about restoring the ego to the world from which his systematic doubt had torn it. . . .
>
> But notice that this ego that is to be restored to its world is

only an abstract ego, the *ego coqitans*, the ego as knower or scientist, and not the concrete self that you and I are. How is this concrete self, with all its physical, sensuous, and emotional life, to be restored to the Cartesian world? And here the problems of Descartes's dualism between body and mind—become particularly acute.

The soul is more inclusive, more encompassing, than reason.[8]

As I was thinking about Descartes's life and thought, the realization that he and Brother Lawrence lived and wrote in the same century and endured many of the same political and intellectual upheavals was quite forcefully borne in on me. The contrast in the two is remarkable. The conclusions Descartes comes to through intellectual reasoning, and the joyous knowledge of how man is linked to God that Brother Lawrence comes to through prayer and the practice of the Presence illustrates so well the trouble we get into when we try to think about reality in separation from an inner knowledge of it.

After Descartes, the split between thought and experience (the two minds: head and heart) steadily widened into the chasm it is today. From the understanding that God had "thought" them into existence, creating them in His image, Christians and Jews alike began with Descartes to try to think themselves into existence. They lost the vital incarnational understanding of the co-inherence of all things (the "God-centered universe of order, hierarchy, purpose, and 'dance and harmony'"), including those faculties that made up their own inner cosmos. Descartes's dictum became the basis of Enlightenment thought, and the full shift from a God-centered to a man-centered cosmology was secured.

In this way, the Christian incarnational view of man and reality (including, of course, a truly Christian spirituality and its concomitant psychology) has been almost entirely lost to us—even in great part to those who continued faithful to the Scriptures. The man in the church pew, along with his fellow in the classroom and on the street, has lost even the terminology with which to speak and meditate upon it.

Christianity is incarnational. We are linked to Ultimate Reality by His Presence within. Christian epistemology is unique in that our way of knowing is rooted in Christ's incarnational Presence. To any degree we depart from this understanding, we substitute the means for the end—religion for God Himself—the letter of the law for the Spirit that quickens—church buildings and organizations for the fellowship of the Body—aesthetic appreciation (our own sentiments and feelings about beauty and truth) for the Truth—theology (our ideas about God) for God. The Sacraments, rather than being perceived and received aright, are thus either emptied of meaning or become churchly idols. "To a phenomenal degree, appearance has replaced reality," states John A. Mackay in his classic on this subject.[9]

Christ in us and we in Him: this is the concrete reality. God was incarnate of Mary by the Spirit of Christ; man is indwelt, in-gifted, in-graced, in-godded.

This is why our eclecticism (so prevalent in the Church today, as many non-Christian ideas flood in) will not work. Herein is the (dreadful to some) exclusiveness of the Christian truth and reality that we are to proclaim. There is no possibility for eclecticism in it. In the Presence, unless they will to remain separate, men are born anew. Moslems, Hindus, Hebrews who walk into the Presence and power of the Holy Spirit are quickly remade. They become Christians.

"By definition," says Charles Williams, "Christendom cannot fundamentally admit the right of an Opposition [to its dogma] to exist: to refuse the co-inherence [of God and man by His Spirit] is to separate oneself from the very nature of things."[10]

To be separate from the Presence is indeed to be separate from all that is ultimately real. Only as the Church cries for incarnation, for the Presence and power of the Holy Spirit in her midst, can she hope to reach those who are in fact separated from the very nature of things.

Protection from false ideologies, philosophies, and mysticisms resides in our living in this truth experientially and with understanding. How can we know truth? Ultimate Reality? The great liberal arts institutions were founded to pursue this very question. This was, historically, what the university student sought to know. We know Ultimate Reality, not by theological ideas about it, even though these are necessary, but by union with it, by taking our place "in the Cup," in Christ's death and resurrection—by knowing that we are centered in God and He in us.

Due to the loss of an incarnational understanding of reality, the Christian imagination has long been eclectic; that is, it has to a great extent been resymbolized. It is not enough merely to have an intellectual grasp of Judeo-Christian truth—that is, to have head knowledge of the Scriptures. We must also have an imaginative grasp of Christianity—that is, a heart and imagination baptized in symbolic truth, a deep knowledge of all reality as incarnational. Failure to integrate the intellectual and imaginative aspects of Christian truth puts us at the mercy of other symbolic systems. Dr. Donald G. Bloesch opens his book *The Battle for the Trinity* by saying: "Two decades ago the principal issues in the church were whether the Bible should be demythologized (Bultmann) or deliteralized (Tillich). Now the main issue is whether the Bible should be resymbolized."[11]

The Judeo-Christian Scriptures are the great guardian and repository of the Christian (that is, the thoroughly incarnational) symbolic system. The modern Christian, reading the Bible, is all too often blinded to great parts of it, and simply screens out the portions for which his mind no longer has an imaginative category with which to think. But the Spirit, working with the Word, has always the chance to open the eyes of the reader to the true nature of reality. To those who accept a resymbolized Bible, however, the final hardening in the shift from a God-centered to a man-centered cosmology will have occurred. The old Gnosticisms with their occult ways of knowing will come in new dress (such as has occurred already in Jungian and feminist Gnosticisms) and will permanently blind them. The present push to resymbolize the Bible is a push to irreversibly harden the eighteenth-century shift in thought, one that is already critically difficult to reverse in the human psyche. Psychological and emotional healings through prayer have to do with a miraculous resymbolizing of the human heart, one that restores to it the Scriptural, incarnational view of reality.

With the Christian's loss of the Judeo-Christian symbolic system, new systems rich with alien symbolic imagery have flooded in. The symbolism of Free Masonry, the occult, and the various Eastern, pagan, pantheistic and Gnostic (feminist, Jungian, New Age) systems now informs the minds and hearts of many churchgoers.

Misguided reactions to this problem can be quite as harmful to the Body of Christ as the problem itself. Certain Christian groups and individuals, noted for their anti-intellectual and anti-imaginative stances, have misunderstood symbol and the symbolic mind altogether. Terrified over the influx of these alien symbolic systems, they rise up as cult-hunters lumping together the false and the true, whether of an intellectual or an imaginative nature. These groups and individuals do not realize that they too are victims, thoroughly modern and given over to dwarfed Christian symbolic systems. Their warped views lead them to label as heretical or occult all they do not understand. Ironically, their highly rationalized religious systems—with the intellectual drive toward power not balanced by the deep heart's wisdom and love—are even more dangerous to the Body of Christ than some of the manifestly un-Christian systems they condemn. This is because, to paraphrase C.S. Lewis, if being Christian does not make one an awful lot better, it can make one an awful lot worse. Such a one becomes a religious tyrant who, in the name of a religious cause, has a great deal of power to do harm.

To sum up, then: the understanding of how we know Ultimate Reality is lost to modern man, which is another way of expressing Pope John Paul's words, "The sense of the presence of God is vanishing from the earth." Furthermore, we have lost even the language and the imagery with which to express this truth. This is, of course, why Christian students have such difficult times in institutions of higher learning, and why great Christian scholarship is not accepted.

Incarnational Reality has to do with the embodiment of spiritual reality in material form: God in union with man. Sacramental reality exhibits the principle of the Incarnation; it has to do with the Presence of God being channeled to us through material means. God does not despise matter; He deigns to come to us through the womb of Mary, through the baptismal waters, through the Communion Cup. As Charles Williams has said, "The Incarnation has forever hallowed the flesh." Hatred or fear of the body, the imagination, the intellect, or any part of ourselves is not Christian. As C.S. Lewis has said, "If the whole man is offered to God, all disputes about the value of this or that faculty is, as it were, henceforward out of date."[12]

In my trek through the university (both Christian and secular), I chose the Communion Cup, with all its meaning, as a symbol of Incarnational Reality, and I kept it before me as I studied. I measured the systems of this world (philosophies, religions, mysticisms) and their meaning against this great symbol of Christian truth and reality, and there they all fell short. Of every great philosopher, mystic, and artist I read, I asked, "What for you is Ultimate Reality, and how do you say man knows it?" This made the writing of critical papers exciting indeed, and forced me into naming and comparing their symbolic systems. How puny and insignificant those systems, how without hope and meaningless, in comparison to the Christian reality of Christ in me, my hope of glory, my way of knowing and of being linked with ultimate truth and reality.

A Brief Biographical Sketch of My Discovery of the Christian Reality

> For to me, to live is Christ. . . . I no longer live, but Christ lives in me. (St. Paul, in Philippians 1:21; Galatians 2:20)

It took three major lessons in Incarnational Reality, two of them extremely painful, before the full meaning of Paul's words ("Christ . . . in me") sank permanently into my soul.

The first lesson came when I was a young girl, yet in grade school. My aunt took me to a church service that featured several speakers. I have no idea what was preached, but the prayers of the people permeated the place, and the Holy Spirit was there. I was a believer, but felt drawn toward the altar that night as the call to receive Christ was given. Kneeling there, praying with all my might (only an unction from the Holy Spirit could enable a person, much less a child, to pray like that), I had what would now be described as a most remarkable baptism of the Spirit. The Spirit descended upon me and into me. There is no describing that experience. I can only say that the living Presence entered as a holy fire throughout my being and, filling me, ascended both as a holy shout and as a holy wine, bubbling up in sheerest, most incredible joy. Later, sleeping between my Aunt Maude's fresh, crisp linen sheets, I felt exquisitely "clean" (purified and holy) to my very fingers and toes.

I lived in the glow of that experience, but as it turned out, I had not the understanding to go along with it. Several months after the sensory experience faded, I began to try to "recapture" it. As a child and on into my early teens, I feared that if I did not sense God's Presence in some way, He was not there. After adolescence, and in early adulthood, I gave up striving to experience God and gradually lost my way. This is the very lesson C. S. Lewis learned and wrote of so well: the taking of the eyes off the object from which the joy comes, and onto the experience or track it leaves in the sensory being. To keep one's eye on the object is the only way. At any rate, this was the lesson that would elude me for a number of years, years when I left the path God had intended for me. During those years, though, there was in my memory, however dimmed and obscured, a time when I knew the reality of "Another in me."

The time came when, humbled and brought to the end of myself, I knelt in obedience before God. Remembering with sinking heart the fruitless striving to apprehend God in my youth, I prayed, "Lord, if I never know Your Presence again, if I never make Heaven, yet I will serve You. I will obey You the best I can." That, of course, was what the Lord was waiting for.

> "If you obey my commands, you will remain in my love, just as
> I have obeyed my Father's commands and remain in his love. I
> have told you this so that my joy may be in you and that your
> joy my be complete." (John 15:10, 11)

My eyes would now be solely on the Object. From the Scriptures, I took every command of Christ, personalized it (addressed it to myself by name), and wrote it in a prayer journal. I meditated on these and asked God to show me how best to carry out these commands in the many ways they applied to me right where I was. I was very needy—a young mother, divorced, seeking to make a living and get a full Christian education for her young one. I began to know joy. I grew in Him.

Shortly after this growth began, I had my second big lesson in Incarnational Reality. This occurred when, for the first time in my life, I had a real enemy, one whose actions issued, at least in part, out of a terrible ignorance.

I had grown up in a home with a devout and wise Christian mother. My father had died when I was barely three, and through the tragedy of his early death my mother had come to a fuller knowledge of Christ and an utter dependence upon Him. There was not the least discernible particle of anger, bitterness, hatred, guile, self-pity, envy, or any other vice I can think of in her being. She had no "dysfunctional patterns" to pass on. Because of this, I literally did not know how to act or stay angry. Disillusioned, hurt, disappointed, outraged—all these things I could be momentarily, but these states quickly passed with the proper response to whatever the provocation might be. I can remember thinking how cute my classmates were when they were angry. And once I seriously practiced "being mad" when the situation seemed to call for it. Only I never learned; I seemed to take people just like Mama did: with "a grain of salt," as she would say, or at the worst, "considering the source" (meaning the circumstances out of which "poor so-and-so" did whatever he or she did).

Then, with the advent of knowing what a real enemy is, I suddenly found myself in the grip of a temptation to hate, a temptation so overpowering and strong that I could not throw it off. From this person I had suffered assaults that were irrational and weighted by envy, lying, and slander. But on this day a final act came to light, one that to me was and still is unthinkable, one certainly designed to destroy me and all I held dear. The act went right to the core of me. In pain and amazement, I knew for the first time how in the passion of hate one person could kill another human being. I also knew that if hate came into my heart, my walk with Christ would end.

I fell to my knees and cried out to God for help. "Please do not let me hate," I cried over and over. Getting no relief, I phoned a friend to come over and help me pray. All afternoon, having thrown myself face-down over the living room ottoman, I cried out to God, and my prayer partner cried out with me. There were terrible moments in that interminable afternoon when I wondered what I would do if God failed to help me, if I would simply have to cry out like this the rest of my life. Then came a moment when instantly my pleading was interrupted by an amazing awareness of Christ in me, and from that center where He and I were mysteriously one, forgiveness was extended to my enemy. It was as if Christ in and through me forgave the person (who can explain such a thing?)—yet I too forgave. At the same moment, I was delivered out of the grip of the worst temptation I've ever known, one designed to engender in me the terrible capacity to truly hate another human being.

That night I was awakened by a thunderous Masculine Voice (one I took to be God the Father's), and it boomed out the words of St. Paul: "To me, to live is Christ." I had never understood what these words meant, but as I sat bolt upright in bed, the meaning washed over me, never to depart. It meant letting Christ live in me, letting Him love even my worst enemies through me.

> Do you not know that your body is a temple of the Holy Spirit, who is in you, whom you have received from God? You are not your own. (1 Corinthians 6:19)

Christ had been there all the time. I had only to recognize this and practice His Presence instead of seeking Him as if He were only afar off. It was right and absolutely necessary to look up and out of myself to the Christ who sits interceding for me at the right hand of the Father. He is sovereign Lord, and in this dimension of His presence He is indeed very high above and beyond me.

As we've shown earlier, people get into trouble when, having lost this understanding, usually through a blend of Eastern mysticism, pop psychology, and pop theology, they begin praying to the Christ within. This mistaken way of prayer engenders the kind of man-centeredness that produces false prophets, those who speak their own earthly wisdom and not God's.

But as a Christian, I needed to learn to affirm His immanent as well as His sovereign Presence. Had I done this, I would have prayed much more effectively, and from a much quieter, less frantic place, knowing that Christ had not abandoned me, but was with me in all this. There is a mixture of immaturity and unbelief in our prayer lives until we learn this. It took one more hard lesson in Incarnational Reality before I learned that.

The third lesson came, and this time there was no human enemy, but a demonic one. This bad time seemed to last forever, though actually it spanned about a nine-month period. The suffering was worth it, however, for after it was over, I knew of a certainty what demonic "oppression" (spiritual battle) is, and even more importantly, what the authority of the believer is.

Demonic oppression is always an attack on the mind and thought processes of either an individual or a group, but in one of its manifestations it is an all-out maneuver to "take over" a person's mind, and from there the total person (Christian or non-Christian). The demonic activity consists in lying to the mind, and thereby leveling dreadful accusations at the soul. The demonic goal is to so weaken the mind that it can be taken over. The oppressed person seldom recognizes the source of this activity (the Bible labels the Evil One as "the father of lies" and "the accuser of the brethren"), and that makes the oppression all the more confusing.

New Christians experience this oppression to varying extents and in one way or another, and this opposition is designed to deceive them and either rob them of their new life or at least stop their progress in the Lord. Mature Christians, those who are effectively pulling down Satanic strongholds and bringing in the Kingdom of God, discover the full gamut of the Evil's One's strategems. The way I use the term *oppression*, therefore, is different from being either possessed (that condition whereby demons inhabit and control a person from his central core of spirit) or demonized (when demons have invaded a person's soul and body, but do not yet have full control).

The demon forces that came against me were not within me, but their strategy was designed to lie and accuse the mind until they could, as it were, press it down, weaken it through continual assault, then enter in and take it over.

This sort of extreme experience of the demonic does not usually occur unless one has opened himself up in some way to it. For example, persons who come to Christ out of promiscuous and perverted sexual lifestyles have opened themselves to what the Scriptures term "unclean spirits," and they may not only be oppressed by unclean spirits, but their bodies and minds may still be inhabited by these spirits until they experience deliverance from them. (See the discussion on the renunciation of Baal and Ashtoreth, the male and female idol-gods of sexual orgy in Chapter 14.) Another example is that of missionaries who unwittingly open themselves to oppression by living in areas where witchcraft and other occult practices are present. If such a one, along with his fellow Christians, fails to understand and move in the power of God, he can be in serious trouble. The healing of this could easily be accomplished through laying on of hands, but ignorant as we are of healing prayer, these souls are usually sent to unbelievers for medical and psychiatric treatment instead. Their "oppression" can then turn into a real depression with the possibility of even ending in demonization.

My experience was like the example given of the missionary. At that time, I was a clerical assistant on a top security psychiatric ward that served two hundred men. Here I came face to face with evil: evil as almost a palpable presence. It pervaded the minds, the language, the rantings, the ravings of those who had lost the good of reason, the good of being human. These men heard voices telling them to do vile things; their hallucinations were the very stuff of outer darkness. Many of these men had criminal records. One practiced voodoo, and he would tell the psychiatrist of his hatred for Christians, and of the demon spirits he sent out to attack them, and of how he "watched" this whole thing take place. I knew the darkness within him recognized the Light of Christ with me.

I believe what happened to me had something to do with that man.

At any rate, one day I locked the last door behind me, and something with a "voice" seemed to be sitting on my left shoulder. It said, "Look!" and it must have (who can explain such a thing?) pointed to my extreme left because my head swung around not to "it," but to some distance beyond. There, as a magician might try to raise an apparition with a wand, it reared up a cross, and then said, "How ridiculous!" Just three words, and then an illusion—as if in a different dimension—of a cross. But with that awful "hearing" and "seeing," I threw my hands over my ears and ran across the lovely, well-kept grounds, glistening in the sunlight of a beautiful day. I marveled at how normal and unchanged everything around me was, while at the same time my whole world was altered. I thought, "Oh no! I'm just like the rest of them. Now I'm seeing things (hallucinating); now I'm hearing voices."

From that moment on, when I would walk into a church and look up at a cross or crucifix, I would hear blasphemous voices and see blasphemous things—dreadful impositions of phallic images. At night, when I would kneel to pray I would be terrified by an evil presence, and would have to get off my knees and under the bed covers to pray. It was wholly terrifying, an experience of evil that utterly horrified my soul and threatened to take my mind. I knew of no one to go to for help. Today there are people to go to for prayer for such things, people who understand demonic warfare and how simple it is to free a person from harassment such as this. Back then there were not. My pastor, a faithful minister of the Word and Sacraments, one whom I knew well and had (as an organist) worked closely with, would never have understood what I was going through. I knew that he would not be able to help me, and that furthermore he would rely on the current psychological "wisdom" (wholly Freudian at the time), the effects of which I lived with daily and saw helping no one.

There are mentally and emotionally ill people who hear voices and see things who need the best psychiatric care available, care that has since those days greatly progressed due to increased understanding of how to medicate and bring into wholeness those whose problems are directly related to chemical imbalances and so on. But I knew that my problem was neither physical nor emotional. It was spiritual, and though I had everything to learn in this area, I knew the only answer for me was the grace of God. I cried out for it day and night. I was like a person about to drown, with barely a hold on a lifeline.

It was then that two books by an old evangelical saint, F. B. Meyer, came across my path. One was entitled *The Secret of Guidance*, and the other was *Meet for the Master's Use*. Both ministered greatly to me at the time, and one of them had the answer to my problem. I have long since lost the books through lending them out, but I will paraphrase from memory the passage that helped me so immeasurably. In it, Rev. Meyer told of St. Catherine of Sienna who, surrounded by the evil and the need of her day, went up into a castle turret to pray. As she began to pray, her ears were assaulted by blasphemous words, and she cried out to God, "Oh, look, Lord, I came up here to give you my day. Now look what is happening." And the Lord said, "Does this please you, Catherine?" "Oh, no Lord," she said. And the Lord said, "It is because I indwell you that this displeases you so."

These words brought instant understanding of my plight. I was brought right back to the fact that Another lives in me, and that He is there even when I "sense" His Presence the least. From that day to this, I have never forgotten this truth, or even for an instant relegated it to the abstract. With this knowledge, I also knew that the problem was not a state or condition of my mind or my heart, but that it was harassment from without, from the accuser of my soul. I knew beyond all shadow of a doubt that "Greater is he who is in you, than he who is in the world."

I then cried out to God, "Take it away, Lord. Send this filthy, horrible thing away." But the Lord said, "No, you do it."

It was then that I learned spiritual authority. Centered in God and He in me, I took authority over the evil spirit when it manifested itself and commanded it to leave. After several months of this, a concentrated training in moving from the center where Christ dwells, I was utterly free of this harassment. In the line of duty, I've been oppressed in different ways since that time, but the Evil One knows better than to try to bluff me in this way. He is much more subtle in his attacks now.

As stated in an earlier chapter, there is an illusionary nature to evil. Satan hopes to deceive us. He was at that time seriously bluffing me, and I was terribly afraid and intimidated. Many people, including Christians, lose this battle and are robbed of their minds and all spiritual progress (the exciting and demanding life in Christ) simply because they do not understand the spiritual realm and the provision fully made for us in the Victor. When the forces of evil come against us in this way, they have only the power we grant them, which we do through failure to understand the authority the believer has to rout and send them away.

Prayer for the lifting of demonic oppression is one of the easiest prayers to pray. In cases where demonic oppression is hooked into serious psychological woundedness, it is the latter need where more time and energy is required. We then need to find those places where there is unconfessed sin and a need for repentance, or where there is the need to forgive others who have wounded us.

But the point I want to make here is that I would have been instantly helped and freed had a Christian experienced in the authority we are to move in ministered to me with laying on of hands and prayer. I may not have gone on to learn my own authority in Christ, however, and what it means to move from the center where He and I are one. For that knowledge, the longer, more painful experience was certainly worth it. Without it, I might have needed more than three lessons in Incarnational Reality before finally catching on.

Considering the Human Side of Incarnation: Moral Effort

The reality of *God in us* does not cancel out moral effort on our part, nor our striving to live as Christ taught us. St. Paul, speaking of the strong and decisive action we are to take, admonishes us to *put on* Christ; to *mortify* (put to death) the lusts of spirit, soul, and body; to *put off* anger, strife, jealousy, and so on (Colossians 3). This is something we are to do, and there is grace available to help us do it.

The early Christians regarded baptism as a radical act indeed, and were prepared for it through fastings, laying on of hands, anointings, confessions, exorcisms, etc. In other words, all that we refer to as prayer for personal wholeness (popularly referred to as "inner healing") preceded baptism and prepared the person for his initiation into Christ. There was absolutely nothing "abstract" about it.

> In him also you were circumcised, not in a physical sense, but by being divested of the lower nature; this is Christ's way of circumcision. For in baptism you were buried with him, in baptism also you were raised to life with him through your faith in the active power of God who raised him from the dead. And although you were dead because of your sins and because you were morally uncircumcised, he has made you alive with Christ. (Colossians 2:11-13, NEB)

The early catechumen was to go into the water as one kind of person and come out another. In this act, he deliberately took his place in Christ's death and resurrection. During the first three centuries of the Church, symbol and reality were not so severely divorced as they are today. The early Christians understood that our union with Christ in His death and resurrection is what saves us, and water baptism is at once symbolic of this and a means through which the reality is imparted. The catechumen "died to" his old life, was found hidden in Christ, and rose with him to an utterly new life. Symbolically the catechumen enacted this by casting off his old clothes before going under the waters into Christ's death. Then, upon rising with Christ, he was wondrously covered and enveloped in new white (utterly pure) robes. Try to see with your heart the baptismal imagery that is present (though much more so in the original language) in Paul's letter to the Colossians and especially in the following passage:

> Put to death, therefore, whatever belongs to your earthly nature:
> sexual immorality, impurity, lust, evil desires and greed, which
> is idolatry. . . . You used to walk in these ways, in the life you
> once lived. But now you must rid yourselves of all such things
> as these: anger, rage, malice, slander, and filthy language from
> your lips. Do not lie to each other, since you have taken off your
> old self with its practices and have put on the new self, which is
> being renewed in knowledge in the image of its Creator.
> (Colossians 3:5-10)

As with baptism, so too it is with healing prayer, which is in reality
part of the work of baptism. We go into healing prayer as one kind of person, and we come out another. And in this action, our *will* is involved;
there are things we do. We kill lusts, we cast off the impure and the
unholy, we put on the new. True enough, in His Presence there is grace
to do these things, but *we* do them. You do them. I do them.

From time to time I have someone ask me to pray that God will take
from them a habitual sin such as adultery, envy, anger, masturbation, or
whatever, and I have to say, "No, I can't pray that way. We will go to
prayer right now, and you will look up to God and confess that sin
specifically, by name; then you will kill it. You will cast it off like a filthy
cloak, and together we'll 'watch' you do it." We then deal with this sin
through confession and proclamation of forgiveness, and not just with
words or from the head. We "see," for example, the confessed sin going
into Christ crucified. And if there is a block to letting go of this sin, we
"see" it.

It's amazing the way the heart most truly pictures the reasons we
don't part from our sins! For example, sometimes we discover that we
just plain want to hang on to the sinful behavior, and some of us even
have to face the fact that we then hope to blame God for not "healing" us.
We see right away when we are dealing with a passive will, someone
who lumpishly looks to a counselor or minister or to God to do what only
he himself can do. All such things as these come to the fore, along with
the memories of where the heart opened itself to envy, bitterness, lust,
and so on. Then, in full confession of our sins to God, we acknowledge
our rank foolishness and our basic propensities toward pride and rebellion, and we make a decision about sin.

In cases where the will has long been in captivity, and is not only
passive but is for whatever reason undeveloped and withered, we may
need to pray for its freedom and strengthening, or even for an outright
miracle of restoration. But the will, that most essential faculty of the
human soul, the one that chooses self or God, must then actively choose
life or death, Heaven or Hell. Then, in the strength and grace of God's

Presence, we do not look up and ask God to strike a death blow at any lusts of the spirit, soul, or body that war against the full "putting on" of Christ. We do it. We then, in the practice of the Presence, "put on" Christ.

After such a prayer as this, we are ready to deal with any emotional factors underlying the spiritual ones. For example, underlying the sins of envy and self-pity may be the excruciating pain of the deserted or unwanted baby and an intense fear of abandonment. Underlying the sins of adultery and homosexuality may be intense gender confusion and feelings of inferiority, as well as the symbolic confusion that goes with it. This is where understanding of our inner being, as well as the spirituals (gifts of the Holy Spirit), come in, especially those of healing, wisdom, and knowledge. As we grow in prayer and in understanding, we find the tools to help sincere souls to psychological as well as spiritual healing.

The person who prays this way is soon out of "the healing prayer business" if he doesn't discern when needy souls are failing to act, and are rather expecting to be "acted upon." When a person's problem is related to his failure to make a decision about sin, or to a slothfulness (a deadly sin) that leaves him morally, spiritually, or physically lazy, he may come in wanting someone to say a prayer and magically heal him. The very day of this writing, I received a call from a friend, a young man who has recently begun to pray for others and has been amazed to see God heal even the neediest. But today he felt "simply terrible" about an appointment he'd just made to see someone. This person, recounting his moral problems and bad mental (introspective) habits, ended his call by saying, "I'm a tough nut to crack; you'd better have all your 'powers' going when you see me." Right away. my friend was uneasy about having agreed to see this man, but didn't know why he was so upset over the call.

He had every reason to be upset. This man had shifted the onus of his healing from his own shoulders over to one he expected to magically make him feel better. No one can "heal" anyone of bad mental or moral habits. Such a one is responsible for confessing these and then for "taking them off" and for "putting on the new." Our prayers for that person must be dramatically and graphically toward that end, and it will be, in effect, the work of baptism. The imagery is incarnational. It has to do with taking one's place in Christ and of Christ's resurrection life in us. But this is something the one who comes for healing does, not us, and we will always see God do His part once they've made the decision to put off their sin and slothfulness. In this day of great passivity and emphasis on counseling methods, the counselor or minister must distinguish between those places that are ready for God's healing power and grace, and the other places where the demand for a radical moral and ethical response to God's commands must come first.

In the case of the young man who made the appointment with my friend, he was questioned immediately about his commitment to obey Christ. It was nonexistent. There was in his heart not the least vestige of the imagery of baptism and of the Christian, incarnational view of man. Though he called himself a Christian, he had no intention of changing his lifestyle, and was shocked that this would be thought necessary to his healing. My friend saved lots of vital spiritual energy by calling him to a radical moral decision about sin, one that placed the onus for his healing back where it belonged—on the shoulder of one who could, by making the right decision, become the man God had created him to be.

It is an awesome thing to be a man or woman, God's masterpiece, that human thing that makes up the creaturely side of Incarnational Reality. C. S. Lewis writes of both sides in union, working together:

> Your natural life is derived from your parents; that does not mean it will stay there if you do nothing about it. You can lose it by neglect, or you can drive it away by committing suicide. You have to feed it and look after it: but always remember you are not making it, you are only keeping up a life you got from someone else. In the same way a Christian can lose the Christ-life which has been put into him, and he has to make efforts to keep it. But even the best Christian that ever lived is not acting on his own steam—he is only nourishing or protecting a life he could never have acquired by his own efforts.[13]

> So we have a paradox:

> In one sense, the road back to God is a road of moral effort, of trying harder and harder. But in another sense it is not trying that is ever going to being us home. All this leads up to the vital moment at which you turn to God and say, "You must do this, I cannot."[14]

Besides the fact that we must cease from our own works, we cannot separate "[w]hat exactly God does and what man does when God and man are working together."[15]

> [The Bible] . . . puts the two things together into one amazing sentence. The first half is, "Work out your own salvation with fear and trembling"—which looks as if everything depended on us and our good actions:—but the second half goes on, "For it is God who worketh in you"—which looks as if God did everything and we nothing.[16]

To consider moral effort and man's responsibility is to consider only a small part of what it means to be man, what it means to be gifted with a soul. When Christ strengthens us in the inner man, what is He strengthening? Some of us have, in recent years, preferred to ignore the strictly human side of incarnation: that which thinks, feels, imagines, dreams, symbolizes, remembers, wills, and is the vessel through which the Divine Light is to shine. Just as we feel safe in thinking of Christ in His divinity, but not His humanity, so it is with ourselves. We may even speak rather glibly of Christ's indwelling us (our divine side), but fear to marvel at how wondrously our inner being is fashioned and constituted to receive and pass on this imposition of divine splendor. Our humanity we fear.

Our humanity, in fact, we fail to accept. This is a lingering result of earlier Gnostic incursions into Christian thought, thought which has always tempted us to replace a dying to the old man with a misguided hatred of our souls and bodies, thought which has always tempted us to deny that God would find His dwelling in a temple of flesh. Therefore we cannot celebrate our God, His world, and our own creation *in His image* as we should.

I have ministered to Christians whose chief problem was their ignorant belief that to be a Christian is to cease to be human. They died intellectually, imaginatively, emotionally, and called that dying to the "old man" or old self. On the other hand. there are Christians who make the soul of man everything, calling it man's sole treasure. In union with God, man's soul is his treasure; apart from the God his soul was created to unite with and glorify, the soul is lost.

> For what does it profit a man, if he shall gain the whole world, and lose his own soul? (Mark 8:26, KJV)

The gifts of the Spirit, as we see in this next section, reveal yet another facet of the human side of incarnation and the glorious way God fashioned man to work with Him.

The Gifts of the Spirit: Manifestations of the Presence

> Now to each one the manifestation of the Spirit is given for the common good. To one there is given through the Spirit the message of wisdom, to another the message of knowledge by means of the same Spirit, to another faith by the same Spirit, to another gifts of healing by that one Spirit, to another miraculous powers, to another prophecy, to another the ability to distinguish between spirits, to another the ability to speak in different kinds

of tongues, and to still another the interpretation of tongues. All these are the work of one and the same Spirit, and he gives them to each one, just as he determines. (1 Corinthians 12:7-11)

Today, even as I write, it is Epiphany, the day the Church celebrates with such words as, "Arise, . . . rise clothed in light; your light has come and the glory of the Lord shines over you . . . the Lord shall shine upon you and over you shall his glory appear . . ." (Isaiah 60:1, NEB). The greatest Epiphany, Christ the Light, dawns upon us, bringing salvation and healing. Epiphany has to do with unveilings, disclosures, manifestations of joy, light, truth, salvation, healing. The gifts of the Spirit are of the nature of Epiphany: manifestations of the Presence of our God, dawning upon our heads and wrapping us round with light and truth and joy.

Springing forth from His incarnate life and Presence among us (as the corporate Body of Christ, the Community of God's gathered people) and within us (as individuals) come all the gifts and fruits of the Spirit. Failure to move in the gifts of the Spirit is rooted in the failure to understand Ephipany, the Presence of God dawning upon us, making Jesus manifest in our midst.

The gifts listed in 1 Corinthians 12:8-10 are manifestations (Greek *phanerosis*, "making visible") of the Holy Spirit given to every Christian, for the good of all. They have to do with supernatural energy and power made visible through the manifest words of wisdom, knowledge, faith, prophecies, tongues, interpretation, discerning of spirits, healings, and miracles. They are most often referred to today as the charismatic gifts. We need to be slow in saying, "I have this gift," or "I have that one," for these are rather the manifestations of the Holy Spirit in our midst and we are merely workers with God, used of Him to make first one and then another visible in the Body of Christ. We are merely the vessels through which God sends His healing light and power. It is infinitely truer to say, "We have been given the gift."

Christ, with us, is also our power to *be* and to do the Father's will. We practice His Presence. We invoke His Presence. In the Presence, the potential of any and all the *spirituals*, that term we translate from the Greek as "gifts" of the Spirit, is there as needed. There is the power to *know* (the gifts of revelation): the discerning of spirits, the word of knowledge, the word of wisdom. There is the power to *do* (the gifts of power): the gifts of healings, the working of miracles, the gift of faith. There is the power to *say* (the gifts of inspiration): the gift of tongues, the interpretation of tongues, prophecy. Christ in us, His people, at once gives us access to the mind and power of God.

Throughout my years of ministry, I've felt keenly called to help the people of God to, as I term it, "move in the healing gifts of the Spirit." Though "gifts of healings" are one of the *spirituals*, uniquely different from the other eight, I refer to all nine of them as the "healing gifts" because wherever God's people are free to move in them, God uses them all in various combination in the healing of His people.

To the church in Laodicea our Lord said, "So because you are luke-warm—neither hot nor cold—I am about to spit you out of my mouth" (Revelation 3:16). As the NIV commentator of this Scripture writes, "'Hot' may refer to the hot, medicinal waters of nearby Hierapolis. The Church in Laodicea supplied neither healing for the spiritually sick nor refreshment for the spiritually weary." All this is exactly what is supplied when God moves by His Spirit to heal, and His people are prepared (from the human side of Incarnational Reality) to collaborate with Him. The church in Laodicea, trusting in her material wealth, was no longer collaborating with God's Spirit. Rich in material goods, she knew not her grave spiritual poverty. The church in Laodicea was no longer centered in the Presence.

I once had a theology professor who, claiming the spirituals were not for today, feared and despised the very thought of the gifts of the Spirit. I could be perfectly silent in his classroom, but my very presence (as well as the papers I wrote) bothered him. Challenging me before the class one day, he said, "What do I want with the gifts? I have enough trouble with the fruits." He could hold forth for any length of time on the theology of God's sovereignty, but was in reaction to the idea that God might mani-fest Himself in our midst now, that He might in any way supernaturally dawn upon us now. That the fruits of the Spirit as well as the gifts are exactly as named, of the Spirit, and also have to do with God's immanent Spirit with us, seemed to escape him. His theology was dry and abstract, infinitely boring, and very far from man in his humanness. There was no Incarnational Reality in it.

I answered his question with an astonished, "But the fruits as well as the gifts are incarnational," meaning that neither are something we rev up on our own strength; they have to do with the Presence of Another. He never did know what I meant, and I spent the next several years trying to verbalize what I knew the Scriptures taught and what I daily experienced as true.

We are all to move in these manifestations of God's Presence with us. They are foundational tools with which we do the works of God. When we lose the understanding of Incarnational Reality, God's Real Presence with us, then we lose these gifts. Therefore, in teaching people to invoke and practice the Presence of Christ, we lay the foundation for understanding and moving in the gifts of the Spirit.

Ministry Gifts

> There are different kinds of gifts, but the same Spirit. There are
> different kinds of service, but the same Lord. There are different
> kinds of working, but the same God works all of them in all
> men. (1 Corinthians 12:4-6)

Although we need to be slow in saying we have this or that manifestation gift, because we in principle may move in any one of them, depending upon the need at hand, we are far too slow to understand our particular ministry gift. In union with Christ we find our true calling and vocation. In connection with this, we find that we are gifted in a special way, a way that determines how we minister in the other gifts God has given us.

The Apostle Paul, in a letter to the Ephesians, speaks of those gifted to be apostles, prophets, evangelists, pastors, and teachers. They are charged with the preparation of God's people for works of service. In other words, those with these five ministry gifts are key in calling forth the ministry gifts given to the rest of the people of God.

> It was he [Christ] who gave some to be apostles, some to be
> prophets, some to be evangelists, and some to be pastors and
> teachers, to prepare God's people for works of service, so that
> the body of Christ may be built up until all reach unity in the
> faith and knowledge of the Son of God and become mature,
> attaining to the whole measure of the fullness of Christ.
> (Ephesians 4:11, 13)

I have heard many wistfully say, "I wish I knew my special gift." There are three chapters in the Bible where Paul instructs us on the spiritual gifts: Romans 12, 1 Corinthians 12, and Ephesians 4. For the Christians whose ministry gifts do not fall within the five-fold gifts listed above, Romans 12 provides an important key that when turned aright can help unlock the mystery. All can know and appreciate the special way in which God's love and power is to shine through them. Verses 6 to 8 contain this special listing:

> We have different gifts, according to the grace given us. If a
> man's gift is prophesying, let him use it in proportion to his
> faith. If it is serving, let him serve; if it is teaching, let him teach;
> if it is encouraging, let him encourage; if it is contributing to the
> needs of others, let him give generously; if it is leadership, let

him govern diligently; if it is showing mercy, let him do it cheer-
fully. (Romans 12:6-8)

Early on in this ministry, I realized that when the Lord sent me on a
mission, ever so much more got done if someone on the other end where
I was to go not only had the gift of governing ("ruling," as the *King
James* puts it—organizing, as we usually think of it today), but was free
to move in that gift. Since the actual job of organizing seminars is usually
given to women, I would all too often see this ministry gift in a Christian
woman, but would see it operating only minimally since she would be
unfree and unaffirmed in it. I would have to explain this ministry gift,
and show her how it operates in every part of her life, and then encourage
her to "come free" in it.

My prayer partner and fellow team member, Lynne Berendsen, has
this gift, and she keeps our ministry organized and on an even keel.
Through this gift, her other gifts are ordered and made manifest. It is
definitely a ministry of the Spirit. No one could explain, apart from the
supernatural, how we two women manage all the planning and clerical
work of this ministry. With this gift, so much more is accomplished with
each effort because God is in it.

When on a mission, if I'm working with someone who has this gift,
I can safely accept extracurricular assignments that he or she discerns
should be accepted because I know that it will fit into the work of the
mission as a whole and will have God's blessing on it. I know that much
will be accomplished with minimal effort, and that I will not jeopardize
the main ministry through becoming overextended and exhausted. For
example, when someone in charge of a mission who has this gift says to
me, "There is this man or woman in the hospital, and I think you need to
go and pray for that person," I know that the whole thing is bathed in
prayer, that it is part of the schedule of what God wants done in that city,
and that it won't overtax me along with other ministry to be done. I recognize this gift immediately and praise God for it. I quickly become
exhausted in my ministry gift when this one is not fully in operation.

When we observe someone whose ministry gift is that of giving,
here again we see that it is a supernatural gift in operation. To love is to
give, and all Christians give. But one with this particular gift not only
gives generously, but knows just when to give, what to give (whether of
time, money, goods, or whatever), how much to give, and to whom to
give. His or her gift of giving accomplishes miracles in the Kingdom of
God.

For many years I have observed a woman firsthand whose ministry
is characterized by this gift, and have seen her develop it to the maxi-
mum. She has never destroyed a friendship through giving because she

knows whom to give to. (I've observed other generous Christians give amiss to insecure people or organizations who in turn try to extract more or feel obligated and hate the one who has been generous to them, or become angry when more is not forthcoming. The gift given does not end up glorifying God, but rather stirs up resentment and sometimes envy.) This woman has never, to my knowledge, given through misplaced sympathy or empathy, but only as God, through her own heart, impresses her when and how much to give. I've seen God save the lives and affirm the vocations of many struggling young Christians through her gift. They, in turn, bless the Body of Christ with their mature gifts. Through this gift, this woman's other gifts are ordered and chiefly made manifest.

My ministry gift is one of the five-fold gifts, one that is to call forth the giftedness in others. For years I taught people to move in the manifestation gifts and encouraged them in their vocations without understanding at all what my ministry gift was. Slowly I realized that whether I was teaching freshman English, lecturing on C. S. Lewis, praying for the healing of someone's soul, preparing talks, or writing books, I was always dividing the dark from the light, the bad from the good. I was always crying out something to this effect: 'Look, don't you see the dreadful mixture of good and evil here? Don't you know where it's leading? Think—cast off your sloth—your mental, moral, and spiritual passivity." Then, "Repent; make a decision about this."

I finally realized I was seeing the issues that would be major problems for individuals or for groups in the Body of Christ—inexplicably, long before they or others did. I would call out the warnings, show them the dangerous mixtures. Then I would be immensely uncomfortable because the whole thought or issue would be so new to them. Often they would not understand the issues involved and would not be able to accept what I was saying. I would be involved, time after time, in taking decidedly unpopular or unsettling stands, and would seem narrow-minded (or even a bit eccentric) to some.

I therefore often had to stand alone, and stand I did, until God made the matter clear. This has often taken years! It helped a great deal when I came to realize my main ministry is that of prophet, and that through that ministry gift all the other gifts, natural and supernatural, were and are ordered and operate. I could then understand my life—why the Lord led me away from paying jobs and to full dependence upon Him.

A bishop once told me that if ever a prophet fit comfortably into the Church, he wasn't needed. Though very much a part of the Church, I could not fit into it vocationally, though I tried in every way to see how that could be done. Being a woman, of course, complicated things considerably. I was therefore forced to depend wholly upon God for monies to live, for shelter. Just as God sent the ravens to feed Elijah, so He has acted in utterly incomprehensible ways to care for me. I'm very grateful that I had an innate understanding of "calling" and "vocation,"[17] something so many seem to know little about today, and that I was free enough in Christ to follow the call.

When the concepts of "calling" and "vocation" are missing, or when they are present but separated from the understanding of what it is to move in the power of the Holy Spirit, people will remain confused and unable to find their true ministry gift. It is not at all difficult, provided one is willing to listen and to obey God, but singleness of purpose is required, along with an ongoing openness to the power and infilling of the Holy Spirit.

We've barely broached the subject of manifestation and ministry gifts. *The Holy Spirit and You* by Dennis and Rita Bennett, *The Healing Gifts of the Spirit* by Agnes Sanford, and *Know Your Ministry* by Marilyn Hickey provide foundational insights into these gifts.

The "Naturalness" of the Supernatural Gifts

Though supra-natural, there is a "naturalness" to the *charisms* of the Holy Spirit. This is due to the fact that the capacity in man to receive from God was all there before the Fall. It is our fallenness that is "unnatural" to man, our inability to hear and therefore obey the One who made us. It is also due to the fact that grace builds on nature. Just as the reality of God in us does not cancel out moral effort on our part, so God in and with us in the manifestation of the *spirituals* and the ministry gifts does not cancel out human development and giftedness. Lynne Berendsen had natural organizational gifts before God quickened within her the supernatural dimension of her ministry gift. I had, even as a child and long before God set in the ministry gift, quick discernment as to evil and a sure knowledge that not even a little of it was to be willfully and consciously tolerated. Here again we see the creaturely side of Incarnational Reality, and, insofar as moving in the gifts of the Holy Spirit is concerned, it is wrong to ignore or downplay the more or less natural giftedness. It both limits and aids in the work of the Spirit.

All this pertains solely to the Christian incarnational view of man—that is, to redeemed man's way of knowing, being, and doing. It differs radically from all other views of man, whether Freudian, Jungian, Gnostic, Platonic, pantheist, Stoic, pagan, or simply hodgepodge-modern.

> This is what I have asked of God for you: that you will be encouraged and knit together by strong ties of love, and that you will have the rich experience of knowing Christ with real certainty and clear understanding. *For God's secret plan, now at*

last made known, is Christ himself. In him lie hidden all the mighty, untappped treasures of wisdom and knowledge. (Colossians 2:2-5, *The Living Bible*)

Deceiving Doctrines or Occult Practices Which Replace the Authentic Christian Supernatural

So then, men ought to regard us as servants of Christ *and as those entrusted with the secret things of God.* (1 Corinthians 4:1, italics mine)

St. Paul knew how vital it was that the Colossians grasp the fact that the secret is Christ Himself, and that in Him is all transcendent wisdom and knowledge. He wanted to save them from being misled and deluded by those armed with attractive and even "fine-sounding" but deceiving doctrines (Colossians 2:4). The attempt to add to or replace Christ, the one Way, with another "wisdom" or "knowledge" (another gospel) is always the problem true pastors and teachers must seek to offset.

People then, as now, were attempting to gain metaphysical knowledge, insight into "the secret things," in separation from Christ who alone entrusts us with the secret things, not of darkness, but of God. In doing this, they opened themselves to deceiving doctrines and power. We do not try to add to our intuitive, imaginative, intellectual capacities through attempts to develop ESP (extrasensory perception). That would be to open ourselves up to, at best, the mixed messages and knowledge of this fallen world and at worst the utterly deluding ones. Rather, we receive Christ. We listen to Him. Our intellectual faculty is then hallowed and informed by the Scriptures and indwelling Presence. Our intuitive faculty then is an instrument of the true imagination—one that receives the truth (message, pictures, impressions) that come from God. Thus we have the mind of Christ and can discern the lying words and delusions, as well as the fatal mixtures of the true and the false that always emerge through attempts to know apart from union with God.

Therefore, since Jesus was delivered to you as Christ and Lord, live your lives in union with him. Be rooted in him; be built in him; be consolidated in the faith you were taught; let your hearts overflow with thankfulness. Be on your guard; do not let your minds be captured by hollow and delusive speculations, based on traditions of man-made teaching and centred on the elemental spirits of the universe and not on Christ. (Colossians 2:6-8, NEB)

The desire for knowledge can become a kind of spiritual or psychic lust. Just as we can be given over to physical lusts of the body, so we can be given over to lusts of the spirit or soul. Desire for psychic and spiritual development apart from Christ becomes this sort of lust, and it leads to delusion. St. Paul is saying, therefore, in effect: leave off your spiritual lusts, and give all your attention and devotion to the person of Christ.

> For it is in Christ that the complete being of the Godhead dwells embodied, and in him you have been brought to completion. Every power and authority in the universe is subject to him as Head. (Colossians 2:9, 10, NEB)

Imitation Gifts and Fruits

Satan and his underlings excel in confusing Christians as to imitations (which can be demonic or merely "fleshly"), thereby causing them to fear and eschew the real. When Christians shun the real, which they usually do out of fear of the false, they are inevitably given over, eventually, to the imitation. The supernatural "gifts" that come to man through the principalities and powers of this world not only deceive him, but lead him into tragic and horrendous acts and ends. Besides that, one need only read the messages and lives of mediums and occultists to see how infinitely bleak and boring their "messages" and "cures" turn out to be. It is the kind of boredom that yawns with the breath of Hell itself.

I have long grieved over the fact that the Church, almost totally, goes untutored and in grave ignorance over the spirituals, the tools with which we work the works of Christ. Even within those church bodies that traditionally emphasize them, there is by and large only a very limited understanding and expression of them. The church that does not understand and move rightly in the spirituals is the church that will certainly fail to discern soon enough, or thoroughly enough, the demonic imitations. This is why in our day we have the strange spectacle of "Bible-believing" churches either adopting Gnostic and rationalistic ideas (especially through psychology), or (and this is just as bad) reacting to the same in fearful and un-Christian ways, often confusing the good with the bad in the bargain. Our protection against demonic powers and teaching resides in our appreciation and experience of true spiritual power and the right application of it.

Another successful ploy of the Evil One, however, is that of duping ignorant Christians into exploiting the gifts and power of God, of tempting immature Christians to misuse and dramatize the supra-natural and make it more akin to his imitations.

This does not mean, of course, that God does not move (and that continually) in ways that cause men to respond in quite dramatic and even spectacular fashion. Different healing ministries are characterized by strong manifestations of the Spirit—for example, one way in Kathryn Kuhlmann's, another in John Wimber's, yet another in mine, and so on. The freedom to so respond, and without self-consciousness, is precious indeed (and not at all common in the Church as a whole.) But our point does mean that man's sensory and emotional reaction to God's work in the soul should never be dogmatized, emphasized, or ritualized. It seems strange that this should even need to be noted, but it is perfectly amazing how much loss of healing power occurs through the failure to understand the difference between God's objective Presence and power at work in the soul, and man's subjective response to it.

For various reasons, man's response to the work of the Holy Spirit is at times a mistaken one (for example, exaggerated and/or fearful responses, etc.). This usually requires exhortation so that God's work will not be hindered in the soul. The important thing is not the sensory response, but the work God is doing in the soul. Some exploit and play up the dramatic responses to the healing power of God, and they do this in such a way as to dogmatize, emphasize, ritualize. This is often done in ignorance, often in the hopes of gaining some kind of credence as a "mighty man of God" or in order to fill the collection plates. The result is to distort and dissipate the work of God in the souls of men. This is what I mean by saying that Satan loves to tempt men or women to exploit the gifts and the power of God.

From time to time in my ministry, I've had people come up for prayer and then begin to behave in distorted ways—all in an attempt to *receive* what God was in fact earnestly holding out to them. But they could not simply look to Him and receive because they had been trained in some form of behavior. A misguided emphasis on physical manifestations had them looking to their own bodily response rather than to God and the gift He was freely proffering. They had learned a ritual or "liturgy" of "charismatic" behavior from ministers who either exploited the gifts, or who in ignorance themselves substituted the imitated and ritualized sensory responses for the gifts. Caught in this behavior, they acted it out as if God required it in order to hear and answer their prayers. I always stop this behavior immediately, and so free the soul to respond authentically to the thing God wants to do.

The mightiest acts of God are often strangely hidden to the eye of stubborn unbelief, even when the full panorama of God's love and mercy parades across its vision. Christ repeated over and over, "He who has eyes to see, let him see. He who has ears to hear, let him hear." There is nothing dull, bleak, or lacking in content when God moves, but the eyes of the ungodly cannot see it. These same eyes can often see

Satan's imitations, the effect of which is to further wither and diminish the soul.

Christians, full of the Holy Spirit, should be of all men the most practical, the most down-to-earth, for their spirit is indwelt by Christ, and He rules (when allowed) their willing, reasoning, intuitive, feeling, sensory being. They have the good of reason restored, a cleansed and holy imagination.

To sum up then: all this is not a matter of developing the intuitive faculty, but of worshiping God and being filled with Jesus. To do this is to become a sacramental vessel that wafts continually the sweet aroma of the gifts and fruits of His Presence: those that have to do with Christian man's ways of being, knowing, willing, and doing.

PART III

IMAGERY AND SYMBOL

A right conception of God is basic not only to systematic theology but to practical Christian living as well. It is to worship what the foundation is to the temple.

(A. W. Tozer)[1]

Before the Christian church goes into eclipse anywhere there must first be a corrupting of her simple basic theology. She simply gets a wrong answer to the question, "What is God like," and goes on from there.[2]

CHAPTER 8

Perceiving God Aright

God is not a symbol of goodness. Goodness is a symbol of God.

(G. K. Chesterton)

*O*ur perception of God—how we see (conceptualize and image) His nature and attributes—profoundly affects our psychology—how we see man. Behind the limited and false faces of the psychologies of man we now know and study will be a faulty understanding of God the Father and the way He, through His Son and Spirit, mediates Himself to man.

The work of Freud, Jung, and others who study man and the natural laws concerning the *psyche* have contributed valid psychological concepts and understanding. But their systems are incomplete and faulty because their image of God the Father (and the way He transposes His life to man) is faulty.

Jung, for example, deliberately chose to believe that God is both good and evil, that Yahweh and Satan are polar opposites of one being. He did so under the circumstance of demonic revelation of the very nature I experienced and described in a previous chapter. His reaction was radically different than mine, however, for he chose to attribute to God the revelations of evil accorded him, even naming a phallic image the other face of God, knowing at the time and commenting on the fact that this was a blasphemous thing to do. This false view of God provides the basis for his intellectual framework (Neo-Gnosticism), one that reconciles good and evil not only in the Godhead, but also within the soul of man. (All psychological reductionism ends by reconciling good and evil, but Jung's system, going as it does beyond materialistic assumptions, opens the door to demonic revelation. It is essentially a mystical religion and as such has more power than a materialistic one.)

It is dangerous for a Christian or any other honest seeker after truth to adopt Jung's system, because within it are not only false conceptions (easier to detect) but false images—images that lead astray, often very subtly. These are images that lead us to reconcile good and evil.

From time to time the Church itself has been afflicted with an heretical doctrine of God, and this always spawns a false psychology of man. The following quote from C.S. Lewis points to the connection between a man's ethics, for example, and his view of God:

> There were in the eighteenth century terrible theologians who held that "God did not command certain things because they are right, but certain things are right because God commanded them." To make the position perfectly clear, one of them even said that though God has, as it happens, commanded us to love Him and one another, He might equally well have commanded us to hate Him and one another, and hatred would then have been right. It was apparently a mere toss-up which He decided on. Such a view of course makes God a mere arbitrary tyrant. It would be better and less irreligious to believe in no God and to have no ethics than to have such an ethics and such a theology as this.[1]

The great poets, novelists, philosophers, and saints have bequeathed us immense insights into *persons*, but their view of man (how he is made whole, how he *becomes*) is limited, faulty, and twisted to the degree that their experience and symbolic imagery of God is faulty. It is personally painful to read certain of the great writers and thinkers and see how terribly affected they were, finally, by the transient spirit and mind-set of their own age.

I love George Eliot's work (Mary Ann Evans, 1819-1880), and every once in a while, in rereading one of her books, I find myself crying out, "O George Eliot, what incredible insight you have into the human breast, into persons. If only you had been spared the effects of Enlightenment thinking! The tooth has been pulled from that tiger, but not before it got you! The Church wasn't where it should have been, George, or surely you would have been spared!" I anguish over this great writer and others who emerge from and write out of the milieu of a faltering Church, one with so little Incarnational Reality flowing through it that souls cannot apprehend the true God.

And then one comes to a C. S. Lewis, a man who is probably quoted more often than any other by orthodox Christian writers today. For me it was sheer joy to discover this writer—a man who stands apart from the age, points a finger at it, and impacts it, rather than the other way around.

In his Cambridge inaugural address, he spoke of himself as an old dinosaur, an anachronism in this age. As a great thinker and man of letters, among other men and women of letters, that's precisely what he appears to be. It's as if a real, flesh-and-blood medievalist has somehow survived into our century, replete with a thoroughgoing *Christian* supernaturalist view of all reality. Characterizing himself as an Old Western Man, he said: "It took me as long to acquire inhibitions as others (they say) have taken to get rid of them. That is why I often find myself at such cross-purposes with the modern world: I have been a converted Pagan living among apostate Puritans."[2]

So Lewis, the old dinosaur, understood and experienced God, His creation, and all the great unseen realities as the Scriptures reveal them to us, and not through the grid of twentieth-century materialistic/naturalistic presuppositions, nor through the many other isms that have come down through time and, however camouflaged, presented themselves to us as new *gnoses,* new knowledge. This, I realize, is quite a statement to make, for we are all creatures of our time, all infected by the age in which we live. But Lewis, it seems to me, more than any other great mind of our age, managed to transcend, imaginatively as well as intellectually, the spirit and mind-set of our age. His insights into man and his cosmos, therefore, and the imagery and the symbolism with which he embodied these insights, are profoundly Christian. They are *incarnational.* His work reflects, always and powerfully, the truth that God comes down to us, enters into our closed and alienated minds and worlds, and proclaims Himself to be not a subjective state of our minds or bodies, but the one great Objective Real:

> "I myself am your want of—something other, outside, not you nor any state of you."[3]

This, of course, is the substance and the pattern of Christian healing.

Though C. S. Lewis did not set out to study man's psyche, his insights into persons are true and amazingly comprehensive, because his perception of the nature of God and the way He makes Himself known to man is Scripturally true and comprehensive. In contrast to Jung, C. S. Lewis knew that vital to every soul that needs healing (all of us) is the knowledge that God is absolutely good, and that He loves us with the kind of love capable of radically changing us. Both themes are exceedingly strong in Lewis:

> When Christianity says that God loves man, it means that God *loves* man: not that He has some "disinterested," because really indifferent, concern for our welfare, but that, in awful and sur-

prising truth, we are the objects of His love. You asked for a loving God: you have one. The great spirit you so lightly invoked,
the "lord of terrible aspect," is present: not a senile benevolence
that drowsily wishes you to be happy in your own way, not the
cold philanthropy of a conscientious magistrate, nor the care of
a host who feels responsible for the comfort of his guests, but
the consuming fire Himself, the Love that made the worlds.[4]

On the whole, God's love for us is a much safer subject to think
about than our love for Him. Nobody can always have devout
feelings: and even if we could, feelings are not what God princi-
pally cares about. Christian Love, either toward God or toward
man, is an affair of the will. If we are trying to do His will we are
obeying the commandment, "Thou shalt love the Lord thy God."
He will give us feelings of love if He pleases. We cannot create
them for ourselves, and we must not demand them as a right. But
the great thing to remember is that, though our feelings come and
go, his love for us does not. It is not wearied by our sins, or our
indifference; and, therefore, it is quire relentless in its determination that we shall be cured of those sins, at whatever cost to Him.[5]

The good is uncreated, it never could have been otherwise: it has
no shadow of contingency; it lies, as Plato said, on the other side
of existence. It is the *Rita* of the Hindus by which the gods
themselves are divine, the *Tao* of the Chinese from which all
realities proceed. But we, favoured beyond the wisest pagans,
know what lies beyond existence, what admits no contingency,
what lends divinity to all else, what is the ground of all existence, is not simply a law but also a begetting love, a love begot-
ten, and the love which, being between these two, is also
imminent in all those who are caught up to share the unity of
their self-caused life. God is not merely good, but goodness;
goodness is not merely divine, but God.[6]

These orthodox theological insights, restated for us by Lewis, are
critically important to hear, for one of the strongest thrusts of our age is
toward a reconciliation of good and evil.[7] Being straight on this is all-
important to Christian healing.

I have a friend whose story illustrates the psychological effects of
being very sure of God's goodness and love. Her background was of the
sort that usually insures mental and/or emotional instability in a person.
Yet she is (and has been since her youth) a stable, well-rounded person,
one who would appear to have had the most auspicious of beginnings.

As we know, it is important to have fathers who function as good, loving fathers, not only because they are the ones who one on the natural plane affirm us as persons, but also because they are the ones who symbolize God the Father to us.

Enid could hardly have had a more unaffirming father. Quite the reverse. He was either a very ill man, or a very evil one—perhaps both. Early on, he had deserted the family, leaving them destitute. But he continued to torment them. Once he even attempted to burn down their tiny farmhouse. Enid's mother, a poverty-stricken immigrant woman, hardly knowing even the language of her adopted country, struggled to raise her children on the bit of food she could wrest from a rocky, windswept plot of land.

We know how psychologically damaged people can be, coming out of situations with fathers such as this one. But Enid emerged from adolescence affirmed as a person. Marveling at this, I questioned her as to how such a thing had happened. She wasn't sure, but as we talked the answer soon became apparent.

Her little German mother, a devout woman of prayer, would every day gather her children around her knee, and then would raise her voice in mighty prayer to God. In broken, deeply guttural English, an invocation would rumble up from the depths of her being, one the children knew that beyond all shadow of a doubt reached the Heavenly Father's ears. "Our-r-r loving-g-g Heavenly-y-y Father-r-r-r," she would pray, and His very Presence seemed to fill that humble place. As a result, God the Father was so real in Enid's life that she was not only affirmed as a woman, and as a person, but her mind and heart intuited what true fatherhood and true masculinity are all about. She had a healthy and balanced view of men because she symbolized and imaged her Heavenly Father aright. This is a rare and happy outcome to so tragic a circumstance as she had had with her earthly father and one that is exceedingly rare (as any experienced psychologist or counselor will attest). The Enids of this world, even though thoroughly Christian, usually suffer emotionally for years before coming to a balanced view of men, as well as a true perception of God.[8]

Enid's mother, whose circumstances could hardly have been more severe, even so knew that God the Father is *loving and good*, and that this good streams down to her (note the incarnational imagery here) when she lifts up her face to receive it. By doing this, she saved herself and her family. Enid's brother became a minister of the gospel, and she (now up in years) has for fifty years been part of a vital Christian ministry.

Those of us who minister to wounded souls realize the miracle that happens in the life of a sufferer once he or she gets a true vision of God the Father and the affirming love of the Father starts streaming toward that person. The soul of that person will then begin to see and symbolize God properly; the God of the Scriptures will become his or her full strength and stronghold.

When ministering to others, it is important to keep Scriptural imagery in mind. All stories of healing in the Scriptures, when imaged by the mind, are *incarnational*. Grace is channeled into us. God sends His Word and heals us. The Healing Presence descends into us and does it.

Even as we image *God* differently than a Freud or a Jung, so we image the healing of the *soul* differently than they do. I have noticed throughout the years that immediately, when pastoral people take to themselves the imagery of the soul that is within the various psychological systems, they no longer think in terms of prayer for healing and of grace being channeled into us. They move away from the Confessional, and thus the first two big barriers to wholeness (the failure to forgive others and the failure to receive forgiveness) go uncared for. They no longer move in the healing gifts of the Spirit. Rather, they counsel within a system limited by its failure to image God and the soul of man properly.

We alone have a Savior of the deep mind and heart, One who descends into it and becomes its righteousness, its sanctification, its holiness. Faith, knowledge, love, moral conduct, apostolic courage, hope, prayer, completion: all have to do with Christ in us. This is the way it really is, and the imagery with which our hearts perceive this reality is crucial.

The Scriptural Image of the Heart

The natural (fallen) heart has lost the divine splendor. It is separated from God and from holy converse. It "is deceitful above all things, and desperately wicked," cries Jeremiah (17:9, KJV). "Who can understand it?" he asks (NIV). All the psychologies in the world are attempts to know it.

God knows it: "I the Lord search the heart and examine the mind" (Jeremiah 17:10). The Scriptures name many of the kinds of hearts the Lord finds in His examination: broken, grieved, discouraged, obstinate, proud, wicked, trembling, double, subtle, perverse, sorrowful, haughty, fretting, heavy, unsearchable or unfathomable, cunning, despiteful (insolent, arrogant, and boastful), bitter, stony, uncircumcised, overcharged, troubled, foolish and darkened, jealous, envious, impenitent, evil, whorish, deceitful, hard, scheming, diabolical, covetous, and so on.

These are hearts that are either sinful or wounded and need healing. In their healing, Jesus first of all comes in and stands in the midst of that heart. He who is the Light of the World illuminates it. He then speaks the healing word, one which, if received and acted upon, sets the heart free from all the other dominating voices: those of the world, the flesh, and the Devil.

This is a profound view of man; it is incarnational. Christ is in us, radiating up through us, granting to us the holy imagination, the holy intellect. Our two minds are thus hallowed, as well as our sensory and feeling faculties, our wills, our intuitive faculties, our bodies. As we listen to the One who completes us, we find balance and harmony in all these areas. We find genuine integration of all that we are. We are completed in Him. This is by no means a simplistic view of healing if indeed we believe in the Real Presence—within, without, forgiving and completing man.

We then have hearts such as these, also named in the Scriptures: willing, perfect, tender, soft, pure, upright, clean, fixed, wise, merry, meek and lowly, honest and good, single, true, compassionate, circumcised, thankful, and so on. We have a tiny foretaste of the divine splendor we shall once again know when, at the Marriage Supper of the Lamb. the union of God with His people will be finally and perfectly consummated.

Healing Seminars

After teaching on this in the Pastoral Care Ministry Schools, we immediately go into prayer for healing, putting this Scriptural view of man's heart and God's way of healing it to the test. The healings that we see never cease to astonish us, and illustrate how simply and wonderfully God reveals and then heals the heart of man.

We simply invoke His Presence, then invite Him into our hearts. He shows us our hearts. In prayer for the healing of memories, we simply ask our Lord to come present to that place where we were so wounded (or perhaps wounded another). Forgiving others, and receiving forgiveness, occurs. In prayer for the healing of the heart from fears, bitternesses, etc., we see primal fears as well as the lesser ones dealt with immediately: those fears that the sufferer often has not been aware of, never been able to name—they only know that their lives have been seriously restricted and shaped because of them. We see imaginations cleansed; we see the picture-making faculty of the heart cleansed. In short, in simply understanding God's incarnational pattern of healing, we see miracles occur as easily and as wonderfully as though they are naturally to be expected. And they are.

But in all this we need to understand the way the heart sees and knows: our faculty of symbolizing in order to know, and the resulting inner imagery within our minds and hearts.

CHAPTER 9

Imagery and Symbol:
"The Imagery Really Matters"[1]

Symbols bind up reality for us. When the symbols die, we die too.

(Rev. Alan Jones)[2]

T he Judeo-Christian Scriptures are at once the repository and the great guardian of the Christian world picture—that is, the incarnational symbolic system. A sound understanding of the Scriptures therefore evokes true imagery within the heart, just as it grants a sound theology to the mind. The way mankind in general or the individual heart images God is judged to be adequate or inadequate, true or false, as it lines up with the way the Scriptures image God. The images that come to us from within (our own heart) and from without (the cultural and competing symbolic systems of the day) are therefore always to be interpreted through and by sound interpretation of the Word, the Scriptures.

This is crucial because imagery, symbol, revelation, and experience can be (and are) interpreted by the systems of man, those devised in separation and even (as we have seen in Jung) in opposition to God and His revelation of Himself to us in and through Christ and the Scriptures.

The importance of this cannot be overemphasized because we are mythic beings: we live by and in our symbols. Man is an animal who *symbolizes*, who *talks*.(To talk is to symbolize. Language itself is symbol.) Thus man is set apart from the rest of the natural creation. Symbols bind up reality for us.

When a sound symbolic system (an integrated way of seeing reality) is missing, a lesser one takes its place. When great and good symbolic images of God, the cosmos, fatherhood, motherhood, masculine, feminine, and so on are rejected or are simply absent from the psyche, then lesser images (and even entire symbolic systems) develop to take their place. For a frightening example, one need take only a brief glance at the contemporary heavy metal rock scene and the symbolic meaning in the images it projects. There, the imagery of man and woman created in the image of God has given way to images of men and women that border on the absolute in self-centeredness and evil, including lust, seduction, domination, and sexual perversion. Gender identity, integral to our identities as male or female persons, is either denied through unisex imagery, or is reduced to the unman/unwoman category through portraying men and women as seducers, sadists, and cruel dominators. Our very humanity is effaced, and we no longer share even the goodness of the beasts.

As St. Gregory the Great has said: "If you do not delight in higher things, you most certainly will delight in lower things." This is true of a society, a nation, a world, as well as each and every individual.

> Finally, brothers, whatever is true, whatever is noble, whatever is right, whatever is pure, whatever is lovely, whatever is admirable—if anything is excellent or praiseworthy—think about such things. (Philippians 4:8)

We have a way of becoming (in a sense) what we set our eyes upon. The imagery really matters.

Symbols Bind Up Reality for Us

The following story is an example of what happens to us when the wholesome symbols that bind up reality for us are missing and are replaced by an inner imagery that reflects the loss of true relationship (whether to God, our fellows, or the earth and all creation). This example concerns the gender confusion so prevalent today and the inner imagery that reflects this tormenting condition in the heart.

In this case, the imagery pertains to the homosexual condition, and when properly interpreted it reflects the heart's need and therefore the knowledge of how to pray for healing.

I met with a young doctor (we'll call him Edward), about thirty years of age, who was grievously unaffirmed in his masculinity, and was therefore cut off from a perception of himself as a man. His father had deserted his mother when he was an infant, and Edward had never experienced any kind of attachment either to him or to a father substitute. Though his mother had faithfully cared for him, he seemed cold and unfeeling toward her as well. As his story unfolded, it became clear that during his first months of life she had been far too upset about their abandonment to be able to nurture him in such a way that he could bond with her and arrive at a secure sense of being in her care.

Since age seventeen he had been overtly homosexual, but ceased to act out his sexual compulsions after committing his life to Christ. Although he was no longer overtly homosexual, he complained of making no progress in his spiritual life. With a question or two, I quickly found out why. He yet continuously entertained a homosexual fantasy life, and apparently thought the mental activity to be harmless.

An unhealthy fantasy life (as we have seen) is a killer. It destroys. It wars against and annihilates the true imagination, that which can intuit the real and is therefore creative. When our minds are pregnant with *illusion*, with the lie that disintegrates the personality, and our eyes are set on that, we cannot be impregnated by that which is true and substantive—that which unites the personality and makes it one. Time and again, when a man's inner imagery of himself as a man is either deficient or missing, I find he has an involvement with pornography and with a diseased fantasy life. His outer relationships are diseased or nonexistent, and his inner imagery reflects this. Diseased imagery fills in the vacuum where images of affirming and nourishing relationships should have been.

In this young doctor's life it is easy to see how this inner imagery (a fantasy of uniting sexually with another male) was used as a prop in lieu of having bonded with his own father (and therefore his own masculinity), but also, and very importantly, in lieu of having achieved, early in his life, a *sense of being* or of *well-being*. Like Richard, he had a gaping chasm or void within. He had no home (center) within, replete with wholesome images of fatherhood, masculinity, motherhood, femininity, family: those inner images that make up a healthy symbolic system and reflect and channel beauty, truth, and goodness (the very glory of God and of transcendent good) to us.

As mentioned in the Preface, I once lived in a little third-floor loft, and the tops of a tree that blossomed magnificently reached up to its main window, one through which I could also see Lake Michigan. As if the waters of an inland sea and the blossoms of a mountain ash, changing with every season and with the daily vagaries of sun and cloud, were not enough, the tree attracted all manner of birds. Flocks of orioles and wild canaries never passed up that tree. At times, it seemed to me, there was beauty enough to break one's heart. Scenes such as those help me, in rare moments, to catch a glimpse of what Dostoyevski meant when he said, "Beauty will save the world."

Alexander Solzhenitsyn, just coming out from under Communist rule and the most dreadful kind of ugliness man can know as a prisoner in the Gulag, commented on this enigmatic statement of Dostoyevski in his 1970 Nobel lecture:

Perhaps then the old trinity of Truth, Goodness, and Beauty is not simply the dressed up, worn-out formula we thought it in our presumptuous, materialistic youth? If the crowns of these three trees meet, as scholars have asserted, and if the too obvious, too straight sprouts of Truth and Goodness have been knocked down, cut off, not let grow, perhaps the whimsical, unpredictable, unexpected branches of Beauty will work their way through, rise up to that very place, and thus complete the work of all three?

Images of beauty were missing in Edward's life. Even had he lived daily with such a scene as I described above, he would not have been able to really see it, for his heart was bereft of primal symbols of connectedness and relationship, leaving him empty, depressed, and unseeing. In his healing, his heart would reject the diseased imagery and then open to what I call transcendent images of glory, those inner images and symbols that would blaze a clear path for the straight sprouts of Truth and Goodness to grow into tall trees in his life. And this is exactly what happened, but first there was something he must do.

I told Edward he must renounce the diseased fantasy life in order to find wholeness, and he agreed to do that. We then prayed to this end, banishing the fantasy from his mind. After that, we prayed for the strengthening of his creative, masculine *will*, that which would refuse any return of the old fantasy. We prayed in other ways, such as I describe in *The Broken Image* and *Crisis in Masculinity*, for the healing of his homosexual condition. After I instructed him in listening prayer and Scripture reading, he left greatly strengthened and encouraged.

He call me several weeks later, however, and he was deeply depressed. "I refused the fantasy life," he said, "just like you told me to. But I have never been so depressed. Even when I'm working on a patient, standing over him, it's as if there is nothing there."

This is as good a description as we will find of the failure to come to a sense of being or of well-being. It was this dreadful void or nothingness that his unhealthy fantasy life had been covering and attempting to fill. From the imagery here, I knew exactly what his further need was and how to pray for it.

In our first prayer session, we had addressed the needs he had as one who suffered the homosexual neurosis. The imagery in his fantasy life revealed a man severely separated from his masculine identity and attempting to "connect" with it in a homosexual way. The imagery, that of being sexually united with another male, signaled the fact that he had missed a vital step in the identification process—that of relating to his own father or a father substitute in such a way as to find his own masculinity and personhood affirmed. The imagery also symbolized the fact that he was attempting to meet this terrible deficit the wrong way. This latter is what I've come to term *symbolic confusion*, for from the standpoint of the sufferer, that is what it is. The imagery is telling him the truth, but he is misreading it. As I explained this to him, he immediately understood it and saw the futility of acting out his symbolic confusion. He also understood for the first time why the compulsions were so strong; they had all the power of a deep deprivation neurosis behind them. That was the root problem to be healed, one that our God specializes in.

The strong compulsion he suffered I've come to call the "cannibal compulsion," the twisted way we try to take into ourselves that which we think we lack. In reality, it is that within us which (for whatever reason) is unblessed, unaffirmed. In the cannibal compulsion, we are attempting to unite with that unaffirmed facet of our being, or even the sense of being itself. We project the unaccepted part of ourselves off onto another who symbolizes that lost part, and then we attempt to "swallow" it up in that person; in other words, we attempt to unite with it in the wrong way. In the homosexual neurosis, through homosexual activity and a homosexual fantasy life, that is what is happening, and the symbolic imagery within the mind, when properly understood and interpreted, reveals this.

To begin to understand the imagery is to begin to disengage the power of the symbolic confusion. The homosexual imagery, understood symbolically, was saying, "You are going about this integration in a perverted way."[3] The pedophile, for example, attempts to gain a childhood he never had by "swallowing up" young boys. In his adolescence, he often irrationally resists maturing (still yearning for his lost childhood) by means such as plucking out his own pubic hair and beard. These signs of psychic pain and trouble help us to understand his psychological and emotional needs, and are to be distinguished from what later sinfully happens in him when he acts out his compulsion and becomes addicted to perverted acts, both overtly and in his imagination.

I now knew that more than Edward's masculine identity was at stake. His words, "It's as if there is nothing there," imaged his soul's condition, all that goes along with the failure to come to that most basic sense underlying our identities as persons, whether male or female: that of either 1) a sense of being, or 2) a sense of well-being.

When Edward held the diseased image in his mind, he felt as if there were at least something inside. The diseased image substituted not only for the missing images and symbols of good relationship, but, in this particular case, it also filled in for the lack of an adequate sense of being. Separated from both his masculine identity and a sense of being, he was in fantasy doing what he had actively done before he left off his homosexual behavior. Both were symbolic confusions, attempts to posit his unaffirmed masculinity as well as being itself in another, then integrate with it in a homosexual way.

We need to understand imagery. Images in the mind and heart are symbolic—they mean something. Metaphoric in nature, they are not to be interpreted literally. That would be to confuse the so-called "unconscious" ways of knowing with the more cognitive "conscious" ways. But that is what the sufferer with gender confusion or other emotional problems does. He takes the images literally that should be understood symbolically. Lamentably, all too often so do his counselors.

It should not be construed that everyone with a diseased fantasy life has failed to come to a sense of being or of well-being in the early months of life. Through lust and perverted lifestyles, one can lose an adequate sense of being that one has had earlier.

Edward's need was not, as some would have counseled him, to resume the fantasy life, but to have hands laid on him for a very specific healing: prayer that a sense of being or of well-being be set into him, replacing the void of non-being. He who lacks a sense of being is much sicker than he who lacks a sense of well-being, though both are critical, and I do not use either of these terms lightly. The answer to this prayer is nothing short of miracle, and it is very safe to say that if God does not heal such a one, he will go through life unhealed.[4]

I invited Edward to come back for prayer, and then phoned my prayer team. We laid hands on him and prayed that God, the Source of all being, would find his weak, as it were, center and set into it a sense of being. (In this prayer, I place my right hand firmly on the chest and the left firmly on the back; thus the force of my prayer is directed into his physical center, that which represents the center of his total being: spirit, soul, and body.) We prayed until we could give thanks that the dreadful sense of non-being was (if ever so slightly at first) replaced with a solid sense of being, a true self within. And we thanked God that this work would be completed as Edward walked in faith and obedience. And it was.

With this healing, one gets in touch with the power to *be*, and that in turn helps sufferers such as Edward to get over another difficulty they commonly have—that of compulsively over-intellectualizing everything. This condition is almost inevitable in one as deprived and deficient in the emotional and feeling parts of himself as Edward was. This condition signals an imbalance in the rational mind and the deep heart. It is the active, painful thinking, thinking, thinking of the rational mind when separated from the quiet, still capacity to simply *be*. This, the deep heart, in turn complements and balances the rational mind's power to shape, form, initiate, that for which the painful thinking and endless activism is a substitute.

Images of masochism, Oedipal guilt, and so on are all readable when we are listening to God as well as to the sick symbols that characterize a life. A basic understanding of symbol, and the way the symbolic mind *knows* or understands, together with the guidance of the Holy Spirit, is invaluable in helping these persons.

The Need for Ceremony and Ritual

> Myth [symbol] is necessary because reality is so much larger than rationality. Not that myth is irrational but that it easily accommodates the rational while rising above it. (Dr. Clyde S. Kilby)

Reality is simply far too great to be contained in propositions. That is why man needs gestures, pictures, images, rhythms, metaphor, symbol, and myth. It is also why he needs ceremony, ritual, customs, and conventions: those ways that perpetuate and mediate the images and symbols to us.

It is through ceremony, "one of the particular and crucial ways in which we humans keep alive our particular nature, as opposed to the angelic or the beastial," that, Dr. Tom Howard has said, "freedom, dignity, and joy" come to us as "hints borne from outside ourselves." This, as he says, is "the school of humanness," for "ceremony is the way in which we (all tribes, cultures, communities, from the beginning of myth and history) have given shape to our experience and have ordered it in a structure that bespeaks our hunch that it is all significant and beautiful—not merely functional."

> *We need fortissimo and we need pianissimo.*
> *We need velvet and we need denim.*
> *We need silver trumpets and we need reed pipes.*
> *We need dawn and we need twilight.*
> *We need eagles and we need doves.*
> *We need lions and we need field mice.*
> *We need fire and we need ice.*
> *We need cataracts and we need pools.*
> *We need alps and we need salt marshes.*
> *We need raspberries and we need oatmeal.*
> *We need MAN and we need WOMAN.*
> (Tom Howard)

In Worship the Imagery Matters

> The eucharistic symbols are bread and wine, they are not spinach and pepsi. . . . We need the imagery of humility, and the imagery of splendour to boost us on to the mystery. (Tom Howard)

The glory of God and the splendor of His truth shines through successful ceremony and ritual. One of the prerequisites for successful ritual is that the real be rightly symbolized. God was so concerned about this that He Himself gave the form, measurements, and all the furnishings of the Tabernacle by revelation to Moses. It and everything within it symbolized His holiness and the way He has made for man to come to Him.

Image and apprehension, as C. S. Lewis has said, cleave more closely together than most moderns are willing to admit.[5] The Scriptural image of God the Father, as primarily masculine, is all-important, for example, if we are to understand not only the true Fatherhood of God, but what fatherhood on this plane means. If we believe, as I certainly do, that it is the Masculine Voice we are listening for when it comes time to separate our identities from that of our mother's (our source of being on the earthly plane), and that it is the Masculine Voice that blesses and affirms us finally in our gender identity and as persons, then the words of C. S. Lewis take on critical psychological as well as spiritual meaning:

> [A] child who has been taught to pray to a Mother in Heaven would have a religious life radically different from that of a Christian child.[6]

An interesting phenomenon I've seen repeated in many lives occurred in the life of the young doctor, Edward. He was from a church background rich with Christian symbol. But because faith and active collaboration with the Holy Spirit had been missing in his parish church, those very realities out of which great symbol is born and perpetuated, he is now in reaction to that church and its symbols. (The church he presently attends is concerned lest having a cross in back of the pulpit might be an "excess.") *Formalism* is the word for unsuccessful ceremony or ritual, and at this point Edward sees all ceremony and ritual as formalism.

It is precisely as The Rev. Alan Jones has said: "Protestantism began as a destruction of symbols that *appeared* to have gone dead" (italics mine). We all have a liturgy, and it is good or bad, rich or barren, not only in relation to its theological completeness and balance, but in its capacity to lead us into true worship and thereby mediate to us the Real Presence. No matter how "correct" it is, it is unsuccessful when there is unbelief and a failure to unite with God through it. We are the Fellowship of the Holy Spirit, and we corporately become brimming-over vessels for the Presence in successful worship.

In Statecraft the Imagery Matters

The imagery matters to Nazis and Soviets, Democrats and anarchists, saints and devils. (Tom Howard)

One French historian, explaining to Europeans the success of a young America said: "America is successful because America is good." It was then that our national symbols came into being, and they, along with our ceremonies, reflected goodness, justice, freedom.

Symbols of our goodness died here a while back. They are still extremely fragile and perilously close to dying—because the evil in our society is great.

President Reagan was termed "the great communicator," and to watch his inaugurals closely was to know why he communicated with the American people so well. He made sure that the archetypal symbols of a true democracy were included. He, for a while at least, revived the national symbols of a moral and transcendent good. I remember a large feature newspaper article which prominently headlined, "Reagan Saves the Presidency." And that by a paper hostile to him! Whatever our thoughts about President Reagan might be, or the place he finally finds in American history, there is no doubt that he, momentarily at least, remythologyzed the office of the Presidency. He initially gave it back its symbols of workability, even at times of greatness and authority.

The ceremonies and the ritual of kingship, where the symbols have not died, are a wonderful thing to behold. If we have watched the ceremonies of British royalty, we realize the powerful effect they have on the British people. Some of us might even suspect that when those symbols die, England too will be dead. The ceremonies and the ritual of royalty captivate most Americans, even though they fought hard for their freedom from a British monarch. But such is the power of successful symbol, ritual, and ceremony: it causes our British roots to vibrate and tingle. (It goes without saying that these same symbols work powerfully on others, but in a very different kind of way: say, for example, those of Catholic Ireland.)

As Persons the Imagery Really Matters

We need MAN and we need WOMAN. (Tom Howard)

In regard to the distinction between man and woman, Dr. Howard cries out: "Only persons? Most of you believe them when they tell you that this mightiest and most splendid of all distinctions in the universe—that it is a sexist distinction. I believe that the imagery matters and that this imagery of man and woman is rich and hilarious with liberties and joys so far beyond the gritty vocabulary of struggle and politics . . . that they cannot even be talked about on the same evening."

C. S. Lewis, reacting to the demythologizing of the Scriptures—in other words, the removal of all the supernatural as not being rational—has said truly enough that the same demythologizing process is at work on ourselves as societies, as persons.

Try to visualize a neuter, one who is neither male nor female. Then, in contrast, image the man who best symbolizes the masculine virtues—that is, what it means to be a whole man. He has the power to speak the truth and be the truth; the power to initiate, to exercise authority, to command justice, to pierce through difficulties, to give benevolent leadership. He is in right relationship to woman, and therefore is not only in touch with the feminine principle and grace within her, but those graces within himself are strengthened. The masculine principle is thereby balanced and strengthened. The masculine "drive toward power" in such a man is therefore submitted and responsive to God, and we do not have to fear its egotistical and warlike propensities.

Woman, considered under her symbolic aspect, symbolizes all that is responsive in the universe. In terms of her creation and her capacity to be the mother of life, she symbolizes all that acknowledges itself to be creaturely. In terms of loving God, she symbolizes all that is surrendered and obedient. Imagine, then, the woman who best exemplifies this for you. Just as the masculine must be informed by the feminine, so must woman, in right relationship to man (and nurtured by him), get in touch with the masculine virtues, both within him and within herself. She is thereby strengthened in her capacities to be warmly responsive, yet strong to speak and be the truth and to initiate change where necessary. She has the power to give (or has given) birth, and thereby reveals her special and mysterious connectedness with Nature. She has the power to nurture, the power in her love and feminine virtue to civilize the male. She has the power to participate in and complete the masculine.

These were once powerful images in the Western world, but are now, generally speaking, neuterized. When the great and true symbols of gender die, man and woman weaken and die too.

In a book I wrote several years ago, *Crisis in Masculinity*, I tried to show what has happened to us as a result of the denial of the symbolic mind altogether, what it has meant to run from it. In Karl Stern's book *The Flight from Woman*, he sketches the history of this flight as it can be read through literature and philosophy, along with its terrible effects on men. Men, valuing only the more masculine, analytical, rational, scientific mind, have been in full flight from the more feminine, intuitive, symbolic, feeling mind, both within themselves and within woman. I've tried to show how the loss of the intuitive capacity to see and respond to God that is within us all (God is, after all, so masculine that we are all feminine in relation to Him) has now resulted in the critical loss of the masculine—indeed, in the loss of reason itself.

We cannot lose the good of one mind without eventually losing the good of the other. The masculine and the feminine combine to give us the good of reason, and to lose the feminine is to lose finally the capacity to *know* (be impregnated or penetrated) by meaning at all. This is the flight from woman, the flight which has resulted in a Western world filled with unaffirmed men and women, the loss of the masculine and a headlong fall into the ersatz feminine—a passive, depressed state.

Man and woman, apart from their symbols, die.

At Table the Imagery Matters

"Worship the Lord your God, and his blessing will be on your food and water. I will take away sickness from among you . . . and I will give you a full life span." (Exodus 23:25, 26)

The modern fast track we are on has nearly eliminated ceremony and ritual at table. Think, if you will, of the ceremony or ritual of the blessing that brings down the transcendent, hallowing the ordinary, at table.

How closely does this loss relate to divorce, to homosexuality, to the inability to commit oneself to the opposite sex, and to thereby begin to create family and family life? Or to the ability to fit into the whole family of God at the larger Table, where Christ brings symbol and reality together by saying: "This is My body, this is My blood, given for you, given for all"?

Then too, if you will, think of the single eating alone, year in, year out. Physical health, as well as mental, spiritual, and emotional health, are all at stake where successful symbol and imagery are absent. Then think of the effects on the ritual at table where there is divorce, where mother is absent, where father is absent, where other family members rarely gather, and when they do, only to sit in chilly hostility or even open anger.

In contrast, picture a feast where all the family members are present. There, with candles, prayers, meaningful and traditional rituals, the Sabbaths and all great occasions are celebrated and made real in the life of those who participate. This is one of the important ways the family finds and continues to affirm itself as family. Its reality is rooted in the transcendent as the commonplace is hallowed.

The actuality (the gathered family) and all it symbolizes here is of vital importance: father, mother, son, daughter, grandmother, grandfather, priest, minister, spinster aunt, black-sheep uncle for whom everyone is praying: all belong, all participate, all give, all receive.

With the loss of family, of community, we lose not only the principles involved, but at stake are the primal inner images as well. All that each symbolizes—primal images of motherhood, fatherhood, grandparenthood, priesthood, sonship, what it means to be a daughter blossoming into wholeness—are lost. Imagery and symbol, those things that nourish our inner being, are lost along with the family members themselves.

Sacred Space

Symbol is needed to better apprehend the transcendent in all areas and phases of our lives. As Mircea Eliade says,

> For modern consciousness, a physiological act—eating, sex, and so on—is in sum only an organic phenomenon, however much it may still be encumbered by tabus (imposing, for example, particular rules for "eating properly" or forbidding some sexual behavior disapproved by social morality). But for the primitive, such an act is never simply physiological; it is, or can become, a sacrament, that is, a communion with the sacred.[7]

This is why C. S. Lewis can say that the Christian is much closer to the primitive than to the inhabitant of a "post-Christian" world.

In regard to the sexual act, Eliade says that it was originally "a ritual with transcendent meaning at every point." Dr. Clyde Kilby expresses it this way: "Those who indulge in promiscuous sex perhaps know best the sordidness of its unritual and animal uses. Our world is dispossessed of hierarchy."

Although Eliade believes that man's concept of the absolute "can never be uprooted: it can only be debased," nevertheless, as he says, there are now two modes of being in the world: that of those who believe in sacred space and in bringing the ordinary life into it, and those for whom all space is the same.

This alternative conception of a "completely profane world, the wholly desacralized cosmos," as Eliade says, "is a recent discovery in the history of the human spirit." It is a result of being demythologized, bereft of the transcendent, of thereby becoming absolutely man-centered as opposed to God-centered.

In the eighteenth-century, with the Romantic Movement, our image of ourselves in the cosmos shifted. From a God-centered cosmology (science of the laws which control the universe) of order, hierarchy, purpose, and harmony, we shifted to a cosmology of the psyche: to a man-centered (that is, self-centered) universe. Our world is now no larger that our psyche—that is, our feelings about truth and fact. Our subjective response has supplanted the objective reality. For the modern, there is no objective truth out there, no reference point outside himself. He therefore languishes in the dark chains of introspection and narcissism, the worship of the self. No wonder our symbols or myths are small and insignificant. To lose a God-centered cosmology is to lose, finally, the transcendent dimension of everything: man, woman, gender identity, marriage, sexuality, relationship with God and with all creation.

The Critical Nature of the Christians' Loss
of the Symbolic Mind

Se we begin to see why symbol, the images we carry *within* and we honor *without*, are so important. Symbols of fatherhood, motherhood, family, masculinity, sonship, himself as a man were all dead in the young doctor's life. Therefore, Christian symbols of God the Father, God the Son, and the Church were dead to him, as well as those of earthly relationships. It is precisely as Fr. Alan Jones has said: "Symbols bind up reality for us. When the symbols die, we die too."

When Love Is Disordered There Is Symbolic Confusion

When love is disordered, our relationships disordered, then primal images are missing or they are seriously (as in the homosexual neurosis) confused. This is the tragedy of broken homes where we sustain not only the loss of parents and other family members, but the loss of what these persons symbolize as well. We sustain the loss of symbolic images of wholeness that continue to nourish us.

Edward was a man alone in the world, separated from father, mother, family, sonship, woman, man. His inner vision of himself, though fairly successful as a professional man, was utterly desiccated. He had been unable to find God because the symbolic significance of *relationship* was missing in his life. The diseased imagery was a substitute for the meaningful primal images within and meaningful relationships without. What was he to do? What was to be done for him? The answer is exciting indeed.

The Healing Answer

Edward was to be remythologized. He, like Bultmann's Scriptures, had been demythologized.

How are we remythologized? Through listening prayer, through reception of the words and the pictures that come from God. Through learning to practice the Presence, thereby bringing every thought of the mind, every imagination of the heart captive to Christ. Through exchanging every negative word coming from the world, the flesh, and the Devil for the word that God is always speaking. Through baptism in the Holy Spirit. All of this presupposing, of course, regeneration and conversion of the will, and fellowship with God's people.

Edward's task in all this? To come present to God, and then to do what we all have to do. "Set love in order, thou that lovest me" (from Dante's *Divine Comedy*, St. Francis in the *Paradiso*). St. Augustine prayed fervently: "Set love in order in me."

Alan Jones, in a lecture on Dante's *Divine Comedy,* the greatest of poems, shows it to be an allegory of the spiritual journey we all take (allegory is interpretation of experience by use of picture). It is, as Fr. Jones states, a poem about *right order*. Divine justice is "concerned with right ordering." Christian discipline is for the purpose of the right ordering of our loves.

We love confusedly, we fallen ones; the journey of life is for setting love in order.

In the setting of love in order, the true imagination (our capacity to intuit the real) is all-important. Our capacity to fasten the eyes of our hearts on God and all that is real outside ourselves, loving it, becoming incarnate of it, is crucial. God is love, and to practice His Presence is to become filled not only with Him, but with primal images of glory. We end, no matter how empty we were before, in fullness of being.

The prescription for Edward was to be filled with God. He was, and is. The primal images of God, fatherhood, motherhood, family, love, what it means to be a man—all these symbols that were missing in his life he is now gaining through meditation on the Scriptures, listening prayer, the practice of the Presence, and fellowship within the Body of Christ. He is getting to know all kinds of people—young and old, male and female, good-humored and crotchety, homespun and cultured. He is today exuberantly learning to relate to others—all the many varieties one finds in a loving church fellowship. He is learning what a grandmother is, and will therefore have a wholesome concept or image of what grandmotherliness is. Through fellowship with others, he is learning what normal is. He is, in short, being remythologized (divinely symbolized) through setting love in order.

The imagery, within and without, really matters.

CHAPTER 10

The Terrible Schism
in the Heart of Man

*C*hristians use such phrases as *head and heart* and *head knowledge versus heart knowledge* to distinguish between discursive reason on the one hand, and intuitive, symbolic, feeling ways of knowing on the other. The latter has to do with the way of faith and love, prayer, worship, the Sacraments, and repentance. This language acknowledges the terrible schism in the heart of man that Kierkegaard cried out about when he said that we have forgotten how to exist, and can only think and talk about being.

This way of speaking, making the *heart* a metaphor to stand for the neglected faculty, is deeply imbedded in our terminology. This has much to do with our history—a history of slowly losing the Christian supernatural, and therefore the vital Christian "myth" or symbolic system.

Throughout this book and the other books I have written, I've used such phrases as "mind and heart," "intellect and heart," "the cold intellect", "the schism between head and heart," "the way the heart sees," "it is with the heart that we see the Unseen Real," "the way the deep heart knows" (meaning the more "unconscious" reaches of our being). All this is a way of expressing the schism we moderns suffer due to the false separation between reason and faith, that which is behind the elevation of the rational faculty (making it to be the whole mind) and the denigration and even denial of the intuitive, feeling mind.

The pagan world distinguished between the educated, rational mind (the elite) and the mind of the masses (the common man). The elite were initiated, so to speak. On the one hand, they had access to the best that practical, moral reason could come up with (which is considerable), and on the other, as with the Gnostics and so on, they had their secret doctrines, the *gnoses*, fueled more often than not with the power of dark ways of knowing. All of this knowledge, of course, fell short of divine wisdom, the dimension the Jews as a people in communication with God had.

Then Christ, the Light of the World, dawned upon the Greco-Roman world, and His gospel was the same for all—educated and uneducated, rich and poor, free and slave, male and female, Jew and pagan. He differentiated between the wisdom of this world and the wisdom that comes through communication with God. At the foot of His Cross, the elite and the common alike can find the one true wisdom. And that wisdom, because it has to do with God living in us, changes all of life. There was to be no more *elite* as opposed to *common*. There was to be one body of men in Christ. Initiations into secret doctrines were out. Great moral teachers would learn from the unlearned, such as Peter and John. Repentance, belief, and initiation into Christ through baptism replaced pagan rites and *gnoses*. The power of the Holy Spirit (the Christian supernatural) and the light of the gospel overcame and replaced superstitions and the dark powers and ways of knowing.

As stressed earlier in this book, we practice the Presence of Father, Son, and Holy Spirit, and we are not to lose sight of any one of the Three. But another extremely important thing to keep in mind is the fact that it is through Christ that we know the Father and the Spirit. The Church that knows God the Father and God the Spirit is therefore Christocentric. In the history of the Church, as the ecclesiastical structures grew, the Church became increasingly theocentric, and there came a time when the Church was no longer Christ-centered. Its mysticism therefore ceased to be Christocentric (Christ in and with us, the way of knowing God and the divine supernatural). Though theocentric (God-centered), in its failure to "practice the Presence of Christ with us" it lost its relationship to God the Father as well. In other words, God seemed very far away. He became an abstract—the kind of God the pagans acknowledged—rather than a personal God.

People then, as now, could not live in such a meaningless gap. It was at this point that pagan thought began to infiltrate the ranks of Christendom. Having lost Incarnational Reality, personal fellowship with God, the Church had no defense against such thought. Pagan spirituality and mysticism began to replace and war against what was left of the knowledge of the Presence and the Christian supernatural.

It was here that the controversy between faith and reason began. As C. S. Lewis and Thomas Molnar point out, the pagan worldview always lurks just beneath the Christian. It is, as Lewis says, the natural religion of man, the man without faith. And this is where the schism between the "two minds" or ways of knowing (as we experience the rift today) began.

The separation of faith and reason began plaguing Christian speculation . . . when large doses of Greek philosophy came to the attention of medieval Christian thinkers through the Arab-Syrian rediscovery of hitherto unknown texts.[1]

The problem of faith, as Thomas Molnar points out, had no precedent in the pagan world. The Greeks examined knowledge from every angle except faith. The reason for this, of course, is, "faith can only arise with a personal God." "The root of faith," as Oswald Chambers reminds us, "is the knowledge of a Person."[2] We can't obey an abstraction. We can't even pray to one. We may meditate (think) on one, as Plotinus and the great pagans did, but we cannot have faith and trust in one. We begin to look for other answers, other "wisdom," new *gnoses* to speak meaning and "connectedness" with the cosmos into our being.

The Church, then infiltrated with Greek philosophy, was unable to reconcile faith and reason. According to Thomas Molnar:

> It was finally the Arab world that produced an answer known as the doctrine of the "two verities," usually attributed to Averroes. In the Arab philosophers' own words: "Of the things which are too hard for ordinary believers to grasp, God gave them signs and symbols. . . . Thus divine things are divided into the exoteric ones (accessible to the masses) and esoteric ones reserved for the philosophers."
>
> Though the doctrine of the two verities was unacceptable to the church, it was eagerly seized upon by the philosophers at the University of Padua, which subsequently became known for this option while continuing, nonetheless, as a center of Aristotelian studies. From Padua, Averroism spread to many places in Europe, particularly by the end of the fifteenth and sixteenth centuries when Italy was opened to the outside world through the wars on its soil by Spaniards, Germans, and the French. Partisans of the Averroist doctrine, leaning on the authority of Aristotle, who, so the saying went, "could not err," possessed a great advantage from the point of view of the "paganizers": they could pacify church authorities with assurances of orthodox faith, yet free themselves for the elaboration of a materialist system.
>
> Here we see the tragic effects of syncretism: Officially the Paduans discovered two parallel ways of interpreting religion. But in fact, there was not much question of parallel ways since the faith dimension was abandoned to the nonthinking orthodox

and to the untutored masses. The philosophers held as valid for themselves only that area on which reason could operate unobstructed. This led, in time, to two divergent courses. One was fideism, in which faith renounced the claim to understanding and was therefore encouraged by the Paduan philosophers as a safe blind alley for the religious minded; the other was rationalism, which, if well directed, could lead to science. The scientific enterprise was thus freed in advance from religious interference. Instead of reconciling reason and faith as advertised, or at least recognizing the validity of the respective paths, the Paduan teaching effectively drove a wedge between the two, depreciated the value of faith, and thereby broke the medieval harmony between theology and philosophy.[3]

All this was further solidified in the seventeenth century with the philosopher Rene Descartes's dictum, "I think, therefore I am." In the Cartesian world that followed, only the cognitive, scientific mind was recognized, and we have now come to that tragic place where we are paying the full spiritual and psychological price for such false thinking as this.

From this brief historical overview, we see why we speak of "head and heart" the way we do. Our language reflects at once the historical schism, as well as the attempt to overcome it and explain the knowledge of faith and the imaginative-intuitive-symbolic ways of knowing. But I want to make it clear that this language is a concession, a necessary one in that it acknowledges this historical ideology which has resulted in a psychological schism (between thinking and being) within the souls of men and women everywhere. But it is unfortunate terminology in that it too can seem to divide what should only be differentiated, and can therefore mislead us into the opposite error of undervaluing the discursive reason, its symbolic capacities, its power to complement and balance the intuitive-feeling mind. It can and does lead to differentiations in the "two minds" that are inaccurate and therefore misleading.

The Bible knows nothing of the schism we have suffered, so it does not use the metaphor *heart* in this way. "In Biblical language," the heart is "the center of the human spirit, from which spring emotions, thought, motivations, courage and action—the 'wellspring of life.'"[4] In the Scriptures, therefore, the *heart* of man refers to both "minds"—or as we say today, to "head knowledge" as well as "heart knowledge." It also refers to both the spirit and the soul in man. Therefore, rather than speaking of healing the head in contrast to the heart, the "conscious" in contrast to the "unconscious," or the spirit in contrast to the soul, it speaks very simply of *cleansing the heart*. This cleansing radically starts the transformation in every faculty, preparing the total inner man for a *transposition*—an infilling of God's Spirit.

This means, of course, just as in any number of cases in the English language, that we use a language symbol in more than one way. When we say "head and heart," we acknowledge the schism that is in man and has to be healed. But in terms of prayer for healing, we hold firmly to the Scriptural metaphor which rightly speaks of man's inner being in this integrated way. We are then less likely to be tempted to make the healing of man more complicated and difficult than it is.

The incredibly wonderful thing about all this is that God's way of cleansing the conscience works. It sets right the "two minds" that have been at such loggerheads, and thereby sets the stage for their further maturation and sanctification. We may need special prayer help or special counseling and therapy to help remove the blocks to our acceptance of all that Christ's blood (atoning death) has wrought for us. But once we finally receive it, we receive the basic healing, that which forms the basis for bringing into balance the whole of man. "Blessed are the pure in heart, for they will see God" (Matthew 5:8).

"Remember," says Oswald Chambers, "that vision depends on character—the pure in heart see God." The mind of man, including his spirit and entire soul, are either cleansed and wise (in balance), or evil and darkened (unseeing), depending whether or not there is confession of sin and fellowship with God through Christ.

So the Bible, while acknowledging the differing faculties of the heart, does not speak of its "two minds," but of one heart with two mindsets.

> Those who live according to the sinful nature have their mind
> set on what that nature desires; but those who live in accordance
> with the Spirit have their minds set on what the Spirit desires.
> (Romans 8:5)

"Lift your eyes and look to the heavens" (Isaiah 40:36). "I looked and saw the glory of the Lord" (Ezekiel 44:4). "Those who look to him are radiant" (Psalm 34:5). The "elementary organ of new vision," then, is "that faculty for looking up."[5] This is the secret of the true imagination in its highest sense.

CHAPTER 11

The True Imagination

Thou wilt keep him in perfect peace whose imagination is stayed on Thee.

(Isaiah 26:3, RSV)

*I*n the Presence, listening, our souls are remythologized. The words and the pictures that come from God replace the old, negative, lying words and inner images that have their genesis in the world, the flesh, and the Devil—all that underlies out need for healing and salvation. This new experience (our remythologization) has to do with the true imagination, the way we as creaturely receivers "see" and "hear" the inaudible, the invisible. It involves our loving and receiving from God, and from all that He has made and calls good.

Imaginative Experience
The truly imaginative experience is defined therefore as an intuition of the real. It is an acknowledgement of objective realities (those outside the self) in their transcendent, unseen dimension (perhaps we could say, in their essence). It is that which, when received, enlarges and completes us, for it speaks to and unites with some lonely facet of our own being. All true worship, knowledge, and art come out of this.

At its highest level, the truly imaginative experience (intuition of the real) is the experience of receiving from God, whether by word, vision, or (greatest of all) an infilling of Himself. In philosophical terms, this would be an intuition of the real from the realm of absolute reality (the Uncreated). There are two other realms, both created, from which truly imaginative experiences arise, and they are 1) Nature, and 2) Super-Nature (the created nonmaterial, such as angelic beings, and the mind, the rational and imaginative in man). Wonderfully, these three planes or realms correspond to spirit, soul, and body: our tri-partite nature. Man, in his body, participates in Nature; in his psyche, he participates in Super-Nature; and through his spirit, the whole of him can be linked beyond all Nature and Super-Nature to absolute being.[1]

Awe

Man is properly awed in the presence of that which is mysterious or majestic, or that which is greater than he. Beauty, greatness, genius, love, sheer goodness—all these, objectively real, inspire in the beholder (the intuiter) the awe due them. With an intuition of the Holy—that is, of God Himself—or of unfallen angelic beings, the numinous awe one feels is profound indeed. In this Presence, man's creatureliness is exquisitely realized and acknowledged. He knows the fear of God and finds, as the Scriptures promise, the reward of a wisdom that does not originate in himself.

> The fear of the Lord is the beginning of wisdom; a good under-standing have all those who practice it. (Psalm 111:10, RSV)

To "practice" this fear, of course, is to practice the Presence—to call to mind often the objective Presence of the Unseen Other—whether or not there is an active intuition of Him. The Divine Object draws awe and worship from the subject. Man's creatureliness is affirmed.

C. S. Lewis asked one of his friends if the conception of creatureli-ness was part of his philosophy at all, or if his system was not in fact anthropocentric (man-centered). If one's system is anthropocentric, he simply will not have the categories with which to understand this view of the imagination in man or of the creative process as it involves the human maker. A full acknowledgement of our creatureliness, of our-selves as subject, and of ourselves as intuiters of that objective truth that lies outside ourselves is all-important to understanding the truly imagi-native experience.

> [T]he value of the individual does not lie in him. He is capable of receiving value. He receives it by union with Christ. There is no question of finding for him a place in the living temple which will do justice to his inherent value and give scope to his natural idiosyncrasy. The place was there first. The man was created for it. He will not be himself till he is there. . . . To say this is to repeat what everyone here admits already—that we are saved by grace, that in our flesh dwells no good thing, that we are, through and through, creatures not creators, derived beings, liv-ing not of ourselves but from Christ.[2]

The Word *Imagination*

For most of us, the word *imagination* is a vague one. For many Christians, raised on the *King James Bible,* the word may hold distinctly negative connotations, for it was used in that translation to denote a scheming or devising mind. This may be one of the factors behind the irrational fear of the imagination which we find in some Christian circles. The imaginative faculty, like any other human faculty, can be used for good or evil. To ignore or fear it is dangerous, and is a kind of evil, just as misusing it is evil.

The dictionary defines *imagination* as "the action . . . of forming a mental image or concept of what is not present to the senses." Another definition denotes the imaginative faculty itself by which these images or concepts are formed. A third meaning refers to the "power which the mind has of forming concepts beyond those derived from external objects (the 'productive imagination')." This power refers not only to fancy but to creative or poetic genius, "the power of framing new and striking intellectual conceptions" (*Oxford English Dictionary*).

This last definition, in its reference to creative or poetic genius, approaches our definition of the true and higher imagination. A thing to note here is that the dictionary definition is, from our point of view, necessarily a truncated one, for the imagination is defined there from the standpoint of man only. His power to form images or concepts within his mind and imagination is made clear, but not his status as receiver of that which is other than himself.

Religious and Poetic Awe

As receivers, the awe we experience differs as the kinds of reality (whether that of Nature, Super-Nature, or the Real Presence of God) to be intuited differ. It is in the object, that which invokes the awe, that the difference lies.

When the heavens were opened and the prophet Ezekiel saw "visions of God," he fell upon his face in worshipful awe. In the midst of this he heard a Voice speaking: "And when he spoke to me, the Spirit entered into me and set me upon my feet." Ezekiel was then indwelt by the object. This is religious awe, and the object that inspired it was God. No one is ever the same after an experience like that. When Saul was knocked to the ground by a Light from Heaven and heard Christ speaking to him, that was a life-changing encounter with the Unseen Real, "an intuition of the real" that drastically changed his life, instantly and forever. It blinded him for a time. He was renamed Paul. Experiences like these bring instant healings, and instant cripplings as well. Jacob stood up after such an encounter, one in which he wrestled with the Almighty and was wounded in his thigh. But the wound became a sign to him, and to those after him.

When the object that inspires the awe is from the realm of Nature, its very essence seems momentarily revealed to the artist. While observing a flower, a whale breaching the water, a human face, a mountain, he may suddenly be overwhelmed with the disclosure Nature yields; or we might say, with the universal or even transcendent meaning behind the particular he is seeing. For example, in seeing a particular whale, its alien and thrilling otherness, its whaleness, might be revealed to him. In a woman's face, he may be confronted with the transcendent and eternal feminine, and know thereafter more of what true womanhood is, what womanness in contrast to manness is.

These experiences differ from Ezekiel's in that the objects giving rise to them differ. But the parallels to religious awe are there. Looking to the object, the artist has forgotten himself, and in loving that which he sees, he finds it has opened itself more fully to him. He has become totally "absorbed" in it. Possessed then by the creative idea, he feels compelled to transpose it into material form. This is poetic awe, capable at any moment of becoming not less, but more than poetic awe. This is so, and could not be otherwise when we consider that all that exists is created by God; it has transcendent dimensions, those that go beyond Nature. Its roots are in the heavenlies. The overlapping between Nature and Super-Nature is obvious here, for immediately, as Nature makes such a disclosure, we are into another realm. And when God discloses Himself through Nature, we are into the realm of absolute being.

When the eyes of God's people are opened to see angelic beings, they are seeing into the realm of Super-Nature. The awe one experiences in the face of an unfallen, though created, angelic being, is exquisite. There are different degrees in these "intuitions of the real," though I hardly know how to explain it. For example, angels have appeared and given their messages or their comfort and guidance through dreams and visions (waking dreams), but in addition there are times when another spiritual plane is opened, and in that case the experience of an angelic being has an astounding immediacy.

On a number of occasions, I have discerned the presence of angels. Once while in earnest prayer for guidance from the Lord, a huge angel was suddenly with me, and my eyes were opened to *see* him.[3] I felt a distinct physical change in the power of my eyes to focus. The awe at the "degree" of his presence and the seemingly superimposed spiritual plane was such that it remained for weeks (and seemed even to spill over on to the few others I shared the experience with). I realized (only afterward) that this angel had brought me the knowledge of where to go, and even whom to contact, though he had not spoken to me. I did not even see his face, for he was huge and I was too awed to look up. After the visitation, I simply had the answer.

During this experience, as I continued in prayer and worship, I sang in the most incredible tongue, one that seemed to chime (bell-like) and resonate with the very sounds of Heaven, one that I believe to have been an angelic language. There simply are no languages like it on earth. (C. S. Lewis and J. R. R. Tolkien, in their Christian myth, have an uncanny way of portraying these experiences. Tolkien, writing of the Elves and of the glorious singing in the Elven languages, comes as near to capturing the experience of this singing as can be done.)

This, as all true experience does, has its unfortunate counterpart in the world of darkness. When spectators who are naive about the world of Super-Nature watch an occult ritual in which a person becomes possessed by demons, they may find themselves speaking in demonic tongues. They have stepped into a circle of darkness and are themselves now infected (even demonized) by it. In prayer, worshiping God, I was in His circle, replete with angelic hosts that continuously sing to His glory. They imparted, if but for that once, their song to me!

When the spiritual being that one sees or intuits is a fallen one, such as an evil angel or an unclean spirit (demon), the feeling is one of intense revulsion. Even so, this has to do with an intuition from a realm other than that of the sensory, of Nature. It is from the realm of Super-Nature. (Here again, there are different degrees of these "intuitions," of discernment of the unseen. My eyes have been opened—always for a needed purpose—to "see" these things in all their revolting "forms," while at other times the same discernment is there without the actual "seeing" into another realm.)

As our minds and hearts are opened to intuit angelic beings, so they also are opened to the great revelations of the mind. Einstein's great theorem danced as figures before the eyes of his mind. It was purely a "given," a product of the true imagination from the realm of Super-Nature, as are most all the great discoveries of the human mind and heart.

Some of these discoveries are best described (it seems to me) as simply mythic. In an intense moment, the greater meaning of a thing is disclosed to us. We've met it before, perhaps, in some of its isolated particulars, but now its meaning floods in upon us in an overpowering way. We may not understand just what happened to us, as was the case with a young, expectant mother who was troubled and confused over her seemingly excessive reactions to the death of her canary.

From a condition of calm repose, with her family (as well as the family cat) milling quietly about, she was startled by her bird's cry. She raced upstairs to see this cherished pet, affectionately named Tweety Bird, breathing his last—a bloody gash in his throat where Tom Cat had caught him. She let out a scream that no one in the house will ever forget. The hearers were not just transfixed; they were, in their words, almost irreparably unhinged. Linda was embarrassed. "How," she asked, "could I have screamed such a scream?"

I knew instantly what had happened to her. She who was carrying life within her womb experienced for the first time the true meaning of death. I said to her, "Linda, you've had a mythic experience. Somehow, with this traumatic thing you experienced the universal meaning of death, the Fall, the meaninglessness of it all. It was a cruel shock to see something so beautiful and full of joyful sound as your canary blotted out of life for no good reason. The cat wasn't even hungry. But your experience was far more than merely the sorrow and shock over Tweety Bird. The essence of sin, darkness, pain, and its annihilation of life, beauty, harmony, was somehow revealed to you." And it was.

We prayed for the healing of the trauma, and for the quieting of the babe within her womb. For her, after that, there was a new dimension in appreciation of the Cross, of why Christ died to overcome the meaninglessness that man knows apart from eternal life. That one experience distilled for her the essence of death itself, its mythic, universal meaning.

The following is chiefly an experience of the Real Presence, but it is similar to the above in that the universal meaning of a thing was imparted. In this case, the meaning of divine love (rather than death) was imparted. My mother was praying when a wave of love (in its essence, or so it seemed to her) washed over her and into her as the Shekinah Glory. (How would she know what the Shekinah Glory is? But she did.) She experienced waves of it, waves that came in vivid colors beyond her power to describe. She shared this with very few people, which is wise. Joy has a way of dissipating when shared indiscriminately, while it multiplies in its healing effects (even to others) when rightly garnered and stewarded. Mother was never quite the same after that, for she had grasped, if but for a moment, love in its universal essence and meaning.

Connie Boerner, singer and songwriter as well as beloved prayer partner and team member, wrote and recorded "Hind's Feet," a song I never tire of hearing her sing. She awakened one morning hearing the song chanted by a choir of black singers! She simply wrote the words and the music she heard. Here we have religious and poetic experience coming together.

We could write endlessly on these things, but I think my point has been made. It can only be in awe and humility that the saint, the artist, the great scholar, or scientist begins to work with what has been given unaccountably from outside. Often the recipients are flat on their faces with the feeling of utter inadequacy as to how to pass the vision on to others. To one who is not an artist it seems incredible that Michelangelo felt himself to be a fumbler! Always there is the gap between that which is seen and heard and that which can finally be captured—on canvas, in word, in stone, in poetry, in melody.

As a way of summing this up, then: An intuition of God differs only in degree from the sudden intuition of a truth in Nature or Super-Nature—but the manner in which the revelation comes and the intuitive and experiential nature of the *knowing* is much the same.

This is the true imagination at work.

It is from the receiver's side an intuition of the real, and from the object's side a revelation imparted.

The spirituals, such as the gifts of knowledge and of wisdom, are part of it. Listening prayer, incarnation, and baptism in the Holy Spirit are part of it. C. S. Lewis calls it joy. There is little wonder, then, that Oswald Chambers has called it the greatest gift (faculty) we have—the faculty of receiving impartations of that which is other than ourselves.

Thinking Imaginatively Without Images

God sends us pictures and He sends us words. Pictures—that is, metaphor, symbol, myth, dreams, and visions—are a vital part of the language of the heart. We need to understand this symbolic language. But one can think imaginatively without images. Knowledge, wisdom, understanding come to us as *word* (i.e., more nearly as concept) as well as in picture form. As I once heard Dr. Paul T. Holmer say, to be truly imaginative does not mean to have "a train of images coursing through one's brain." It is the intuition of the real that matters, and it can come as thought or as picture. For many, including myself, the imaginative insight and/or revelation comes more often as thought than as picture. For Lucy Smith, another beloved prayer partner and team member, it comes almost always as "seeings," and often there is a succession of pictures in vivid color.

It should be clear by now that the imagination is not active only in the "gifted" person, but is a necessary part of everyone's life. I hope it is equally clear that the power to visualize, as a physiological and psychological phenomenon (like thinking and breathing), differs from the truly imaginative experience.

Though the power to visualize is not imagination in the higher sense, it can play a part in the creative process. It can and often does serve the true imagination in healing prayer. For example, when I ask someone to see with his heart Christ on the Cross, the capacity to deliberately visualize it is one thing, but to be very good at visualizing it (the attempt to make a mental image like one in the outer world or to produce a way of seeing close to the conscious, literal way) would get in the way of true imagination. It is the casting of our eyes upon God and, in this case, that which symbolizes His salvation that matters. When we look to Christ crucified, then the picture our heart makes (Christ on the Cross) acts in its full capacity as symbol and becomes a vehicle for all the saving power of God to come to us. It opens us to meaning. Meaning streams to the deepest reaches of the unconscious (the deep heart) through it. Thus, in that one symbol the entire theology of the Cross has come together with experience (reception) of its grace.

Symbol is the key for the fusion of thought with feeling. The symbolic mind, working properly, brings together head and heart. What starts out as a deliberate visualizing of the Cross becomes an intuition of the real. God sends His healing grace, a thing we could never have deliberately visualized.

This is exactly what we see commanded in the Scriptures time and again: "Lift up your eyes on high, and behold who hath created these things" (Isaiah 40:26, KJV). We cast our eyes upon God as Father, as risen Savior, as Shepherd, as coming King—the many ways He has revealed Himself to us. When we do, good things start to happen.

Oswald Chambers understands the heart's need to focus on God and the interchange that begins between God and man when this happens. Commenting on Isaiah 26:3, "Thou wilt keep him in perfect peace, whose mind [imagination] is stayed on thee" (KJV), Chambers asks:

> Is your imagination stayed on God or is it starved? The starvation of the imagination is one of the most fruitful sources of exhaustion and sapping in a worker's life. If you have never used your imagination to put yourself before God, begin to do it now. It is no use waiting for God to come; you must put your imagination away from the face of idols and look unto Him and be saved. Imagination is the greatest gift God has given us and it ought to be devoted entirely to Him. If you have been bringing every thought into captivity to the obedience of Christ, it will be one of the greatest assets to faith when the time of trial comes because your faith and the Spirit of God will work together.[4]

Commenting on Isaiah 40:26, "Lift up your eyes on high, and behold who hath created these things" (KJV), Chambers says:

> The people of God in Isaiah's day had starved their imagination by looking on the face of idols, and Isaiah made them look up at the heavens, that is, he made them begin to use their imagination aright. . . .
> The test of spiritual concentration is bringing the imagination into captivity. Is your imagination looking on the face of an idol? Is the idol yourself? Your work? . . . If your imagination is

starved, do not look back to your own experience; it is God Whom you need. Go right out of yourself, away from the face of your idols, away from everything that has been starving your imagination. Rouse yourself, take the gift that Isaiah gave the people, and deliberately turn your imagination to God.

One of the reasons of stultification in prayer is that there is no imagination, no power of putting ourselves deliberately before God. . . . Imagination is the power God gives a saint to posit himself out of himself into relationships he never was in.[5]

This has everything to do with believing in God, a supreme Ultimate Reality outside ourselves, and with understanding that our sole avenue to Him is "through prayer, sacrament, repentance, and adoration" (C.S. Lewis)—through the intuitive way the heart sees and hears. It has nothing to do with inducing some sort of psychological (untrue or merely wishful) mind-set upon ourselves.

Without true faith and obedience and knowledge of what we are doing, we can misuse any good thing. Christians can and do use to little effect or even misuse visualization in healing prayer. Under such circumstances, the methods do not open the way for true communication with God or for integration of thought with feeling. The rift between head and heart, intellect and imagination, spirit and matter is left intact. Obviously, these techniques, insofar as the psychological is concerned, can be used to great or ill effect in the secular world as well. They may involve little more than the inducing of a psychological mind-set. Even worse, when used in the service of darkness, they can be an opening for false revelation from demonic powers, evil thoughts, and fantasies. The same goes for the reasoning faculty. Apart from the experience of truth, its machinations also end in futility, or even worse, as we see in the end of those overly influenced by such thinkers as Nietzsche in philosophy, Bultmann in theology, or B. F. Skinner in psychology. To think or to picture apart from God is to inherit darkness. But we do not stop thinking because there are deluded thinkers. One can only speculate where we would be today had St. Paul not used his great mind, if St. Augustine had not used his, if in this century we had not had a C. S. Lewis. These men used both the head and the heart to full capacity in defense of the gospel.

In the history of the West, by and large, it has been the intellect, separated from the heart and moral good, that has most often led us into darkness. And, as history so often reveals, the imagination of the thinker, as well as those he has influenced, becomes darkened as well.

To deliberately image or visualize, then, is not the true imagination in action, but it can play a part in opening us to the truly imaginative experience. Time and time again, I've had people brought in for prayer who are in the midst of a mental and emotional breakdown. Inevitably they will say to me, "It's no use to pray. I can't believe. I've tried so hard, but I can't." Their difficulty, of course, is that this trying and believing has all been in the head, and the major difficulty is in the heart. The conscious, analytical mind has finally collapsed in its attempt to repress or handle the difficulties erupting from the deep mind and heart. Right away I say something to this effect: "That's O.K., you just let me do the praying for you." Then we kneel down before God and with my arm around the sufferer, I ask him or her to look up and see Christ on the Cross, dying to take into Himself whatever is amiss in his heart. Invariably, within a matter of minutes, the "diseased matter" within starts surfacing. It comes right up and is given to Him. I ask them to see with their hearts this being done, and it is amazing what they see. All that they have never been able to receive through painful thinking and striving now comes with "interest" as God does over and above what they were able to think or imagine. The connection is now made between the heart and God. As this healing takes place, peace and healing comes to the conscious mind and mental processes as well.

Another thing to remember is that even the pictures our hearts make of the real are not themselves the real (just as the word *apple* is not the real apple but a symbol for it). Our pictures are simply the language of the heart, and like icons are merely images through which the real is to shine. If the image is mistaken for the real (the icon for God), then it becomes "self-conscious" and misleads. It becomes an idol.

As an illustration, consider the Apostle Paul's vision of a man of Macedonia standing and begging him, "Come over to Macedonia and help us" (Acts 16:9). He understood this symbolically, as any Jewish man in his day would; and it's a good thing, for what did he find when he got to Macedonia? Not a man begging for help, but a successful businesswoman named Lydia. She in turn introduced him to a number of other women. Paul taught them, and out of their witness the word spread in Macedonia. He knew full well there was no conflict between his vision and what actually occurred, for he did not mistake the image for the real. It is amazing how difficult this is for some moderns to grasp. I even heard one minister say that Paul got the vision wrong!

When an angel appeared to Joseph in a dream and told him that the Holy Spirit had conceived Mary's child, Joseph's heart intuited the presence of the angel and the angel's message aright. Had he not understood the symbolic way the heart knows, he may have thought the "picture" his heart made of the angel was akin to the way we see an outer image. He might have said: "All angels look like the one who appeared in my dream." He may even have lost the true message in an attempt to make it more akin to the way we see and know with the discursive reason.

Another illustration: On one occasion, I was praying with a person, and I "saw" an evil eel-like thing slithering away. I knew that it was a demonic presence—a "stubborn spirit." Now had I said, "I saw a demon, and it looked like a dreadful eely snake, and all stubborn spirits look like that," I would have mistaken the symbolic form (the picture) for the thing itself. Should I have an occasion to discern another "stubborn spirit," it will most likely be in a different form. But the discernment will be the same.

C. S. Lewis, writing on the nature of mental images, states that they play an important part in his prayers.

> I doubt if any act of will or thought or emotion occurs in me without them. But they seem to help me most when they are most fugitive and fragmentary—rising and bursting like bubbles in champagne or wheeling like rooks in a windy sky: contradicting one another (in logic) as the crowded metaphors of a swift poet may do. Fix on any one, and it goes dead. You must do as Blake would do with a joy, kiss it as it flies. And then, in their total effect, they do mediate to me something very important. It is always something qualitative—more like an adjective than a noun. That, for me, gives it the impact of reality. For I think we respect nouns (and what we think they stand for) too much. All my deepest, and certainly all my earliest, experiences seem to be of sheer quality. The terrible and the lovely are older and solider than terrible and lovely things. If a musical phrase could be translated into words at all it would become an adjective. A great lyric is very like a long, utterly adequate, adjective. Plato was not so silly as the moderns think when he elevated abstract nouns—that is, adjectives disguised as nouns—into the supreme realities—the Forms.[6]

The Use and Misuse of Guided Imagery

There is nothing wrong with the use of guided imagery in prayer for healing as long as these precautions are taken. First, the one being prayed for needs to be completely aware of the philosophy and purpose of the one who is guiding. Second, the one doing the guiding must understand imagery and symbol and learn how to deal with any confusing or frightening *unbidden* imagery that comes up. Jesus, through story and parable, led the people in this way all the time. He did not have to teach visualization or the use of guided imagery. It's something humans normally do. The tendency of modern people to be cut off from the imaginative in metaphor, symbol, story, and parable, and from the capacity either to intuit or to visualize is abnormal. This is why psychologists and therapists use imaging as a method. They are attempting to help people who suffer the rift between head and heart, between the conscious and the unconscious. Having said this, I think that Christians would do much better to teach true prayer and then dispense, for the most part, with the method.

I use guided imagery when the situation calls for it, but I do not teach imaging or visualizing as such because it would be superfluous. When I ask people to look up and see the Lord and to hear Him with their hearts, they get in touch with the higher imagination (the capacity to receive whether by thought or picture). Then blocks to the lower (i.e., the physiological) capacity to image are removed. I make it a point to state the difference between visualizing and the true imagination. If people do not know already, they learn easily enough how intuitions of the real differ from their power to visualize as a physiological and psychological phenomenon.

It is, of course, unwise to conduct others in imaging methods if one is unfamiliar with his own soul, the souls of others, and some basic principles about the soul's makeup and motions. But it is foolish and even sinful to fear imaging. As fallen beings we are subject to bad images just as we are subject to bad thoughts. The bad in either case is to be discerned and replaced with the good. This is eminently the field of the Christian, and we should be leading the way in helping people to bring every thought of the mind and every imagination of the heart into subjection to Christ.

When a person (the one seeking help) with diseased imagery and symbolic confusion begins to visualize, he will quickly get in touch with these. This is what scares people who do not understand either the imagery or how to help the person who suffers it. This, however, is a vital part of healing prayer. The diseased imagery is to be discerned. If it is from the world, the flesh, or the Devil, it can be renounced. But if it wells up from an unhealed psyche, it provides the clue to what needs healing.

For example, I ask a woman for whom I am praying to look up and to see with her heart Christ on the Cross. When she does so, she is horrified by obscene images. I will not (as some do) stop asking people to look up to God, thinking it to be a dangerous practice. I will immediately know that this is not the true imagination at work, but that she needs another kind of prayer, another healing, before she can conceptualize God aright. Her identity may be eroticized through sexual molestation, incest, or sinful sexual acitivity. She may be unable to see a male figure in any other way. She may need to renounce Baal, the god of sexual orgy (see Chapter 14). In any case, we have before us an image from an unhealed psyche, and we now know how to proceed. We discern the true problem and tackle that. The image that has so horrified the person is telling us something about her need.

Just as I was writing this paragraph, I received a letter from a girl who has come out of the lesbian lifestyle. She is beginning to deal with the truly awful memories of abandonment she had as an infant. She is already listening to God and praying with great effect for others who have known the depths of psychological illness. She writes:

One young woman for whom we prayed has had considerable blocks to healing nearly every step of the way. She had previously been a Satan worshiper and then part of a legalistic church. She's a lover of C. S. Lewis and, in my estimation, has a strong intuition for the real—but also has countless unhealed images, confusion, and demons harrassing her. The first time that [ ] prayed for her, she reported that thereafter, she could do what was "right." Prior to that, she said she simply could not choose the right. She had to do the wrong. . . . She began to get truly honest after that, willing to do what was right, but more inner turmoil followed till one night in group I felt that [ ] and I needed to minister to her in prayer right then for her to get some freedom and relief. She had no useful imagery of God which she could embrace: a male persona was definitely out [not unusual with certain forms of lesbian neurosis such as this woman suffered], . . . and without a concept of God I was truly blocked in helping her.

I had asked a few nights previously, though, what was an acceptable and useful image to her. She'd said she really liked Aslan—Lewis's God-character. I encouraged her to think of God as Aslan, because He is the Lion of Judah. This particular night in prayer, we leaned on this imagery heavily, and the task in the prayer time seemed to be that she desperately wanted and needed Aslan to come and breathe life into her like he had the statues in the witch's courtyard in the first Narnia chronicle. (I don't quite remember how we got to the realization of what the task was. To me, it just seems to become apparent as I talk with people or hear what the Lord is doing in their visualization experience. [This is precisely the way it is with those gifted to pray with others. The gifts of knowledge and of wisdom usually operate at almost an imperceptible level.] Anyway, she could envision very little without our prompting and help. And especially when "Aslan" would come to breathe life into her, he would instead walk away or disappear. I had not yet heard your tape on how sometimes a person has virtually only unhealed images in their psyche, but I sensed and assumed that something like that was going on, and so I tried something, because I felt it was important to bring [the girl] through this and give her her first solid images of the real. So, with her O.K., I began to lead her in a visualization, describing her standing there frozen, seeing Aslan out of the corner of her eye and him coming up to the statue, how he nuzzled her—something like that till I got to the point where I was describing how he brought her to life, and she broke in and said, "No, that's not how it is," and she proceeded to describe how Aslan was handling her! [This points out the value of guided imagery: when used in true healing prayer—prayer anointed by the Holy Spirit—the real invariably breaks in.] Well, we rejoiced, because Aslan tipped the statue over and let it crash into pieces, and he did that several times with successive statues inside the first one till he came to the real, living, warm [girl]—who happened to be an infant in this picture. Then she was able to climb up on his back and be enfolded in his fur and mane and nestle in. . . . She described it in an unusual way—as being both warm and cool—something like that.

Here is guided imagery to great effect. There was a wonderful breakthrough for one who had not been able to receive loving words from a loving God. Only those who work with the deeply wounded know how great a healing step this was. It was the necessary breakthrough before the next step toward wholeness could be taken.

The writer of the letter later shared what happened with a group in the church. The leader of that group, whom she greatly respected as a Bible teacher, rebuked her for "dealing in the soulish realm," for using visualization and animal imagery. (That "animal imagery" was mentioned is particularly distressing because it indicates a crucial loss in the understanding of metaphor and symbol.) This sort of misunderstanding within the Church leaves people vulnerable to non-Christian groups that have empathy for the unhealed psyche. Those heavily into Jungian spirituality, the New Age, or some other form of Neo-Gnosticism and paganism know the language of the heart. They recognize that this language is metaphoric and symbolic. They are not afraid to visualize.

Christian groups that practice visualization as a method, however, rely on it either too heavily or in exclusion to sound teaching and get into trouble sooner or later and lose the good of reason. They become too subjective. There is an overemphasis on the intuitive and an underemphasis on objective truth and the rational mind's capacity to interpret, edit, and shape.

The greatest misuse of imaging in Christian circles is related to false teaching. Everywhere in churches and retreat houses, naive Christian prayer groups are being taught by priests, ministers, and therapists who have a mixture of paganism (whether materialistic or Gnostic) in their Christianity. These groups are seriously endangered. They are in effect being "resymbolized."

They invariably end up anthropocentric, man-centered, and so fall into a reconciliation of good and evil in matters pertaining to the soul. The teacher who has synthesized the false with the true in his Christian faith passes it on to his listeners through guided imagery. But beyond that, he cannot in any effective way invoke the Presence of God and point people to the Holy One. The very sense of the holy will be lost to them. Therefore, these teachers, rather than bringing people into identity in Christ and into an authentic understanding of the way we intuit the real, will be teaching them self-actualization and psychological methods. These leaders will also lack discernment when those they guide are at the mercy of images from the world, the flesh, or the Devil. They often will have some valid insight into the images that well up from an unhealed psyche, but their interpretation of these, as well as the healing they aim for, will be merely man-centered. It will be "soulish" in the very sense that the leader quoted above meant when she described imaging as being soulish. (Hidden within her concern is a seed of Manichaeism: hatred or fear of the body and the soul and its motions; also, true discernment of what is merely "soulish" and therefore harmful is missing.) Misuses of imaging, then, are chiefly related to an insufficient experience and understanding of the Christian real—the loss of a truly Christian theology and symbolic system that can withstand the current incursions of Neo-Gnosticism and materialism, and of the man-centeredness resulting from both.

Leaving this weightier cause for concern, we can go on to the more mundane mistakes we make simply because we are untutored. In genuinely Christian prayer groups, the misuses of visualization in prayer for healing are related to ignorance of the intuition of the real. This intuition is, in its outworking, the operation of the authentic gifts of the Holy Spirit. There is also a failure to understand symbol, and therefore the language of the heart. In place of the real we may be treated to someone's idle fancy—a thought or picture that happened to flit through the mind when it began to rove around for a helpful "word." Along this same vein, rather than fixing their hearts on God in prayer, others may get into a "stream of consciousness," or "unconsciousness," and begin to share some of that. Such activity may reveal some interesting things about the one who is doing the speaking, but that's another matter. All of this has to do with trying to "receive" pictures rather than with the use of guided imagery, but one can see that visualization methods adopted in such a group would be ineffective.

Most will be aware that these are not the kind of utterances that minister the healing word to anyone. There is nothing inherently wrong with these activities unless we try to call them something they are not. Within the context of healing prayer, these things do mischief, especially if the one putting forth the images is clever about superimposing them on another. These and related types of activity I stop right away. The Holy Spirit's gift of exhortation is used to wonderful effect here, and I find that few are ever offended by it. Rather, they are grateful for the learning experience and eager to learn how to pray for others effectively.

When there is trouble between head and heart, there will always be imagery within the mind that reflects the trouble. Banning visualization in order not to have to learn about and pray for people with frightening unbidden imagery really doesn't work. They need help. Avoiding visualization itself doesn't work because imaging is a physiological thing. It is always happening. We may cease to share the images that plague us, but they just get worse.

We as Christians must regain our souls and the knowledge of the truly imaginative. We then must teach others. We will make mistakes, but the greater mistake is to ignore and deny the soul with its incredible giftedness in the areas of reason and the truly imaginative.

CHAPTER 12

Introspection versus True Imagination

"Friend," said the Spirit, "could you, only for one moment, fix your mind on something not yourself?" [1]

*T*he disease of introspection has to do with what I've before called the "two minds"—the more "conscious," rational one turned in on and analyzing (thereby paralyzing) the more "unconscious," intuitive, feeling one. In this activity, there is a failure to understand the "two minds" and their differences, and there is therefore a grievous loss of the proper complementarity between the two.

The two minds, so very different, are both vital in the creative process of living—one as *the intuiter of the real* (the matrix of the creative idea and the mythopoeic imagination); the other as *the seat of the rational powers* which must, after the creative idea is given material form, bring to bear on it a shaping critique. The two minds do not work in ways at all comparable. Intuitive revelations of Nature, Super-Nature, and God are one thing; conscious thinking about them is quite another.

C. S. Lewis's life was changed once he recognized this, and his artistic, religious, and emotional life was preserved because of it. A beloved professor of mine, Dr. Clyde S. Kilby, used to say to the men in his classroom, "Fellas, you can't kiss your girl and think about the kiss at the same time." You can't experience life and think about it at the same time without losing the good of both experience and thought.

As thinkers, we are cut off from what we think about; as tasting, touching, willing, loving, hating, we do not clearly understand. The more lucidly we think, the more we are cut off; the more deeply we enter into reality, the less we can think. You cannot

study Pleasure in the moment of the nuptial embrace, nor repentance while repenting, nor analyze the nature of humor while
roaring with laughter.[2]

Our dilemma, because the conscious intellect is incurably abstract, is
"either to taste and not to know or to know and not to taste—or, more
strictly, to lack one kind of knowledge because we are in an experience
or to lack another kind because we are out of it."[3]

As Dr. Kilby restates this: "We intellectualize in order to know but,
paradoxically, intellectualization tends to destroy its object. The harder
we grasp at the thing, the more its reality move away." He goes on to
explain this power of abstraction gone awry:

Our present one-dimensioned age in particular is convinced that
the main avenue to knowing is the making of statements. Yet all
statements whatever, indeed all systems, in becoming statements and system, become self-destructive. One is at sixes and
sevens to translate a language of one hundred thousand words
into a language of one thousand words. This is man's predicament. What man is, what he feels himself to be, makes a waste-
land of language. Yet because of man's insatiable desire to know
he requires some sort of verbal actualization. He is like the old
woman who said, "How do I know what I think until I hear what
I say?" Yet man's saying, i.e., his systemizing, is always inadequate. The more he defines, the more he abstracts, the farther a
satisfying reality seems to fly.[4]

We have valued and developed the mind's power to abstract and analyze, while at the same time we have ignored (and even denied) its imaginative ways of knowing: those with which we apprehend the Unseen
Real—the higher good, including meaning and the power to be itself.

The disease of introspection has many levels, some more lethal than
others. There are times when I have to tell a person that healing his
depression, his homosexual neurosis, or whatever, will be as easy as
falling off a log—once he is healed of an advanced case of introspection.
It is amazing how perfectly and methodically some persons can go about
destroying every experience of life (i.e., the power to be), even every
thought experience, through turning an introspective, analytical mind to
bear on it. I have even seen pride connected with this, as though it were
some kind of advanced intellectual activity. Actually, it is the annihilation
of the intellect.

Stan's story, in *The Broken Image*, is a classic example of this disease at its worst. He was almost destroyed by it, being at the point of sui-

cide when I first met with him. He was a bright young man who had spent years developing the rational mind, while neglecting the weightier matters of the heart. His emotional needs were very great. He had not accepted himself while going through puberty and was unaffirmed as a man. When his sexual and gender inferiority began to show up as symbolic confusion in the fantasy and dream life, lust entered in and he suffered a moral and spiritual fall—something for which he could not forgive himself. His mind was then held captive not only by a demonic imagery,

> but by a vicious and continuous mental obsession that contained two elements: a constant analyzing of himself, an exercise in which he was continually looking inward to find some sort of a personal truth or reality, and a constant analyzing of what he had before accepted as true. This inner dialogue was full of an irrational sophistry that could only tear concepts apart, but could never put the fragments back together in any kind of satisfying whole. Another way to describe this is to say that his thought, severely introspective and full of doubts about what is or is not true, was agonizingly painful and circular. This is the disease of introspection, and Stan had it to a fearful degree. He was in fact floundering in serious mental and spiritual darkness and was filled with fear when he first sought help through prayer.[5]

It is not unusual, as in Stan's case, that the first step is to command the powers of darkness to release the mind and depart from the sufferer. To turn in so severely on the self (a "practice of the presence of self" in lonely insolation from God and other selves) invites demonic participation at some point. I hasten to add that the Holy Spirit's gift of discerning of spirits must be in operation before such a prayer is made. The relief this prayer brings, once the demonic is truly discerned and sent away, is immediate.

The next step for Stan was prayer for the healing of the mind. Under the Holy Spirit's leading, we pray according to that person's individual need. Usually in a case like this, however, I anoint the forehead with oil, making the sign of the Cross on the forehead. Then, laying my hands on the head (or sometimes gently pressing both temples), I ask Jesus to enter in and to heal and quiet the mind. I picture (see with my heart) this being done, and wait, quietly praying, as the Lord does it. (When we open our hearts to see, God can send us further direction on how and what to pray; He often sends us wisdom and knowledge via picture and word.)

After this prayer, the person is ready to make his confession and receive the needed cleansing and forgiveness. He is also ready to face honestly his psychological and emotional needs and get the counsel and prayer that will enable him to come present to his own heart (emotions, feelings, etc.) and to what it is experiencing and saying to him. He comes present to his own heart only as he comes fully present to God. Then, listening to Him, he replaces every diseased attitudinal pattern with the word God is sending. Stan did this, and his mind-set was changed. He looked up to God, and in so doing came present to his own heart and to the heart of God. He is now so healed he can hardly remember his pain. But had he not gotten this help, he could easily have committed suicide. Today he is a most gifted intellect and artist who leads a full life and leads others in creative directions.

You may be thinking that introspection especially afflicts students and scholars and those gifted intellectually and artistically. But I find this "disease" everywhere. The schism between mind and heart affects the ditch-digger as well as the college professor, the store clerk as well as the artistic genius.

In every healing service I conduct, some there are fighting a life-and-death battle with the dreadful twentieth-century disease. I have to tell them right away that "Just as no one can accept you for you, no one can fight against this habit for you. And that's what it is, a bad mental habit, but one that happens to be narcissistic, one that can destroy you and perhaps others who love you."

Here is an example of introspection at a level not as advanced as Stan's, but devastating nevertheless. I met with a young man who had just been awarded a full fellowship in a graduate program at one of our finest universities. He had done very well in school, but had some serious mental and emotional conflicts in his life. He, like Stan, was unaffirmed as a man and unable to accept himself. He was attracted toward certain young men and fearful of the emotional dependency he got into when close to them.

He had read my books and had heard the taped teachings on introspection, but never thought of himself as having that particular problem. However, he had told me, "I stand back and look at myself and logically go over everything I can't stand about myself—my walk, the way I look, my mannerisms," etc. This young man constantly did this. Just as a scientist studies a bug or a flower by dissecting it, so this young man regularly pinned himself to his own dissecting table, fragmenting himself in the process.

His healing would never come until he stopped this pernicious activity. I told him in no uncertain terms what he was doing and led him to repent and turn from that diseased emotional view of the self. Then I taught him the kind of prayer that enabled him to take deep draughts of the Spirit of God (the ultimate in the Ojective Real outside himself) *back* into him. His difficulty was, he had never accepted himself, and his self-criticism and even self-hatred manifested itself in this way. The cure? Teaching him to look up and out. "But as a Christian I have to examine myself, don't I?" he asked in some amazement. He was right, but as I always say to these sufferers, in looking up to God—that is, asking Him to come in and shine His light into my heart—I get involved with *real* things, what's really there. And I receive an *objective good*, either for-giveness or illumination. I am not indulging in diseased attitudes toward the self.

All the great saints and teachers know and teach this out-directed-ness in one way or another. Dr. Clyde S. Kilby expressed this understand-ing in a series of statements he printed for his students:

At least once each day I shall look steadily up at the sky and remember that I, a consciousness with a conscience, am on a planet traveling in space with everlastingly mysterious things above and about me.

Dr. Kilby delighted in teaching the works of C. S. Lewis, J. R. R. Tolkein, Charles Williams, George MacDonald, and the poetry and liter-ature of other great minds and hearts that were on to this truth in ways that transformed their art and their philosophy. He knew it to be the secret of their greatness. Of C. S. Lewis, one writer has said, "He had a greater actuality of soul than most men." Once Lewis conquered the sin of introspection, and recognized it as pride, his soul never stopped grow-ing and expanding, because he never stopped loving the things above and about and all around himself. His awe in the face of the great and the mysterious, the beautiful and the true was never dimmed or extinguished by a turning inward to analyze the self. He learned early that to do this was to destroy the capacity to experience, to be, and therefore the ability to accomplish the work he was born to do.

Early in his life he had destroyed his prayer life by turning from God, the Object of his worship and conversation, to analyze the self who was doing the praying. He later began to destroy his creative capacities in the same way, by taking his eyes and his love from the object (the work to be written about) and instead fastening his attention on the self who was doing the writing. In turning to see if that self was really praying, or really being "creative" or "original," he gradually realized how fatal this disease of introspection is to the artist, the saint, the person on the street. He understood the many malignant levels this disease could operate on and why we moderns are particularly cursed with it. As a consequence, he wrote with the keenest insight about what occurs between head and heart when an analytical and introspective practice is maintained.

Here we have the schism, so fatal to the personality, that runs between *being* and *doing*, and it has erupted into warfare. One "mind" is devouring the other, until both are finally paralyzed.

To have the capacity to simply *be* is to be centered within, and therefore in touch with the soul's capacity for serene contemplation, that stance whereby we *experience* life firsthand. For those who can't quite understand what is meant here, I love to use an analogy out of my own experience. Have you ever traveled abroad with someone who is a camera buff? By this I don't mean someone who takes a camera along and in special moments gets a valued shot, but one who painstakingly sets up a tripod, snaps literally hundreds of pictures, and is consumed with the responsibility of capturing as much on film as possible. The companion of such a person will be delighting in seeing Europe and its museums firsthand, while he is seeing it only through the lens of a camera. He will have to come home in order to relax and see Europe, and his films may or may not reveal very much of the real thing.

How much of life do we see firsthand? To fail to be centered is to "walk alongside ourselves," a stance whereby we live out of an activism separated from *being* and therefore from *meaning*. A person split in this way can never live in the present moment. He can only live for a future that never quite arrives, one that he is perhaps feverishly trying to control in order to avoid the pain of his past.

A high percentage of Westerners (as well as Easterners affected by our atheistic materialism) are thus caught in a ceaseless *doing* and can only *think about* life, but never experience it. Don Miguel Unamuno, the great Spanish philosopher and writer, speaks of the effects of this schism on the soul:

> Those who drink only pure ideas end up suffering from spiritual cretinism. The soul that lives on categories remains a dwarf.[6]

This is the schism that makes the disease of introspection the dreadful and prevalent twentieth-century malady that it is. The disease itself represents a still greater step backward, and is the inevitable conclusion when for reality itself we substitute merely our intellectual ideas about that reality.

Clyde Kilby, understanding both the schism and the painful disease, did not lecture his students on it. Rather he pointed his finger alongside Lewis's toward the *mystery*, toward the greatness that enlarges the soul and always eludes one in self-analysis. This mystery is far too immense to be put into words and requires therefore the best of the saints' and poets' symbols and imagery to try to talk about it, to try to "uncover" and "disclose" it. This is why Dr. Kilby says:

I shall not turn my life into a thin straight line which prefers abstractions to reality. I shall know what I am doing when I abstract, which of course I shall often have to do. . . .

I shall open my eyes and ears. Once every day I shall simply stare at a tree, a flower, a cloud, or a person. I shall not then be concerned at all to ask *what* they are but simply be glad *that* they are. I shall joyfully allow them the mystery of what Lewis calls their "divine, magical, terrifying and ecstatic" existence.

I was Dr. Kilby's assistant, both during my undergraduate and graduate studies. The *is-ness*, the celebration of *being* he pointed his students to, he personally celebrated until he died at age eighty-four. He had an unusual relationship with plants and animals. His birds flew free in his home, and seemed to gain almost human characteristics through the rare relationship they had with him.[7]

No faithful canine ever greeted its master with more joy and energy than Dr. Kilby's birds as he returned to his rooms. I've had to duck on more than one occasion to get out of the way of a certain parakeet named Peter, who made the straightest swoop for the professor's shoulders and resented any other body that got in his way. He would nuzzle Dr. Kilby's ears, talking incessantly into them, and competed mightily with me for the good man's attention.

Dr. Kilby delighted in the very "soul" or "is-ness" of that bird, the very "is-ness" of his flowers, and he never ceased to be awed by them. One day he saw a squirrel turn a backward somersault which he later declared to me was "just for sheer joy, Leanne, just for sheer joy!" I have no doubt he was right, for Dr. Kilby knew joy when he saw it. Furthermore, though the squirrel was full of life for a number of reasons, one of them was certainly because Dr Kilby was there, and he had long delighted in the "is-ness," the being, of that squirrel. There was joy and respect between them.

I've been especially privileged to know two persons with such extraordinary relationships to Nature, and it came out of their capacity to love God and all He has created. The other was Agnes Sanford.

When she was in her eighties, she would leap for joy at the sight of a friend. Her relationship to earth, air, sea, water, and all that moves in it was as close to the Green Lady's as I ever expect to see this side of Heaven. Her respect and love for even the inanimate creation—the very earth and its rock structures, for example—was most remarkable. She would hold up a seashell, one she had discovered years before, and continue to marvel over it. Looking at its design she once exclaimed to me: "Can you believe that written into [what was] this little creature was the 'mind' to create such a design!" She was marveling over the genetic makeup that could "think" or create such beauty, and she often looked at that shell in awe. One has only to read her book *Creation Waits* to see the unusual reverence and relationship she had to the earth and all God's creation.

She and Dr. Kilby were always, even into their eighties, "the child of the pure unclouded brow, and dreaming eyes of wonder." *Here we are privileged to see the Eternal Child, and it is in starkest contrast to the immature, hurting, complaining, lost child*, the one whose center is the illusionary self, the one whose center is a complex of diseased feelings, attitudes, images, and symbols that have nothing to do with our new substantive, outwardly-oriented selves in Christ.

Clyde Kilby and Agnes Sanford had learned to love the great realities outside themselves, to be able to *be*, in contrast to only being able to analyze and *think about being*. The latter (the discursive reason) was highly developed in them, but was not in conflict and out of balance with the former. I should probably add here that they were both so genuinely human. There was not the slightest hint of their ever having donned the noble or the self-important or the pious *persona* of scholar, artist, or saint. Neither seemed hurried or unduly pressed, and this was because the considerable power to think, to act, and to accomplish for each was rooted in and issued out of the capacity to be.

To be is to experience life firsthand, to live in the present moment. The person who has the disease of introspection, who thinks painfully, constantly, and in circles about life, lives always in the painful past and for the future. In this way, he squanders his present by trying to figure out a more secure or less painful future. The future, of course, never arrives, for it is in the present moment that we "live and move and have our being."

> I shall not allow the devilish onrush of the century to usurp all my energies but will instead, as Charles Williams suggested, "fulfill the moment as the moment." I shall try to keep truly alive now just because the only time that exists is now. (C. S. Kilby)

Because Heaven and earth are crammed with living creatures and concrete things, awesome to know in their reality, man is only becoming whole while reaching out to them—i.e., when he is outer-directed. He can only know himself by knowing others—by coming to taste, in a manner of speaking, the incredible variety of *is-ness*, of *being*, that resides outside himself. Solomon expresses this point by his proverb: "As iron sharpens iron, so one man sharpens another" (Proverbs 27:17). So it is that we are "sharpened" by all that *is*. The outlines of who we are (our own inner reality and *is-ness*) become sharper and clearer as the eyes of our souls are opened to see and rejoice in the realities outside ourselves. Love is the way: love for the object rather than concentration on oneself, the subject.

We come to know even ourselves, not through turning inward to study and analyze, but by turning outward to love all that is real and other than ourselves. There is a true examination of our hearts and minds, as we have already said, but it is never made in separation from the Presence of Another—the One who illumines and forgives. The person who is turned inward has not accepted himself, so there will always be various degrees of the wrong kind of self-hatred involved, and that only grows worse as he concentrates on himself. He has a problem with himself, and he's looking hard at himself trying to solve it. The disease of introspection is always a lonely business; it is carried on by the self in isolation from love.

To lift our eyes from ourselves to others is a decision we can and must make. It is, at first, a minute by minute kind of discipline, then hour by hour, and so on. We learn to pray, "Lord, love someone through me today," when we are unhappily meditating upon ourselves and our imagined or real shortcomings. We then deliberately set out to help everyone else that crosses our path—not for what we get in return, but humbly, knowing that our own needs are not the center around which this world spins, but God is. I recall my first glimmer of understanding this. It was as an adolescent, going into large groups, and finding myself painfully aware of *me*. I remember the conscious decision I made to think about others and their needs when unhappily concentrating on myself. The rewards were immediate.

If we have the disease of introspection very badly, we will then start introspecting about what we are doing, or looking to see if we "feel" love, for example. We must stop that activity right away, knowing that our feeling being needs healing (it is wounded through self-hate, etc.), and knowing besides that love is not a feeling. Love is willing the best for others.[8]

How do we get a self? How do we become persons? Not through cognitive skill, not by trying to think existence. Not through learning one personality theory after another. Man becomes as he obeys. Knowledge of oneself and others as selves is dependent upon moral and spiritual development—and this comes through obedience to truth, to the way things really are. We *become* as we are obedient to the best we know at one level, to the words that come from God on the highest level. "Listen," the Scriptures admonish us—listen to that word that is coming to you from outside your isolated position, "that you might have life."

To love the good, the beautiful, the just, the true is, mysteriously, to be drawn up into them—or to use another image, to become incarnate of them, to participate in them. To love God, for example, is to be drawn up and out of ourselves (the hell of the self-in-separation) and into Him. In loving Him, I become incarnate of Him. The imagery here is of ascending and descending. God descends into us, and we are drawn into Him. This is a profound thing to think on, for it is the way we get in touch with all that is real. If I come to know and understand justice by loving it, I receive it into myself. If I rejoice in the beauty of another's face, I become more beautiful.

This is precisely why the capital sin of envy is so deadly a destroyer. By envying what we feel to be more beautiful, just, good, true, etc., or trying to possessively hold it for ourselves through jealousy, one of the dread daughters of envy, we cut ourselves off from becoming. To envy is to hate. It is to attempt to reduce all we fear to be brighter or better than ourselves to a size whereby we can be a master (a god) over it. We thereby cut ourselves off from receiving into ourselves (by loving them) the very things of which we are envious. The disease of introspection, perpetuated by deep feelings of rejection, often has this deadly vice in its train. All that is real is incarnational. In loving the real, I (as it were) am drawn up into it. I unite in a wholesome (not a possessive) way with it; it descends into me.

There is nothing more draining to work with than an advanced case of the disease of introspection. It is like a black hole in the cosmos that swallows stars. In this case the black hole is inside the person, and the person is the disappearing star—falling into the hell of self—and he or she would pull the unwary in after him or her.

The healing? We point these souls upward and outward. We teach them to practice the Presence, to listen to God and exchange their negative attitudinal patterns for the word that He is sending. (In cases where this activity has led to clinical depression, and these souls are unable to look up and out, the first step after prayer with them will be to point them toward the best psychological and psychiatric treatment available.) This is the activity of the true imagination and fullness of being as over and against the disease of introspection and emptiness.

To sum up: The disease of introspection occurs when the rational, analytical mind turns in on the intuitive, feeling mind, and the proper complementarity between the two is lost. This introspective mode has various levels of intensity, but in the more painful stages a painful activism (painful doing and thinking) has annihilated the power to be. Finally, a depression can ensue that will wipe out the power to act or to think.

The power to be has to do with the power of being at home *within* the present moment, of being centered, of living serenely and contemplatively from the true center. In such a stance, one experiences life more directly—that is, one lives in the present moment.

This is in contrast to the activism that annihilates or eats up time—that annihilates the power to contemplate, to be. When we live in the present moment, it may be, even as the poet Coleridge, has said, that we don't so much live in time as we take time into ourselves and give it a soul.

With Christ, we remain the Eternal Child and can say, "I love the Father, I do what I see Him do, He has crowned me with glory and honor." Loving all that *is*, we learn to die daily to the introspective, self-conscious self.

CHAPTER 13

Incarnational Reality:
The Key to Carrying the Cross

*Now I rejoice in what was suffered for you, and I fill up in my flesh
what is still lacking in regard to Christ's afflictions, for the sake of
his body, which is the church. I have become its servant by the
commission God gave me to present to you the word of God in its
fullness—the mystery that has been kept hidden for ages and
generations, but is now disclosed to the saints. To them God has
chosen to make known among the Gentiles the glorious riches of this
mystery, which is Christ in you, the hope of glory.*

(Colossians 1:24-27)

As he is so are we in this world.

(John the Beloved)

"*N*o man is worthy of me who does not take up his cross and walk in
my footsteps. By gaining his life a man will lose it; by losing his
life for my sake, he will gain it" (Matthew 10:38, 39, NEB). Thus Jesus
instructed His twelve disciples; thus He instructs every disciple. The
image here, of taking up one's cross, immediately conjures up the idea of
extreme suffering.

We have had strange and distorted notions about what this suffering
is. These notions carry with them heavy emotional and psychological
baggage. Many of our beliefs and inner images about "bearing our cross"
are not thought through; they are irrational, confused, distorted. This cultural baggage, coming as it does out of various religious backgrounds,
accounts for certain predictable strains of distortions. They have several

things in common, however, the chief being the failure to understand the walk in the Spirit. We do God's work by collaborating with His Spirit, not by passive notions of self-abnegation or by "being crucified."

Other tragic mistakes arise out of this failure to understand active collaboration with God. Rather than taking a passive, uncreative stance, we become tyrannical and move into sinful activism. For example, rather than moving in the power of the Holy Spirit to deliver witches, we, in our hysteria and failure to trust in God, burn them at the stake. The Spanish Inquisition, as another historical example, illustrates all too well that the flipside of a passive self-abnegation can be a murderous activism.

Practicing the Presence of God and listening for the word He is always sending, we actively heal in the name of Jesus rather than indulge in mistaken forms or notions of self-denial. We are not to fall into weakly passive notions of self-sacrifice.

The following example, an actual case, illustrates a common erroneous emotional view of what it means to carry one's cross. Although this view comes down through the Catholic tradition, it is not orthodox Catholic dogma, as their own scholars point out.[1] Rather the notion has its roots in an unbalanced medieval asceticism.

A certain priest saw God as utterly transcendent. Because this clergyman was unhealed inside, he was fearful of an immanent God. He was terrified lest Christ come any closer. He had dreadful pictures in his mind and heart of what it means to take up his cross. Miserable, but wanting to fully commit himself to God, wanting to help his people, he began to read some of the old books on suffering. These books were full of the notions of substitution (dying for other people, taking into oneself the demons or the sicknesses of afflicted people) rather than of the power to heal.

He became more and more fearful of "taking up his cross" and more and more fearful of God. In addition, the Christian life seemed increasingly dull, gray, and boring to him. He began to beg, "Please pray that I will be faithful." His mind and heart were filled with images of suffering, all separated from joy, the possibility of healing, and the heroic excitement of a life dynamically empowered by Christ. Even though he would deny this, he had always to strive, to move in his own strength.

He felt guilty because he couldn't "commit" himself more fully to his erroneous ideas about God and about what it means to carry the cross. There was no freedom of spirit in him; there was only a fearful, guilt-ridden immaturity.

He did not believe his own notions and images on a rational level; i.e., none of this would show up in his stated or written theology. But he believed them emotionally, and suffered accordingly. Here we see the double bind such error leads to. Although this deceptively passive state caused increasingly serious bouts of depression, he would not submit to healing for it because, he said, "This suffering is my cross."

The next example is typical of the Protestant tradition. Nona, a lovely, young Bible college student, came for help. She had two problems. First of all, she loved to design and sew and wanted to create beautiful dresses, but she felt guilty for doing what she loved to do. Why should she make more clothes than she could or should wear? Even though her parents had the money, she would deny herself. She didn't know what she would do during summer vacation, but she wouldn't do that.

Her second problem, and the main reason she sought counsel, was a persistent, nagging fear. She had been terribly overweight as a young child, and she feared the weight would come back. Her two problems were related, though she didn't know it.

I asked her, "What is your definition of carrying the cross?"

She immediately responded, "Dying to self."

Nona's desire to die to self-centeredness (which is what dying to self means) was commendable. But she was unable to distinguish between the creative motions and desires of the soul (much less those of the new self in Christ) and the principle of evil and selfishness common to fallen people. A second problem was her misunderstanding about what authentic Christian suffering is. She was succeeding only in putting the *real self* to death. Fearful and unhappy, she was practicing the presence of self.

What we see here in Nona is a young girl full of creative energy and the capacity, perhaps, to become a great dress designer. She, in the image of her Creator, is a maker. She was astounded when I told her to go home and make all the lovely creations her heart desired—and then give them away as she liked! She was afflicted with false guilt for doing what she loved to do—what would help bring her up out of the self, frustration, and the disease of introspection. This is part of the value of the arts and all our work. In creating, we are drawn up and out of ourselves. Even beyond that, as some of the wise monastics discovered, work done as unto the Lord can be a form of prayer. "Commit thy works unto the Lord, and thy thoughts shall be established" (Proverbs 16:3, KJV) is a proverb I regularly turn into a prayer of petition. I ask that all the work of my hands and heart will be as a prayer to God. He delights in establishing our thoughts; in fact, He waits to be so petitioned by the Christian.

Nona could easily turn this proverb into a personal prayer and find the very designing and making of her dresses a part of the practice of the Presence of God! This was foreign to her, however, and a strong work ethic (striving to be heroic and perfect in all she did) substituted for the understanding of vocation and calling. Work that is at once creative, disciplined, and responsible, yet joyous and free because we are doing what we were born to do, always glorifies God.

The creative drive needs to be expressed. If not, it will break out in lower levels. Nona's fear about her weight was related to her false guilt and false notions about what it means to die to self and "take up one's cross." When one puts the real self, that creative person made in the image of God, to death, then one is liable to the odd temptations peculiar to unfulfilled lives.

I gave Nona my definition of what it means to carry the cross. It means to practice the Presence of Jesus and allow His love to flow through us to others; it means that we are to carry the life of Christ to other people and say to them, "The Kingdom of God has come to you."

Nona said, "I never heard that definition before!"

One has to understand the work of the Holy Spirit in us and among us to understand the positive character of what it means to carry one's cross. He comes into us and does it!

Christian Suffering

There is most certainly the true, authentic, and specifically Christian suffering we undergo in the carrying of our cross. When we allow Christ to live in and through us, we find ourselves in the conflict of spiritual battle. His Light in us collides with the darkness in the world—the ignorance, hate, lies, and delusions within the souls of men and women, and therefore within the cultural, institutional, and governmental structures they create. When we, as carriers of the Kingdom of God, meet the lies and delusions of a darkened, fallen world, we know conflict. Every voluntary suffering we undergo as channels of His life constitutes the "carrying of our cross." Therefore joy and peace, not martyred looks and long faces, characterize the true cross-bearers.

This suffering is redemptive in the sense that we literally carry His love and forgiveness into the lives of others. Such sufferings end in an "eternal weight of glory," the Scriptures tell us, and we should rejoice when we take part in Christ's suffering (see 2 Corinthians 4:17 and 1 Peter 4:13).

We should not be surprised when we experience persecutions for righteousness' sake, revilings and slander, false accusations, scourgings for Christ, rejection by the world, hatred by relatives, martyrdoms, shame for His name, imprisonments, tribulations, stonings, beatings, being a spectacle to men, misunderstandings, necessities, defamation, despisings, troubles, afflictions, distresses, tumults, labors, watchings, fastings, and so on—all these are mentioned specifically in the Scriptures.

In this suffering Christ is with us; He suffers too.

> In all their distress he too was distressed, and the angel of his presence saved them. (Isaiah 63:9)

Dear friends, do not be surprised at the painful trial you are suffering, as though something strange were happening to you. But rejoice that you *participate in the sufferings of Christ*, so that you may be overjoyed when his glory is revealed. (1 Peter 4:12, 13, italics mine)

Mistaken and unclear notions of what Christian sufferings are leave persons such as the priest and Nona liable to passive sacrificial behavior that puts to death the creative real self and leaves them, finally, in the clutches of the old self. The true self, in full communion with God, is required to effectively carry one's cross. When this is the case, there will be authentic, redemptive Christian suffering—that which comes about because we are channels of the life of Another.

Authentic Suffering Preferable

If you are insulted because of the name of Christ, you are blessed, for the Spirit of glory and of God rests on you. If you suffer, it should not be as a murderer or thief or any other kind of criminal, or even as a meddler. (1 Peter 4:14, 15)

Authentic Christian suffering is greatly preferable to that which comes through failure to accept and live from the locus of the true self. The one fearing to take up his cross often fails to see the flipside here—the suffering produced by conviction over our sins and separation from God when we dwell in the old self. There is suffering aplenty that comes from the self-centeredness, the bentness toward the creature, the greed, and the failure to know God or one's own heart. I'll take the suffering that comes with standing in the vertical position with Christ any day. I would rather endure suffering that comes from actively listening to and obeying God than the suffering that comes from being separated from God's purposes for me. I've suffered enough for my own sins and foolishness, my own pride and willfulness. Therefore, it would be extremely difficult for me to put on a long face over sufferings that come through obedience to Christ and the word He is always speaking.

Remedial Sufferings

There are sufferings that have to do with ours and the world's bentness. We suffer headaches, stomach ulcers, all manner of derangements in our minds and hearts due to fears, hatred, bitterness, resentments, lusts, anxieties, rebellion, and so on. We suffer due to the sin of others and their inability to care for us. We suffer due to the corporate sins of mankind—environments full of hate, anger, ignorance, pollution, poor or insufficient food. We suffer the deprivations and injustices of a fallen world. But these are remedial sufferings. They are not due to the life-giving work of carrying the cross. Therefore we do not hold to any of these sufferings and diseases, saying, "This is my cross," but we pray in faith for deliverance and healing from such distress.

When we suffer due to the sin of others or to the corporate sins of mankind, we can ask God to transform these sufferings into healing power. This God gladly does. For example, we forgive those who have sinned against us, and we accept the circumstances of our lives. Then we go on to make prayers of confession and intercession for ourselves and others. (As an example of a prayer of confession, study Nehemiah 1, and note the incredibly fruitful outcome of Nehemiah's prayer.) We also pray on behalf of our environment. As we pray, that which is redemptive is accomplished. Right action ensues, even that which brings in the Kingdom of God. Furthermore, our own souls are healed.

An example out of the healing ministry is apropos here. The abused or abandoned child reaches adulthood and realizes his depression and intense inner suffering is directly connected to childhood experiences in a dysfunctional family (whether due to alcohol, chemical or sexual addiction, mental illness, deprivation of basic needs, overt or subtle evil on the part of parents or those around him, etc.). Then that adult will not call his or her suffering the carrying of the cross. His affliction is surely a cross to bear, in the popular sense of that metaphor, but it is not the cross he is to take up as he walks with Christ. Rather, if he is to be whole, he must take this cross of pain and suffering to Christ's Cross, and there acknowledge that Christ died to take into Himself this very suffering.

Patsy Casey, a remarkably gifted fellow minister of healing prayer and my trusted prayer partner and friend, bears the deepest scars as the adult child of alcoholic and deeply depressed parents. In her most intense periods of suffering, those associated with abandonment, she at first was unable to take her place at Christ's Cross and there identify with Him in his suffering for her. In order to be whole, her intense fear, grief, shame, anger, need for love, and so on had to be acknowledged. And she needed professional therapy in order for this to happen. She could no longer repress and deny these feelings or the causes of them.

But next is the matter of what we do with these feelings once they surface. Not knowing how to allow Christ to take these feelings into His dying for her, she projected them outward onto those closest to her. Then she turned them inward again with intense anger toward herself.

A thing to remember here is that every rejection we experience, until forgiven and healed, we will project onto another. Such pain and anger has to go somewhere. Due to her grief and some conflicting messages regarding "getting in touch with one's feelings" that she was getting in therapy groups, it took Patsy a while to grasp this key.

Patsy was fortunate in that she had good professional help and therapy from those who understand the mechanisms the child of the alcoholic adopts to survive. But somewhere along the line, she got stuck in acting out her feelings. She would, in her pain, descend into the "angry child" or the "grieving child" or the "rejected child," and would become immersed in the feelings. When living out of the "angry child," she would project her anger onto others. When living out of the "grieving child," rather than acknowledging the valid need to grieve and be willing to stand and hurt in Christ until relief and healing came, she would be at the mercy of these feelings. They would get turned inward again, and self-pity, anger, and even thoughts of suicide resulted.

Powerful in the healing ministry herself, she would at these tough times live unconsciously from the immature, hurting, and powerless center of the "wounded child." To get in touch with and experience those feelings again was to suffer over and over again the same wounding.

One day I happened on the key for her by saying, "Patsy, one of the big differences between what you do when you hurt and what I do when I hurt is that I stand up straight and hurt, praying to God until help comes. It may take a while, but eventually help comes. It simply never occurs to me to project it outward in the way you do—to be angry with others, with the Church, and even with God, which is a very dangerous and foolish thing to do." (Some of her spiritual directors in the past had seemed to encourage this latter practice.) She had grown up in a home where these kinds of reactions to pain were the norm. I had grown up in a home where my mother, no matter what the suffering, stood without a trace of anger or self-pity, face upward toward God, ready to stand like that till kingdom come if necessary.

I explained again how it is one stands and hurts. "See the Cross, Patsy; see yourself standing and hurting, acknowledging all these feelings, but this time let Christ take them into Himself. Let them flow into Him, just as you would sins you have confessed."

Just as we take our place in Christ's death, dying again with Him to our own sins, so we die to these diseased feelings by allowing Him to take them into Himself. And we learn to wait, still suffering if necessary, until relief and healing come. But we do it from our true center, not from an immature or false one. This Patsy has now learned to do, and if ever one's wounds have been turned into healing power for others, Patsy Casey's have.

As we learn more about the processes of healing within the soul, we often find that the power to feel the pain is itself a vital part of the healing. The sufferer has repressed this heretofore and denied it precisely because it was so painful. But now he has to get it up and out. He needs to understand that, if he will stand in the Cross and hurt, there is a place for it to go, an end to the pain. This seemingly endless pain is the way he gets in touch with and names the heretofore repressed grief, fear, anger, and shame underlying his depression. In order to come out of certain types of depression, one must feel the most appalling pain and grief. It often seems that death would be easier. But repressed grief and sorrow and loss remain to afflict us in other ways until we grieve them out. It is a wonderful thing to stand in Christ, identify with His suffering for us, and grieve out our griefs and yield up our angers, naming them and forgiving others at the same time.

Patsy said, "In all my years in the Church and in all my time in therapy, I've never heard that." To this day she reminds me in almost every seminar we conduct to share with the people how to stand and hurt.

It is likely clear by now why Patsy at first could not hear the answer. A gifted psychologist who had been to a Pastoral Care Ministry School and saw the healings there asked me why it was ever necessary to send her clients. I answered right off the top of my head, "We send you those who are unable to hear." Right away she understood. There are other things that have to be taken care of first.

Patsy was unable to quietly listen to God, for this required the capacity to simply be in Him. Her pattern of response to the inner pain was one of compulsive, almost frantic activism. She couldn't effectively practice the Presence or listen to God at these times, even though she knew that this quiet resting in Him would eventually bring her to safety and healing. She never lost her confidence that this would happen. Yet, as she said:

> I was far too chaotic inside to listen to God at these times. I couldn't sit still or get quiet long enough to simply be in Him. I was too intensely afraid to face the feelings inside. These nearly pushed me over the edge when I was a baby; I feared they could yet push me over the edge. And I was used to the intense activism, I was so at home with the patterns of running, running, running when the pain inside got unbearable. I knew Calvary was there, I had already experienced my salvation there, and many healings, many deliverances from fear. But I had to get to the point where I could face the inner chaos without terror. I needed additional insight in order to understand and deal with the inner chaos.

Time and further insight were required before she could fully hear the healing answer. It has been one of the great blessings of our prayer cell (Lynne, Lucy, Connie, and I, along with Patsy) to see her face and name the dreaded feelings and deal with, one at a time, the underlying root causes.

Nothing points more strongly to the need for God to bring His entire healing team together than the suffering of people as a result of trauma in infancy and early childhood. We are here dealing not only with a need for healing of memories from out of people's preconceptual past, but also with the complicated survival mechanisms these persons have adopted in order to live. Medical doctor, psychologist, and prayer-counselor alike are humbled in the face of needs like this. We all must be prepared to help, working together if possible.

Those Unoffended by Suffering

Whether or not the suffering is remedial or that produced through the redemptive activity of carrying the cross, we need to understand that "blessed is he, whosoever shall not be offended in me" (Matthew 11:6, KJV). F. B. Meyer refers to this as "the beatitude of the unoffended, of those who do not stumble over the mystery of God's dealings with their lives."[2] It is the blessedness of those who, though they do not understand the trial, yet "rest in what they know of His heart."

> God's children are sometimes the most bitterly tried. For them the fires are heated seven times; they suffer, not only at the hand of man, but the heavens seem as brass to their cries and tears. The enemy of souls has reason to challenge them with the taunt, "Where is now your God?"
>
> You and I have perhaps been in this plight. We have said, "Hath God forgotten to be gracious? Has He in anger shut up His tender mercies?" We are tempted to stumble. . . . But it is then that we have the chance of inheriting this new beatitude. If we refuse to bend under the mighty hand of God—questioning, chafing, murmuring at His appointments—we miss the door which would admit us into rich and unalloyed happiness. . . .[3]

The matter of suffering is seldom dealt with today in such a way as to help us either understand or undergo it. Some of the popular drivel we hear seems almost to deny that the Christian does suffer. Especially hurtful is the strange teaching that all hurts within the soul are healed at the moment one comes to Christ. The same thing would not be said of a broken limb or cancer. This is one more example of the modern's estrangement from his own soul. On the other hand, we are prone to take in the psycho-babble about suffering that leads to sinful reactions. Either extreme represents shallow comprehensions of the mystery of suffering and of God's ways with us.

Mario Bergner, beloved colleague and team member in this ministry, just ministered to a black woman whose history included such poverty that the mother had attempted to kill her at birth. After receiving much healing (actually a trauma of birth healing), she looked up to Mario in tears without the least taint of bitterness or blaming and simply asked: "Why?" Mario's heart was thoroughly wrenched within him. As he did not answer the question, she again asked, "Why?" Then, "Why did my whole family have to experience starvation?" He felt helpless to answer her and simply continued to comfort her in Christ's name. The next day he got down on his face before the Lord with the same question, asking why she had to suffer this way. Before long he heard these words: "Blessed are those who mourn, for they shall be comforted. Those who mourn ask, why?"

He then reflected that Jesus on the Cross asked the Father, "Why have You forsaken me?" And then he knew, deep within his spirit, that we may not get the answer, but *we shall receive the comfort.*

Continuing to think about this, Mario thought that perhaps the fact that Christ had to ask why is the source of one of the greatest blessings for those who mourn. That is because it opens the way for us to ask, and then to listen. Mario knew that "because Christ asked it of the Father, we too can ask it of the Father." Mario saw that three days after Christ asked the question, the Father replied, not with an answer to the question, but with the comfort to the pain. He did this through resurrecting His Son. After this answer to his question, Mario joyously concluded that our job is to minister resurrection power to those who ask why.

It seems good, therefore, to consider Rev. Meyer's prayer:

Forgive our sins, our faithless tears, and our repining murmur. Lift us on the tide of Thy love into fuller, richer, deeper experiences. May we know what it is to have Christ in us, the Hope of Glory. Amen.[4]

O God, Thou hast revealed Thyself to us in Thy Son, Jesus Christ our Lord. We love Him, because He endured the Cross, and despised the shame in order to save us. May we follow Him by the way of the Cross, bearing His reproach, sharing His griefs, obedient even unto death, that we may also live and reign with Him here, and more perfectly at last. Amen.[5]

Christ's Sufferings
Christ's suffering consists in the fact that "He became the way of life."[6] He channeled (by dying) His life to us. Our suffering, as we have already

pointed out, consists in the fact that we become a channel of His life. His life and light in us overcome the evil and pain in the souls of men. This is where the battle lies, and this is where we experience suffering for Christ's sake. Jesus has overcome sin. We appropriate His life.

> Something which has existed since the beginning, that we have heard, and we have seen with our own eyes; and we have watched and touched with our hands: the Word, who is Life—This is our subject. (1 John 1:1, *The Jerusalem Bible*)

To carry the cross is to appropriate His life and carry it. In the power of His life, we destroy Satan's strongholds in the souls of men, and therefore his strongholds in the world. The imaginations, intellects, entire inner and physical beings are cleansed and set free. This is what carrying the cross is.

Agnes Sanford asks why Jesus would need to carry His Cross, why He would need to die, if His becoming incarnate and His teaching would have healed us. There are many great teachers of the conscious mind—Confucius, Plato, Socrates, and so on. There are many ladders to perfection, but, as she writes, there is always a problem at the top. The last rung of any ladder we try to ascend always comes short of communion and union with God. It is much more sensible, says she, to "merely sit down on the bottom step and howl for help through Jesus Christ."[7]

At the bottom or the top of any ladder we try to ascend, we need a Savior, not only to teach us, but to pour His life into us.

> He can enter below the level of consciousness, can project his life back through time in me and heal my oldest and most hidden memories, so that as His power works in the submerged mind, my conscious thoughts more and more conform to the image of His joy and light.[8]

His teaching illumines me, but He, the very Word, incarnates me.

Dying to the Old Man

> The natural life in each of us is something self-centered, something that wants to be petted and admired, to take advantage of other lives, to exploit the whole universe. And especially it wants to be left to itself: to keep well away from anything better or stronger or higher than it, anything that might make it feel small. It is afraid of the light and air of the spiritual world, just as people who have been brought up to be dirty are afraid of a bath. And in

a sense it is quite right. It knows that if the spiritual life gets hold of it, all its self-centeredness and self-will are going to be killed and it is ready to fight tooth and nail to avoid that.[9]

The "old man" is what we call that drive toward evil that is in our old fallen nature. Dying to this nature is a kind of suffering; it can even be violent. Yet it is not the carrying of the cross. It is a corollary to it. As we abide in Christ (practice His Presence), we die to the old man, that bent toward self-centeredness, self-will, becoming our own god.

I find this following concept important in counseling all who sincerely desire to follow Christ:

Purity is not a long struggle against that which is impure or forbidden. Rather is it singleness of heart. Catch the great thought that from Him, the Father of Lights, comes every good and perfect gift, and therefore nothing outside of God is worth having or craving.[10]

I wonder about all this business of "detachment" as taught in some spirituality courses. If we just practice "attachment" to God, the detachment from all that is amiss in our lives will take care of itself. In fact, I am more and more impressed with the danger of "emptying out" without "filling up." We seem much more proficient at leading people to empty themselves than to fill themselves.

Just as we resist the Devil by drawing near to Jesus, so we stop practicing the presence of the old man by practicing the presence of the new. In this practice, we put away the deeds of the old man, we bring captive every thought of the mind or imagination of the heart, in submission to Christ. This involves a kind of suffering.

The full acting out of self's surrender to God therefore demands pain: this action, to be perfect, must be done from the pure will to obey, in the absence, or in the teeth, of inclination.[11]

In the practice of the Presence, more of the true self is being apprehended and Christ is being given more of me.

In his novel *The Great Divorce*, C. S. Lewis sketches a number of remarkable pictures of this old man we must die to.

In one sketch, the old man appears as a seedy old actor, a tragedian (Chapter 12). From personal experience, we fallen ones recognize him only too well. The thesis of this book is that Heaven and all it contains is of such solid reality that the unredeemed (those who have chosen self and Hell) can never be at home in it. Lewis pictures those refusing life as insubstantial, ghostlike. These "ghosts" choose Hell because they cannot stand the utter reality of Heaven. Even the blades of grass on the outskirts of Paradise prove too much for them, as these are of such solid reality that they pierce through their shadowy feet.

In this particular sketch, a lovely, bright spirit appears—one who on earth had chosen joy and Heaven. She was Sarah Smith, lately of Golder's Green. She had been the wife of the pompous old actor. "Love shone not from her face only, but from all her limbs, as if it were some liquid in which she had just been bathing." As she runs over the green turf on the outskirts of Paradise, "the invitation to all joy" sings "out of her whole being like a bird's song on an April evening." She is in starkest contrast to the shadowy ghost she has been sent to help. He appears to lead a tiny dwarf ghost, but we soon realize that the tall theatrical figure is the illusory self, and the tiny dwarf is all that is left of the man. The dwarf figure holds a chain attached to the collar of the tall one.

Sarah Smith, the bright spirit, appeals only to the dwarf ghost, all that is left of the real Frank Smith. She looks and speaks solely to it—ignoring completely the big tragedian. But the dwarf ghost will not speak to her or even look at her. Instead he yanks the chain of the shadowy tragedian, and he answers her. Try as she might, she cannot get past this large inflated "self-image" to the dwarfed figure of Frank. But "the abundance of life she had in Christ from the Father" flowed out of her, and the dwarf ghost became more real when once he did look at her. However, the life the dwarf received from the one who in life had been his wife reached him against his will. With each of his bad choices, the dwarf diminishes. Finally he is swallowed up in the illusion—the persona of the dramatized self which Frank in life had adopted and into which he had disappeared. The last image we see is that of the dwarf ghost growing smaller and smaller, crawling up the chain around the neck of the tragedian, the illusory self.

Anyone with a valid ministry to sin-sick souls will recognize the powerful psychological insight Lewis has into the hearts and minds of those who choose Hell. I shall never forget one deeply unrepentant man who had an important post in the church. He came to see me, not for help, but as I found out later, to try to discredit the ministry of healing prayer with its strong message of repentance. In good faith I saw him and, not comprehending his motives at first, I proceeded as I would with anyone. I invoked the Presence of God and invited him into that awesomely holy and therefore healing Presence. In spite of himself, true insight and healing entered into his soul, and I saw him grow more real and solid for a moment. He had begun to forgive another, and with that a healing started that was beginning to lift from his mind and heart a very dark condition.

His surprise at what God was so willing to do was quite visible. It was not difficult to read the conflicting motions of his soul at that moment. But he quickly willed to hang on to malice and unforgiveness. He left extremely angry with me because he had almost forgiven a parent he hated.

The history of this person since that interview has been tragic. His willful sin destroyed his family, and then the churches he pastored, and finally it destroyed him. Sometimes we see someone get more help and healing than he or she came for or will accept. And we, though deeply saddened, cannot force the person's will. We can only paint the most glorious word pictures we can of what it means to choose Heaven and the real.

The unredeemed, in choosing self rather than God, Hell rather than Heaven, choose inessentiality rather than an incarnation of radiant life. They refuse Incarnational Reality, the infusion of the Spirit of God into their insubstantial and inessential lives.

In ministry to a person (in carrying the cross), we learn from Sarah Smith of Golder's Green always to appeal to the real person. We do not converse or in any way interact with the seedy old actor, the old man. We do not help this person when through misplaced sympathy or empathy we fail to recognize carnal strongholds in his life and name them. We do not help him when we engage in long months of conversation with his "illusory self." When we do this, we simply practice with him the presence of his old man. "Love," says Lewis, "is something more stern and splendid than mere kindness." Some come for mere kindness—sympathy or empathy—and are amazed to find God's love shining on them instead. God's love names the rebellion they are in and calls them to a radical repentance. His love then begins to separate them from the darkness within and without. But, like the ghost dwarf, only against their will do they give up their greed, their lusts, their fantasy lives, their jealousies and envies, their hatred and bitterness.

Those who are sick—psychologically, physically, or spiritually— because they hate, envy, covet, idolize, commit adultery, fornicate, practice homosexuality, and so on—are sick because they practice the presence of the old man, the illusory self.

To die to this self is painful; it is remedial pain, not what carrying the cross is. I must will to die this death; I must choose it, knowing that "[a]nything outside the system of self-giving is not earth, nor nature, nor ordinary life, but simply and solely Hell."[12]

The True Self Carries the Cross
As we appropriate the life of Christ and carry it, we know with St. Paul that even as we do not suffer alone, so also we do not do battle in our own strength.

> Weak men we may be, but it is not as such that we fight our battles. The weapons we wield are not merely human, but divinely

potent to demolish strongholds; we demolish sophistries and all
that rears its proud head against the knowledge of God; we com-
pel every human thought to surrender in obedience to Christ. . . .
(2 Corinthians 10:3b-5, NEB)

As we practice the Presence of Christ, we make every thought "our
prisoner, captured to be brought into obedience to Christ." Our entire being
is thus consecrated to God, wholly committed, given over to Him. We
become channels of His life; we carry the cross.

This life manifests itself as both fruit and gift of the Spirit. As fruit of
the Spirit, the character and the nature of Jesus is shown—kindness, faith,
humility, love, joy, peace, patience, gentleness, discipline. As the gifts of
the Holy Spirit, this life manifests itself as the power to say, to do, and to
know. Such are the tools with which we work the works of Christ. The
fruits are the way of love, that most excellent way in which all the gifts are
to operate.

Presence-Oriented, Not Gift-Centered

The gifts of the Holy Spirit, then, as well as the fruits of the Spirit, have to
do with God's Presence with us. There is Another who lives in our midst,
and He has the Spirit without measure. With Him are all the gifts and all
the fruits of the Spirit. Because Jesus, the Gift, lives in and with us, the gifts
and the fruits of His life are present and can radiate through us. Thus are
we empowered to preach, teach, and heal.

The authentic gifts and fruits, then, have to do with the Real Presence.
When our eyes are fixed on Christ (and not our gifts), our fruits will be
genuine. We are never to be gift-centered or even fruit-centered, but
Presence-oriented. In this way we abide in Him; in this way Incarnational
Reality and humility go hand in hand.

The Corinthians, forgetting the presence of Jesus with them, were having problems with experience. In their Eucharist, they no longer discerned
the Lord's body (1 Corinthians 11:29), His Presence with them. Though
they did not "lack any spiritual gift" (1 Corinthians 1:7), they had become
unspiritual.

Brothers, I could not address you as spiritual but as
worldly—mere infants in Christ. I gave you milk, not solid food,
for you were not yet ready for it. Indeed, you are still not ready.
You are still worldly. For since there is jealousy and quarreling
among you, are you not worldly? Are you not acting like mere
men? For when one says, "I follow Paul," and another,"I follow
Apollos," are you not mere men? (1 Corinthians 3:1-4)

The Corinthians were behaving as our human nature leads us to
behave when we do not act from our true center—in union with Him.

They had become too impressed with the merely human in wisdom and knowledge, forgetting about the one thing needful—the continued grace and Real Presence of God in the midst of Christian fellowship and the Christian Meal. They were therefore making wrong judgments of their leaders. Envy and strife had accompanied their pride in this "new *gnosis*," this ladder to perfection via new knowledge .The new way bypassed the Way of the Cross, the way of Jesus first dying for us and then giving us new life. Therefore they squabbled over which leader to follow. Schism had occurred. They were unspiritual and immature. Their gifts jangled.

The Corinthians were no longer "carrying the cross," no longer channels of God's love. They no longer understood their union, their at-one-ness with God and unity with others.

The Matter of Judging

The Corinthians apparently were making wrong judgments about matters other than leadership. They had become tolerant of the wrong things and proud of that tolerance. Failing then to judge the sin in their midst, they had apparently come to believe that it was an "elitism" to accept a man who was unrepentant and living in sin.

As William Barclay reminds us:

An easy-going attitude to sin is always dangerous. It has been said that our one security against sin lies in our being shocked at it. Carlyle said that men must see the infinite beauty of holiness and the infinite damnability of sin. When we cease to take a serious view of sin we are in a perilous position. It is not a question of being critical and condemnatory; it is a question of being wounded and shocked. It was sin that crucified Jesus Christ; it was to free men from sin that he died. No Christian can take an easy-going view of it.[13]

The Apostle Paul had to teach the Corinthians that we in the Body of Christ are indeed to judge ourselves; that we are to judge the sin that is killing us.

> *In keeping silent about evil,*
> *in burying it deep within us,*
> *so that it appears nowhere on the surface,*
> *we are implanting it,*
> *And it will rise up*
> *a thousandfold in the future.*
>   (Aleksandr Solzhenitsyn)[14]

One cannot effectively carry his cross apart from exercising right judgment. One of the sad things in today's church world is the inability to confront sin and call sinners to repentance. This is where some of the worst psycho-babble comes in, that which reconciles good and evil within the soul of the person who needs to repent and be healed. In addition to needing healing, often this person is being consumed with his own rebellion. Fortunate is such a one who has the minister, priest, or bishop who will in the power of the Spirit call him to repent, hear his confession, and pray for the healing of any emotional difficulties underlying his aberrant behavior.

Often these unfortunates find themselves in the hands of those who have a *new gnosis*, a new kind of false light or love. It smiles broadly with a compassion that is as cruel as death, for it leads to the death of the soul that continues in willful sin. It opens the Church to a darkness she can no longer judge as evil.

The people of God go unprotected, not only because the leaders fail to judge sin, but also because they all too often deliberately "desensitize" the person in the pew to the nature of sin, and bar him from a right judgment as well.

Many, therefore, are afraid to rightly discern and judge evil. The evil, then, as Solzhenitsyn says, rises up a thousandfold in the future. This is a part of the present crisis in masculinity and authority that affects us all because it is ingrained in our culture. We live in an age that reconciles good and evil, and that therefore has no moral measuring stick for judging. A passive compassion (that does a great deal of harm) is easier for the modern Christian than a decisive action that proves to be, in the end, the only loving thing to do. Because of this blindness, Christians can hear our Lord say, "Do not judge, and you will not be judged" (this regarding unjust, hypocritical judging—Luke 6:37). But they find it hard to hear Christ's command to "Judge not according to appearance, but judge righteous judgement" (John 7:24, KJV).

There is a right as opposed to wrong judging, and we who follow the Way of the Cross must learn it. We do not judge or act apart from the Spirit of God; we do not fail to judge or fail to act in obedience to God. Paul's letter to the Corinthians provides a wonderful study on the matter of judging. A point to be made here is that he was writing to a people who "did not lack any spiritual gift." He was writing, then, to a people who were self-centered in the use of the spirituals. He was writing to a people no longer Presence-oriented but experience-oriented. There are few souls more dangerous to the Church and her mission than those in whom the gifts still operate but clang.

Jesus in me, as I carry my cross, will never misuse the gifts in ministry. Rather, as I collaborate with the Holy Spirit, He will always point to Christ. Christ will be honored. He will be glorified.

In His Presence, listening, we find that every need for healing is unique and different. Therefore the gifts of the Spirit are never ritualized. They vary, they overlap, they intermingle. We plainly see in the Scriptures that with Jesus there were never two healings alike; there is no way to learn a system. One acknowledges a Presence and listens to Him.

No Substitution

"Are you able to drink the cup that I drink, or to be baptized with the baptism with which I am baptized?" (Mark 10:38, NASB)

When someone asks to take upon himself the pain, illness, fear, or even sorrow of another, he is not carrying his cross, but is voluntarily practicing substitution. He may or may not be influenced by the unbalanced practices and beliefs of some medieval Christians who first learned a false asceticism of compassion. They afflicted themselves "no longer so much to fight and overcome the power of sin through Christ and by His power; it was rather to suffer with Him, as if to bring some alleviation to His suffering by taking a part of it"[15] on themselves. They ultimately developed an asceticism of substitution antithetical to the doctrine of grace as taught both in the Scriptures and in all orthodox tradition. We are not redeemers—only Christ is great and good enough to die on the Cross for mankind. Substitution is wrong.

I don't remember even once teaching on the dangers of substitution without finding several persons needing both the information and healing as a result of their own involvement in substitutionary practice. The following example is dramatic. An attractive seminary professor, on hearing me strongly assert that substitution or proxy healing is dangerous and falls short of Christian healing, immediately asked for prayer.

She complained of numbness in her left arm and shoulder and of pain in her left hand. At the same time, she had experienced other more alarming internal symptoms that had finally proven to foreshadow kidney and thyroid trouble. At this time she still needed medication for the kidney infection, and she had undergone a thyroid operation for the glandular problems. I had known her previous to this time as an exceptionally healthy person, active beyond average both intellectually and physically. But now she was obviously not nearly so energetic and was clearly concerned about the symptoms in her body.

She began telling me of her practice of "sitting in proxy" both for the healing and the deliverance of others. By deliverance was meant the casting out of demons, and this would be guesswork, not a true discerning of spirits since the person prayed for would not even be there. Such a practice constitutes the practice of the presence of demons, something bound to end in malevolent consequences. Wanting to help the sick and oppressed, she would ask to take their sickness, darkness, and even demonic oppression into and upon herself. Others in her prayer group would then pray for her as the proxy for the healing or deliverance of the person who was either too far away or unwilling to come.

She was in frightful need of release from the oppression that she had in error invited upon herself. I was astounded at the almost violent emotional and physical reactions that occurred as we began to pray for her release. Before laying hands on her and praying for her healing, I asked her to confess the sin of pride by saying: "Lord, You only are the Redeemer, and I ask Your forgiveness for trying to take on myself what You have already done. I have focused on the darkness and on the need rather than upon You. Forgive my foolish pride, O Lord." Then I asked her to renounce the substitutions.

When there have been only a few substitutions, I ask people to renounce each specifically. But in her case there had been many. Therefore, I simply asked her to renounce the entire practice of substitution and all her previous substitutions along with it. At the moment she did this, she was thrown quite forcefully to the floor by the conjunction of two powers. God's Spirit was flooding in to heal as the evil, oppressing spirits fled. After this, her physical and spiritual problems cleared up "miraculously."

She right away began to pray with others in her prayer group who needed this same healing. The practice of substitution was eliminated in their congregation and in sister congregations to which it had spread. This is an extreme example of a conscious and deliberate practice of substitution, but unfortunately even these situations pop up from time to time.

Less conscious and deliberate substitutions, however, are not uncommon. Nuns and mothers seem to lead the field in terms of who needs healing from them. Their healings are fully as remarkable as the one recounted above. Seemingly instantaneous healings of cancer and emphysema, as well as other problems, have occurred. A number of years before attending my conference, a well-meaning mother, praying for her son's salvation, asked to take his emphysema and bear it for him. Her son was still unconverted, though free from emphysema. She had it so badly she could hardly walk a block. Before the end of the conference, she climbed the foothills of the California mountains where our conference was held.

The following excerpt is from a letter a nun wrote after she and a group of her sisters had received unexpected and truly remarkable healings once they renounced the practice of substitution. This, I think, typifies the majority of instances we deal with:

I heard your message so strongly because all my life I can recall times when I felt moved to pray in this way: "Lord, please don't let Mom be sick; if someone has to be sick, let me be—not her." When these thoughts came, I really didn't enjoy saying prayers like that because I was afraid I would be taken at my word. But as I look back, I probably felt like a martyr or some kind of a hero offering myself for the sake of another.

Just lately, I find myself doing the same thing—asking the Lord to heal my friend of cystic fibrosis and afflict me in his place—some such weird idea. When you began explaining this as substitution and wrong, I saw for the first time how I was really sort of making myself God—determining who should be sick or well, and proudly offering myself. I saw how insidious a temptation it was and how un-Biblical and unworthy of our God it is.

That's about as clear as I can explain it. I see it now as based on false theology and dangerous. If there are any articles I could read which would clarify even more in my mind, I'd be grateful if you'd tell me about them.

When one inadvertently takes into or upon himself the symptoms of one for whom he is praying, this also is substitution, "an involuntary over-identification with the patient and an under-identification with Him," as Agnes Sanford says.[16] When first learning to pray for others, Agnes attempted a substitution and in her novel *Lost Shepherd* she showed it in a positive light. But she learned better and renounced the dangerous practice.

We who are concerned for the conversion and healing of others easily fall unwittingly into substitutionary practices. Mostly it results from ministering out of our own emotional being (rather than from Christ *in us*). For instance, in one seminar a woman came up asking for prayer for her eyesight. She had been ministering to a blind woman. She explained, "I felt so sorry for her, and I asked to take on the burden of her blindness; now I'm having trouble with my eyes."

Dark spiritual forces aside, when we do something like this, we send the wrong message to our soul and body, a command that says: "Disintegrate." What an awe-ful thing to do. But also, when we look solely on the pain or suffering, we forget to focus on Christ. From looking to the Savior, and pointing the suffering one to Him, we try in ourselves to find the strength and efficacy to "save" them.

Recently a nun came forward after my teaching on substitution and gratefully hugged me. She had often been tempted to practice substitution. In particularly hard cases she would say to herself, "Oh, I wish I could carry this," and then would feel vaguely confused and guilty for not doing so. She was laboring under some of the old notions that if one were really loving and Christlike, one would want to suffer vicariously for another. "Now," she said, "I know what is happening when I fall into this."

Substitution occurs when we forget the distinction between being a savior-redeemer (something only Jesus could ever be and do) and being His disciple, a sacramental channel through whom His life is to flow. To substitute is to attempt to do the work Christ has already finished, and at the same time to miss one's own proper work. To take upon or into ourselves (as mediators) the darkness of others is at best based in ignorance, at worst based in pride. Either way, we've fallen into a messiah or savior complex and will have to confess pride to get out of it.

The greatest danger in substitution has to do with the fact that spiritual forces we do not understand or discern can be directly involved in sicknesses of spirit, soul, and body. In the case of demons, these don't mind "transferring" themselves from the sick one to the one who prays for the healing. The first time I realized this, I was ministering to persons who had come forward to the altar for prayer. One of these persons had an excruciating stomach pain. As sometimes happens in churches, ministry can be going on around the altar while others, not in prayer, chat among themselves (never a good practice when serious prayer is occurring). At the very moment this woman was prayed for and released from the pain, a woman visiting with a neighbor a few rows from the altar rail suddenly screamed out with a stomach pain. We then had to pray for her. This unsuspecting woman had experienced a completely involuntary "substitution."

The well-publicized movie *The Exorcist* did not feature an exorcism at all, but a substitution. A priest, failing to exercise the authority of his office, took into himself the demonic force afflicting a child. The movie ends with the priest leaping from a window to his death. This illustrates most graphically that in substitutions there is a price to pay. This price is not true Christian suffering, nor is it carrying our cross.

There are current doctrines embodied in powerful and beautiful literature that recommend substitutionary practices as the way of love. Poets and novelists, following the Muse rather than the Holy Spirit, can cause a lot of mischief, especially when they are Christians. Charles Williams, well-loved friend of C. S. Lewis and T. S. Eliot, formulated a doctrine of substitution which has great appeal to the romantic imagination, and it has led many astray.

The good characters in Williams's novels are convincingly good, a real plus for him. But the imagery he uses is that of truly good persons absorbing the fear, darkness, or evil of others into the lucidity of their own light-filled spirits (what only Christ can do). This imagery in his imaginative works is true to his doctrine of substitution outlined in his theological books and essays—that of good swallowing up evil.[17] Williams wrote:

> To take over the grief or the fear or the anxiety of another is precisely that (the way of Love); and precisely that is less practiced than praised.[18]

Because Williams combines this doctrine with truth about the real work of the Christian disciple (for instance, bearing another's burdens), it is difficult to sort out the erroneous extremes. One of his approved examples, however, would jolt most of us to recognize the truth and shows that Williams believed in his doctrine so unreservedly that he did not shy away from even the sorest extreme:

> It is said (among other examples of substitution in the Church) that the blessed St. Seraphim of Sarov laid on a certain nun the ascetic discipline of death, that she should die instead of her sick brother Michael, whose work was not yet done.[19]

To lay death on a person is not only un-Scriptural, it is diabolical. Where was the Church's gift of healing for the priest whose work was not yet finished? One can only quake at the thought of how the nun must have reacted to this dreadful laying on of hands. The very psychology of the thing, if received into the deep mind, would start the process of death in the soul believing it. This is the medieval asceticism of substitution, the influences of which still come down to us in one way or another. It's amazing to me that Charles Williams's doctrine could blind him to the extent that he would include this example in his writings.

Until Gethsemane and Calvary, Jesus never took upon or into Himself anyone else's fear, sin, illness, or darkness. One has only to look at His prayer life and at every instance of his healing ministry to see that this is so. Rather, *as a man* limited by His flesh body, He healed the same way He has authorized us to do. Listening always to the Father, doing only what He saw the Father do, what He heard the Father saying, He perfectly obeyed the Father and collaborated with the Holy Spirit to heal sickness and to cast out devils.

In an era when Christians shy away from the power of God and fail to understand the healing gifts of the Holy Spirit, we fall into false notions about Christian work and Christian suffering. Then, rather than exorcising witches, we hang or burn them. Rather than bringing people in to the saving Presence of Christ, we merely analyze them to see why they haven't "realized an integration of their personalities." Rather than healing the sick and casting out devils, we neglect them altogether or attempt some sort of substitution.

Charles Williams did not live in an era when the Church experienced or even desired much of the healing power of the Lord. Yet he longed to see this "old knowledge" of love working. For this reason and many more, he is not to be judged by me. I am convinced that in the Judgment both he and I and all others will be judged, not on what we've accomplished or on our theologies and methodologies, but on how well we have loved. That is to say, how much we have sought and recognized Christ's Presence, how much we have received and given His love. In Charles Williams's determination to know and give only love, he must have succeeded to a phenomenal degree. Those who knew him report that his spirit burned "with intelligence and charity."[20] C. S. Lewis said of him that while lecturing,

> His face becomes almost angelic. Both in public and private he is of nearly all the men I have met the one whose address most overflows with love.[21]

Both because I have quoted Charles Williams in this book and because his doctrine continues to influence others, I've used Williams as an example of one who recommends substitution. Perhaps his followers go further than he himself would go. His letters seem to indicate this, but they also indicate difficulties he got into with people (especially women) whom he taught the way of substitution and exchange.

Williams based his doctrine on the great substitution by Christ ("He hath made him, who knew no sin, to be sin for us," 2 Corinthians 5:21, KJV and "The Lord hath laid on him the iniquity of us all," Isaiah 53:6, KJV). He seemed to have a firm grip (at least intellectually) on what "He in us and we in Him" means. Williams reasoned that we also come into the pattern of Christ's substitution and exchange. He therefore formulated what he believed to be a universal principle: All life, especially that lived in the Kingdom of Heaven, is to be vicarious. The one who truly carries his cross is the one who fully participates in a cosmic pattern of substitution and exchange.

> He was not like us, and yet He became us. . . . He submitted in our stead to the full results of the Law which is He. . . . By that central substitution, which was the thing added by the Cross to the Incarnation, He became everywhere the centre of everywhere He energized and reaffirmed, all our substitutions and exchanges.[22]

This theme runs throughout his novels, poetry, histories, and essays, but is perhaps best seen in his novel *Descent into Hell*. One need read only this novel to see how powerfully this doctrine lends itself to the romantic imagination. One of the great strengths of Charles Williams is his understanding of what happens to the person who cannot give to others. This person cannot enter the Great Dance of order and harmony found on the secular as well as the sacred planes of the universe. Williams's metaphors that describe the descent into the hell of self are so graphic I've had students come running up to me after classes, saying, "Mrs. Payne, Mrs. Payne, pray with me, please pray with me. I am a Wentworth." (Wentworth in this novel is seen descending into Hell through the coils of his own intestines, a really horrifying imagery of what narcissistic self-love is.)

But Williams captures here what is common to fallen man. The imagery he uses can explode the attentive reader out of passivity and get him actively praying for forgiveness and help. I find it an exciting book to teach. But the doctrine of substitution and exchange is there, and I always have to show what these are and warn against them. Even so, I have found it necessary to pray for some who did not hear my warnings and later read the book (apart from the stress of other studies). They had tried "substituting" for some friend or another in trouble. The college professor I wrote about earlier in this chapter was first influenced by the works of Charles Williams. She was "set up" to fall into the difficulty.

C. S. Lewis was also "set up" for it. He had a deep affection for Charles Williams and was familiar with his ideas. In a crucial moment when Lewis's wife was suffering excruciating pain in her leg from cancer, lines from Charles Williams's imaginative works came to his mind. Lewis asked to take her pain. He later lost calcium from his leg as she gained it. From his letters and his remarks to friends, it is evident that this was an inadvertent substitution, more of an emotional desire to help carry her burden in the best Christian sense. But it is typical of what can happen to persons influenced by ideas of substitution at moments when their hearts are deeply moved with compassion and pity.

On March 21, 1957, Lewis married Joy Davidman, a Jewess converted through reading his books. Lewis was fifty-nine years of age at this time. Theirs was an unusual wedding in that it was performed in a hospital where Joy was confined. The doctors had given her at most seven to ten months to live, while her nurses thought she had only a few weeks. As Lewis wrote in letters to friends, an entire femur had by this time been destroyed by bone cancer and her hip was partly destroyed.

In April Joy was sent home to die, but by April 21 her bone trouble first stabilized and then began to heal. Experiencing no pain, she soon was able to walk and except for a limp began to live a normal life. This appeared to be a most wonderful answer to the prayer in that the minister who had married them had also prayed for her healing with laying of hands. At this very time, however, while Joy's bones were gaining the calcium they needed, Lewis's were losing it. His new malady was diagnosed as osteoporosis, and throughout that summer and up until the late fall he experienced excruciating pain.

Lewis for the first time in his life experienced the bliss of wedded love, a love he never dreamed could have been, much less at his age and in view of his and Joy's physical problems. Her reprieve gave them this happiness, and the insights Lewis received through his experience of a truly fulfilling conjugal love have been passed on to us through *A Grief Observed* and, perhaps even more, through personal letters to his closest friends. He came to see this reprieve both in the light of the healing prayer, but also in the light of what he called a Charles Williams substitution. Though Lewis believed his bone disease "a low price to pay" for Joy's release from pain, the substitution was not God's way. It is not a practice that can ever complement a prayer for healing, but will always, in some way, militate against true prayer. Joy died of cancer anyway, and I am convinced that Lewis's life was shortened. It could very well be that Lewis, one of the greatest apologists for the Christian faith in this or any other century, was prematurely taken from the scene because of this substitution. There were other things in his heart to write, and one can only speculate on the wealth of insight and understanding that would have been contained in those writings.

For another thing, there is always a spiritual price to pay when a substitution has occurred. Although there is so much that is great in *A Grief Observed*, and many a grieving person has been extraordinarily blessed by its insights, even so one who has eyes to see can look between the lines to see the spiritual battle Lewis was in. This battle is typical of the aftermath of substitution and is notably untypical of Lewis himself, who had gone through many trials and losses. I am extremely grateful that Lewis came out on the far and the bright side of that battle. (Many a person gets trapped in the doubt and the confusion of such a spiritual battle, and without special help and healing prayer, does not come out of it.) He had strength enough to write the book he had long wanted to write: *Letters to Malcolm: Chiefly on Prayer*. By the time Lewis wrote this, the battle was won.

The practice of "sitting in proxy" and having hands laid on oneself for the healing of another's illness is by no means always a substitution. But it is a mistaken practice, one that confuses the deep mind of the person on whom hands are laid in prayer. He cannot receive the healing for another, even as he cannot take another's darkness or death into himself. He can, however, pray in faith for the healing of that person. In prayer for those at a distance, we do not lay hands on someone else for them. Rather, we can link hands as a gesture that we agree together (the Biblical model) in intercessory prayer for their release and healing. These can be powerful prayers indeed. Some of the most marvelous miracles of physical healings that I have ever seen have come about through intercessory prayer and the prayer of faith released in that fashion. To mix a proxy laying on of hands with intercessory prayer is to seriously weaken the prayer.

To sum up, then, Christ is the Healer. We do not take another's suffering, sin, or sickness into or upon ourselves. This Christ has already done—in Gethsemane and on the Cross. We point always to the One who cried out on the Cross, "My God, My God, why hast thou forsaken me?" We yield up to Him and to Him alone our suffering and our sin. In exchange, He then imparts life and healing. He continues with us, and His life flows through us to others. In His Presence, we help others to yield to him their pain and darkness. But He alone is Redeemer, and His Cross is never the one we carry. From that Cross He cried, "It is finished," and the work that He alone can do was completed. His Cross is not our cross, but the one that enables us to take up our cross and walk in His footsteps.

A number of years ago when writing on Incarnational Reality in the works of C. S. Lewis (published as *Real Presence*), I was meditating upon God as the well-spring or fountain of life. At the same time I was still concerned in my heart about the problem of substitution. Praying to Him as the blessed and holy well-spring of all life, I asked if there was any particular word for me that day. I wrote the following words that came so swiftly in listening prayer. I am still blessed by the message they carry, one that wholly conforms with what the Scriptures teach:

> I am a well-spring within you, welling up into eternal life. You (even now) have eternal life in Me. Eternal life, that I AM within you, flows out to meet the needs of the world. This is, as you have said in your book, Incarnational Reality. I have taken, once and for all, the burden of the sin of the world. I did not practice this as a man among men. I underwent this in Gethsemane. I, the well-spring of life, the author of life, took death into Me—your death—and I overcame it. I came forth from your death victorious, something you could never have done.

In the loss of what it means to truly carry our crosses, we forsake the Lord, the spring of living water (Jeremiah 17:13) and dig for ourselves cisterns, "broken cisterns that cannot hold water" (Jeremiah 2:13, NIV). Truly, we do not overcome death for others. It has already been done.

Conclusion to Carrying the Cross

Christians are merely laborers with God, for the foundation is laid. That foundation is Jesus Christ, and we are an extension of His life.

We can erect two kinds of buildings on this foundation. One is incarnational. We can remember always that Another is with us and allow Him to live through us. In this case, we will have works that will last; they will be of eternal, redeeming value. We can then, in a most astonishing way, bring prisoners out of the prison house, take the chains off of captives. Or we can ignore God's Presence and live from the locus of the old self. We can build to our own glory here on earth.

The Corinthians thought they had arrived. They were pridefully and blindly self-satisfied. But they were failing to discern the Lord's Body. Paul had to reprove them for their carnal division, their factions over ministers and their envying and strife. Factious Christians (denominationally minded rather than Body-of-Christ-oriented) are unspiritual. They operate from a soulish level—one that is at once unloving and prideful. We as the Body of Christ must die individually and corporately to this old man and offer ourselves as channels through which Christ's healing love can flow.

The secret to effectively carrying the cross is the practice of the Presence, the call to appropriate to ourselves the holy. "Be perfect [be completed by my Presence with you], even as I am perfect," says Yahweh to His people. "Walk with Me and do my bidding."

CHAPTER 14

Renouncing False Gods and Appropriating the Holy

"How can you say, 'I am not defiled;
I have not run after the Baals'?
See how you behaved in the valley;
consider what you have done.
You are a swift she-camel
running here and there,
a wild donkey accustomed to the desert,
sniffing the wind in her craving—
in her heat who can restrain her?
Any males that pursue her need not tire themselves;
at mating time they will find her.
Do not run until your feet are bare
and your throat is dry.
But you say, 'It's no use!
I love foreign gods,
and I must go after them.'"

(Jeremiah 2:23-25)

"Make sure there is no man or woman, clan or tribe among you
today whose heart turns away from the Lord our God to go and
worship the gods of those nations; make sure there is no root among
you that produces such bitter poison."

(Deuteronomy 29:18)

"I am the Lord who makes you holy."

(Leviticus 20:8)

D iscerning the problem of evil and differentiating that from the Good, which is finally the Holy One Himself, is what makes the Christian psychologist and counselor different from other doctors of the soul. We have today, however, far too few within the Body of Christ who adequately discern in this matter, and this lack has given rise to the most crucial problem I've seen develop within the Church, that of a very real encroachment of alien gods.

In this chapter, I will address two specific manifestations of this: the rise both of a Baal consciousness and of a new Gnosticism in Christian circles.

Renouncing Baal, the God of Sexual Orgy[1]

So Israel joined himself to [the god] Baal of Peor. (Numbers 25:3, *Amplified Bible*)

Particularly pertinent to those times when I'm asking the Lord to bring people out of sexual neurosis and/or perverted sexual lifestyles, and teaching others how to minister to them, is the matter of *renouncing Baal and Ashtoreth*, the male and female idol-gods of sexual orgy.

Baal, whose name means "lord, possessor," was the supreme deity among the Canaanites and various other pagan nations. He is mentioned at least sixty-three times in the Scriptures. His full title was Baal-Shemaim ("lord of heaven"). Each locality had its own Baal, and the form of worship varied from place to place. He had many other titles, as can be found in at least twenty combined names in Bible indices.

Baal, though originally Phoenician, was the male sun-god worshiped in western Asia among heathen nations as their chief deity. His altars and sanctuaries were located on high places, including the summits of high mountains in order to get the first view of the rising sun and the last of the setting sun. The sun was believed to be the source and emblem of all life and the generative power of Nature.

Ashtoreth was the female idol of Philistia, Zidon, and Phoenicia. She was supposed to be the wife of Baal and the queen of heaven (Jeremiah 7:18; 44:17). The feminine principle was supposed to be embodied in the moon, to which the name Ashtoreth was given. The idol was a female with a crescent moon on her brow. It was set up in the temples and worshiped with the most revolting forms of immorality and sexual perversion. She was worshiped also by Israel in times of apostasy (see Judges 2:13; 10:6; etc). Her priests were eunuchs in women's attire (1 Kings 14:24). Women devotees were prostitutes for males whose lustful orgies formed the main part of the worship, which was carried on in temples, gardens, and high places. The cult of the goddess came from Babylon, where Ishtar was worshiped with immoral rites by bands of men and women.

When there is worship of the sun and moon, of the created, sexual orgies always follow. We either worship the Creator or our own procreative faculties. Finally, a quite literal worship of man's own genitals ensues.[2] Demons, principalities, and powers of the air attend this worship. The dark inroads into human sexuality and personality from this activity are almost incomprehensible. This, of course, is what the Apostle Paul is referring to in Romans 1:23 and following.

In the ministry of prayer for healing, I sometimes have Pastoral Care Schools specifically for those who have come to Christ out of permissive and perverted sexual lifestyles. Once as I came home after such a conference where there were over two hundred afflicted with compulsive sexual behavior of one kind or another, I was acutely aware of the horror of the battle we are in, living as we all do in an age that has forgotten God and now worships the creature. Terribly exhausted, I fell in a heap before the Lord, only to hear Him speak, ever so clearly, these words:

Order your day. Organize the hours. They are precious. . . .
There is no room, no place for the moping, disgruntled prophet.
You are like all prophets in that it is after your greatest victories
that you run and hide and ask to die. But My people are with
you; they have not bent the knee before Baal.
It is Baal worship you are facing and battling—the very
thing the prophets of old inveighed against.
I have given you favor; My favor is upon you. I continue to
give you favor. Gird up your loins (prepare for battle, prepare to
be used) and run the race. You will outrun the chariots of men;
you will run in the power that I give.

I was amazed by such a word as that, and ran to the Scriptures to see what they had to say about Baal. I was even more amazed by the amount of material they contained, and that the import of the material had not struck me more forcibly before then. This latter was especially remarkable to me in light of the demonic oppression I had encountered at the outset of my adult Christian life, one that involved the phallic images. Do you have any idea how much there is about that idol in Scriptures? And of the way the people of Yahweh were always either having to withstand a people who served this idol, or were themselves, when backslidden, under its aegis? He was the god Elijah had his great contest with, for Baal worship was the state religion of Israel under Ahab and Jezebel.

In the worship of Baal, an Asherah (a totem-pole type of god), a pillar or image of wood, was set up with the image of Baal, and was worshiped in libidinous and lascivious practices. Originally the idol was worshiped as a symbol of the tree of life, but later it was perverted to mean the origin of life and was pictured with the male organs of procreation (see Ezekiel 16:17).

The worship of Baal always ends in *phallicism*, meaning the worship of the phallus as a symbol primarily of male generative power, though in the worship of Ashtoreth the symbol sometimes changes to that of the female organ. Such symbols became the objects of worship carried on with all forms of impurity, perversion, and licentiousness by crowds of devotees involved in demonized and obscene orgies. This type of worship centered in the Canaanite nations and then spread. Relics of it are found among all heathen peoples. It led to the destruction of all Canaanite nations and, with other things, caused Israel to be dispersed among the nations.

In ministry to people who need to renounce Baal, we often have to deal with what I have come to call "phallic spirits" (that is how those who are demonically oppressed by them "see" them). Their psyches have openings to the dark world of spirits, and they see these beings in phallic forms. They are likely what the Scriptures refer to as "unclean spirits."

I have discovered, in working with people 1) who have (or have had) a sexual neurosis of one kind or another, or 2) with those who have been involved in perverted or illicit sexuality, or 3) with those whose parents or grandparents have had such difficulties, or 4) even with those who've suffered with pathological frigidity, or 5) even in some cases of those whose parents' chief occupation or problems center around sexuality (frigid or otherwise), that there comes a time when not all, but some of them *must renounce Baal (or Ashtoreth)* by name in order to become free. Before this renunciation, they must make a decision about sin and must repent. There is to be no idol, overt or in the imagination. Then, as those who need to renounce Baal do so, phallic demons leave them. This more often than not is amazingly quiet, for we have prayed to this end. But it can be quite dramatic and even at times noisy.

I have written very little about deliverance or exorcism in my books on the healing of sexual neuroses and gender imbalance (*The Broken Image*, *The Healing of the Homosexual*, and *Crisis in Masculinity*). That is because many people, well-meaning but misguided, have done such great damage to these sufferers by "casting out" demons that were not there. Besides that, as I well know, even when there is an infestation of phallic demons, *until* the emotional-psychological wound that has been the occasion for the demonic infestation is ministered to, the demons will hide. In deeply wounded persons, the *sense of being* itself can be very weak or even non-existent, and the demons seem to realize that the personality itself is too fractured to make an effective decision about sin and therefore a true renunciation of Baal. Such a person will then be much worse off after "deliverance" prayers, so-called, and the neurosis (symbolic confusion within the mind) along with the demonic oppression will be greatly stepped up.

Once the failure to come to a sense of being (or the fear of *non-being* itself) is ministered to by the Spirit of God, the essential personality of the person is made strong enough to make its decision and its renunciation. It is our experience that the phallic demons (who are very subtle and good at hiding) literally race to get away. If there are other types of demons, or an unusually large infestation of these, they may try to hang in there a little while, but not for long. A large reason for their hasty departure is that we use holy water, and these unclean, foul things cannot stand that which is holy, that which has been hallowed and set apart unto God.

Renouncing the Idol-god of One's Father

Many today are in the position of needing to renounce the idol their fathers have worshiped. Their need is like Gideon's of old. Gideon lived in a day when the Israelites were in terrible circumstances because they had not obeyed the Lord their God and had instead worshiped idol-gods. God sent a true prophet in response to their cries, and He also sent an angel with a message to Gideon. The message was: "The Lord is with you, mighty warrior." Gideon was then told by the Lord: "Go in the strength you have and save Israel out of Midian's hand." Gideon argued a bit, reminding the Lord of how small and insignificant he and his family were, but the Lord only reiterated that He was with him. Gideon first built an altar to the Lord and named it, "The Lord Is Peace." That same night the Lord said to him,

> "Tear down your father's altar to Baal and cut down the Asherah pole beside it. Then build a proper kind of altar to the Lord your God on the top of this height. Using the wood of the Asherah pole that you cut down, offer the second bull as a burnt offering." (Judges 6:25, 26)

Gideon did precisely all that the Lord commanded, and after he tore down the altar to Baal, the Spirit of the Lord came upon him and he was mightily empowered to lead the Israelites out of their troubles.

One might say that Gideon, among other things, came into his true masculinity and then led the people of his nation in that same direction. It was in helping men come out of sexual sin and into their true masculinity that I first discovered the principle within Gideon's story, for there were some who had to do the spiritual equivalent of what Gideon did before they could come into freedom.

Joe's story is a good example. He had been seriously hurt by going, as a seventeen-year-old, to a well-publicized deliverance minister. Joe, whose home background was unwholesome in the extreme, had come to Christ in great need of emotional healing. He was thoroughly committed to Christ, and was called to the ministry even then, but was struggling with the worst kinds of symbolic confusion as well as sexual compulsions, shame, and fear. He finally got nerve enough to go to the meeting, and after the "deliverance" he was not only worse, but without hope and convinced he was demon-possessed.

Ten or twelve pain-filled years later, he came to a Pastoral Care Ministry School, and his healing began. As he grew in wholeness and maturity, there was finally a girl in the picture. Since his main sexual difficulty had been with homosexuality, this was for him a major experience, but it brought with it an ugly spiritual battle, one that he was at first ashamed to tell me about. Every time he would think of marriage, a collage of filthy phallic images would come before his face. When he told me of this, and of how it so horrified him that he could not think of marriage and the girl he loved for fear "it" would appear, I said, "Good! Now we know exactly what to do in order to get you on the road to your full heterosexual identity."

I then was led to remind him of his father and his father's behavior. It could hardly have been more sexually vile. By this time we were in prayer and I had invoked the mighty Presence of the Lord, and I said to him, "Now you must renounce Baal, the god your father has always served. You are the Lord's, and He has done so much healing in your life [by now Joe had quite a ministry, bringing people out of gender inferiority and sexual perversion], but the god your father has served is still claiming you. You must renounce him, by name. I'll command that collage to present itself [i.e., command the demon to manifest itself if its there]. Then, as you say, 'I renounce the idol-god of my father, I renounce you Baal,' I want you to look and see with your heart what God does. Our holy God will strike that evil thing, and you will be delivered." And that is exactly what happened. Joe saw fire from God, as though it were a bolt of lightning, pierce through and annihilate the dreaded manifestation. God then set His holiness, His purity, His beauty where this obscene thing had held sway.

This is the chthonic spirit, the underground god not to be named, the numinous in both Freud and Jung.

We now see this happen in large groups where hundreds are set free. But it is not something a Christian leader would begin to do before God has fully prepared him to minister in such a way. It is part of a prophetic ministry, one that has first of all called the people to a radical repentance, and is thereby enabled to minister deeply to the essential spirit and soul of the people. The prophets are indeed the healers, as William Barclay points out, and that is because their call to repentance is clarion-clear. There is no uncertain sound in their message.

I recommend William Barclay's, "On the Emergence of John the Baptizer" in this regard. As he points out,

> John fearlessly denounced evil wherever he might find it. . . . He was like a light which lit up the dark places. . . .
>
> The coming of Christ necessarily involves a separation. Men either accept him or reject him. When they are confronted with him, they are confronted with a choice which cannot be avoided. They are either for or against. And it is precisely this choice which settles destiny. Men are separated by their reaction to Jesus Christ.
>
> In Christianity there is no escape from the eternal choice. On the village green in Bedford, John Bunyan heard the voice which drew him up all of a sudden and left him looking at eternity: "Wilt thou leave thy sins and go to heaven, or wilt thou have thy sins and go to hell?" In the last analysis that is the choice which no man can evade.[3]

In John the Baptist, therefore, as in all the prophets, there is the one demand: "Repent." The Baptist pointed unwaveringly to Christ, whose basic demand was the same: "Repent!"

If sin within the soul is not named and is seen merely as psychological and emotional imbalance and illness, then there is an understanding of man and of his predicament that reconciles good and evil at the core of man's being. The minister who has to any extent reconciled good and evil can never call others to repentance, for the trumpet he blows will give a very uncertain sound. A clarion call like that of the Baptist's or Christ's is required. Once a clear sound goes forth, we can minister to the repentant soul on both the spiritual and the psychological level.

A great many ordained clergy are unable to issue a clear call to repentance today and are therefore into some form of universalism. Barclay speaks to this issue as well. John had scathing words for the Pharisees and the Saducees who were teaching, "All Israelites have a portion in the world to come." This false teaching had led the Jews to believe that "a Jew simply because he was a Jew, and not on any merits of his own, was safe in the life to come."[4]

John the Baptist really demolished that idea (Matthew 3:7-12): Jesus would baptize with the Holy Spirit and with fire. The Spirit of Power would be given—that Spirit who when He enters a man creates and brings the order of God where there has been disorder and chaos. He brings truth, divine certainty, knowledge of what to repent from, the power to repent.

The true teaching of the rabbis, of course, differed from the popular heresies of the day. They taught that "true repentance issues, not merely in a sentimental sorrow, but in a real change in life," and, as William Barclay continues, "so does the Christian." Repentance, completely essential, is always available. "So long as life remains, there is the possibility of repentance."[5]

C. S. Lewis, in *Till We Have Faces*, shows Orual, the aging Queen of Glome, as she goes to the river to throw herself in and die. Fainting with weariness, and sick of what she calls her Ungit self (Ungit is the idol-god of her people), she sees no solution but death. But when she gets to the river, she hears the true God's voice:

> No one who hears a god's voice takes it for a mortal's. "Lord, who are you?" said I.
>
> "Do not do it," said the god. "You cannot escape Ungit by going to the deadlands, for she is there also. Die before you die. There is no chance after."[6]

Incredible illumination and healing comes to Orual as she hears the one true and holy God speak, and distinguishes that voice from Ungit's.

In the Judeo-Christian understanding of reality, there is no universalism. Rather, the soul finds in God the grace to make a radical decision concerning sin, and so he puts it away. He dies to sin and then is himself resurrected, even as Orual was.

Ministers today are having a particularly hard time calling people to repentance over sexual sin, and they are therefore left in the hands of Baal.

About Baal, Alfred Edersheim writes:

> It deserves more than passing notice that the modern denial of God may be reduced to the same ultimate principle as the worship of Baal. For, if the great First Cause—God as the Creator—be denied, then the only mode of accounting for the origin of all things is to trace it to the operation of forces in matter. And what really is this but a deification of "Nature?"[7]

As already stated, Baal was the real deity of Asia, worshipped under different forms (hence the plural: baalim). Molech was only Baal under another aspect, that of destruction, comp. Jer. 19:5, 32:35.[8]

Edersheim points out that the idolatry of Baal quickly gets bored with sex, and will go on to demand more and more to satisfy its appetite for flesh until human sacrifice is the ultimate fare.

It happens only too often now that we minister to someone, under the aegis of Baal, who is almost to the point of beginning to murder his sex victims. It is a great wonder to see them not only set free, but to come into normalcy in Christ. But an even more horrendous and widespread problem, one that has gained legal status and protection by the law in many places, is the vile sin of abortion. We, like the Israelites of old, have our Molechs, our ways of feeding our infants to the fires of Hell.

Baal is the god of sexual orgy, and the soul in his service will later, if not sooner, fall under Molech, his other aspect, as well. This alone explains why in our culture today abortion, and other things too vile to think or write upon, have for many become the accepted order.

Jung and the Service of Baal[9]

Closely related to the reemergence of Baal consciousness within society and even within the Church is the rise of a new Gnosticism. Its main proponent is C. G. Jung, the famed Swiss psychologist and early associate of Freud.

Jung's autobiography, *Memories, Dreams, Reflections*, reveals in a most candid and significant manner the way the pagan psyche, when open to occult revelation, is both informed and develops. It is horrifying in its contrasts, but also in its similarities to the way the Christian soul is informed and develops. The difference, of course, is in the voices that are heard and obeyed.

Jung was all his life oppressed by the demonic, by what some would call occult phenomena. He early in life accepted these revelations (what he himself called "an initiation into darkness"), and interpreted them to mean that God is both good and evil, that Yahweh and Satan are polar ends of one being, and that in similar fashion the psychic life has good and evil poles.

Jung's mother had, according to him, an archaic, "natural mind," the "seer's" mind that Jung himself also had. He believed the insight gained through such a mind was based on instinct, the "peculiar wisdom of nature."[10]. But the Christian who is knowledgable in demonic oppression has only to read the first chapter in his autobiography to realize that her involvement with this kind of "wisdom" easily explains why he had from earliest childhood not only been open to diabolical revelation, but had suffered with depression, social isolation, and severe identity problems.

His first and most influential revelation came very early in life, and was engineered by the phallic god. When Jung was between the ages of three and four, he had a terrifying dream in which he was taken underground and presented to the "Below" god, a horrible enthroned presence in the form of a ritual phallus.

On this platform stood a wonderfully rich golden throne. I am not certain, but perhaps a red cushion lay on the seat. It was a magnificent throne, a real king's throne in a fairy tale. Something was standing on it which I thought at first was a tree trunk twelve to fifteen feet high and about one and a half to two feet thick. It was a huge thing, reaching almost to the ceiling. But it was of a curious composition: it was made of skin and naked flesh, and on top there was something like a rounded head with no face and no hair. On the very top of the head was a single eye, gazing motionlessly upward.

It was fairly light in the room, although there were no windows and no apparent source of light. Above the head, however, was an aura of brightness. The thing did not move, yet I had the feeling that it might at any moment crawl off the throne like a worm and creep toward me. I was paralyzed with terror. At that moment I heard from outside and above me my mother's voice. She called out, "Yes, just look at him. That is the man-eater!"[11]

This was the dream that haunted and preoccupied him the rest of his life. He was afraid to go to sleep after that, and he began to associate the enthroned phallus god with Jesus. This alone would show it to be demonic oppression, for always in such oppression there is the attempt to insinuate the obscene into the holy.

The following illustrates in the life of Jung the "collage" image (see Joe's story earlier) that descends at moments when that which is pure and wholly good is being considered:

The phallus of this dream seems to be a subterranean God "not to be named," and such it remained throughout my youth, reappearing whenever anyone spoke too emphatically about Lord Jesus.[12]

Here we see the tragic and even blasphemous association which was the purpose of the demonic oppression:

Lord Jesus never became quite real for me, never quite acceptable, never quite lovable, for again and again I would think of his underground counterpart, a frightful revelation which had been accorded me without my seeking it.[13]

This dream phallus was introduced to him as the "man-eater," a horror that fed on human flesh. Haunted by this image for years, he later recognized it as a ritual phallus. This and several other such dark revelations shaped his thought and his life and led him to believe and teach that "the dark Lord Jesus," or the dark side of God, and the phallus god are one and the same. His entire system is predicated on this false, demonic revelation.

Equating Jesus with this terrible idol, he asked:

Who brought the Above and Below together, and laid the foundation for everything that was to fill the second half of my life with stormiest passion? Who but that alien guest who came both from above and from below?

Through this childhood dream I was initiated into the secrets of the earth. What happened then was a kind of burial in the earth, and many years were to pass before I came out again. Today I know that it happened in order to bring the greatest possible amount of light into the darkness. It was an initiation into the realm of darkness. My intellectual life had its unconscious beginning at that time.[14]

The light Jung received was a false light, indeed one that synthesizes good and evil. In the appendix of *Real Presence* ("The Great Divorce"), I dealt with this synthesis of Jung's from the standpoint of the orthodox view of good and evil, and though that is extremely important in view of what we are now discussing, I will not repeat that here. Rather, I will consider his synthesis from the standpoint of the Christian's need to renounce alien gods.

The "light" Jung received always leaves the activities of those who serve Baal unnamed and unchallenged. It is interesting to note that his dream revealed that light as it emanated from the enthroned phallus, a light that sadly was never extinguished in the heart of Carl Jung. It affected his personal life, showing up in his relationship to women, as well as in his psychology.

About sexuality, Jung says that it "is of the greatest importance as the expression of the chthonic spirit. That spirit is the 'other face of God,' 'the dark side of the God-image.'"[15]

From his study of ancient mythology and medieval alchemy, Jung, calling this god the "chthonic" or "underground" spirit, sees it as a *numinosum* (a god) in the life and works of Freud. According to Jung, Freud was "emotionally involved in his sexual theory to an extraordinary degree. When he spoke of it, his tone became urgent, almost anxious, and all signs of his normally critical and skeptical manner vanished. A strange, deeply moved expression came over his face. . . ."[16] Later Freud said to Jung, "'Promise me never to abandon the sexual theory. That is the most essential thing of all. You see, we must make a dogma of it, an unshakable bulwark.'"[17] Freud, considering himself completely irreligious, had given up Yahweh, but in Jung's interpretation he thereby only came into the grip of Yahweh's opposite, the underground god or chthonic spirit: "Freud never asked himself why he was compelled to talk continually of sex, why this idea had taken such possession of him. . . . I see him as a tragic figure; for he was a great man, and what is more, a man in the grip of his daimon."[18]

It is ironic in the extreme that Jung doesn't see that he too has bowed down to the phallic god. Under oppression from the same god Freud was under, and in accepting the false revelation it brought him, he too makes of it a numinosum. By attempting to insinuate it into the Godhead, Jung has in fact gone far beyond Freud in making the phallic god a numinosum. This god in his life then prompted him to synthesize all good and evil, a dualism that left him ripe for the Gnostic intellectual framework he later chose.

Gnosticism: Its Syncretism, Dualism, and Capacity for False Revelation

The theologican Harold O. J. Brown, in his book *Heresies*, points out, "The Gnostic movement as a whole and even church-related Gnosticism are really too big and too foreign to the New Testament to be called heresies; they really represent an . . . alternative religion."[19] Gnosticism, then, is not properly termed a heresy except, it seems to me, as it disguises itself and makes its appearance in Christian thought and practice. Due to its chameleon character, its syncretistic nature, it is very good at doing this.

In considering Jung, we need to say a word about Gnosticism, its basic character, and its interpretive methods. To do that in as brief and concise a manner as possible, I will draw from Kurt Rudolph's book *Gnosis*, considered the definitive work on the nature and history of Gnosticism:

> The Church Fathers already were conscious of what was for them the frightening variety of the gnostic teachings; they compare them with the many headed hydra of Greek legend. . . .
> There was . . . no gnostic canon of scripture, unless it was the "holy scriptures" of other religions, like the Bible or Homer, which were employed and interpreted for the purpose of authorising the gnostics' own teachings. . . . *In this process the inter-*

pretive method of allegory and symbolism, widely diffused in the
ancient world, was freely employed.[20] (italics mine)

A statement from a given text, for example, one from the Old or New
Testaments, was in that way given another meaning, a Gnostic one, or
several new meanings, in order to claim it for its own doctrine. This, of
course, is both what Jung and those who follow him do, and the interpretive method of allegory and symbolism is the way in which they do it.
Jung's reductionism, as we've pointed out earlier, consists in treating
supernatural and spiritual realities as merely things within the mind, as
only psychologically real. "Creeds and confessions are regarded as pro-
jections of the psyche. Christianity is then valued not for the truths it
reveals about man and God, but for its usefulness in mapping and explor-
ing the unconscious. Consequently, Scripture is interpreted subjectively.
Christ loses his uniqueness as incarnate Word and mediator between God
and man."[21] It is in this way that Jung not only empties Christianity of its
objective reality, but any other system with transcendent value as well,
and then shapes it into his own perception of psychic reality. His handling
of the Book of Job is as good an illustration of this as one might wish for.

The last statement of the above quote from *Gnosis* points up the
deepest concern we need have regarding Christians, naive about their
own symbolic system, getting into a study of Jung. Starved for knowledge of story, myth, and symbol, starved for acceptance of one's own
soul with its full imaginative, feeling, intuitive capacities, the ordinary
Christian will often have C. G. Jung for his only teacher in this respect
and will adopt, to one extent or another, Jung's reductionistic, interpretive methods of allegory and symbolism. This will not be corrected until
the Church recognizes its unaccountable and irrational aridity and
paucity in this area, and not only catches up with Jung, but far surpasses
him in the understanding of inner reality and its symbolic ways of knowing. Until the believing Church has done this, we must continue to warn
about the Gnostic nature of Jung's spirituality and reductionism.
Returning to Kurt Rudolph in *Gnosis*:

A further peculiarity of the gnostic tradition, connected with
this, lies in the fact that it frequently draws its material from the
most varied existing traditions, attaches itself to it, and at the
same time sets it in a new frame by which this material takes on
a new character and a completely new significance.[22]

This peculiarity we see time and again in the Jungian Christian writings. Side by side with the kind of spiritual and psychological insight that
modern man is starved for will be that which is utterly destructive. This
is why, in writing on the Christian supernatural, one of their leading

spokesmen can mention in a favorable light Edgar Cayce, an infamous medium; or when writing on the matter of homosexuality, he can say that in certain cases homosexual marriage is the answer. This is why he can be writing, ever so nicely, on the unique efficacy of Christ's Cross and Resurrection, and then only a few pages later say that for those who do not find this way appealing, there is yet another way, one that bypasses the Incarnation and the Cross. These things are casually put forward, but are in every book he writes for those who have eyes to see. There is always, if ever so subtly, the introduction of the obscene into the holy, but it is set into a psychological framework by which it takes on for many "a new character and a completely new significance."

Even as the early Gnostic traditions formed out of a synthesis of the Greek and Oriental traditions, so too does the Neo-Gnosticism of Jung.[23] Kurt Rudolph describes the early documents:

> Seen from outside, the gnostic documents are often composi-
> tions and even compilations from the mythological or religious
> ideas of the most varied regions of religion and culture: from
> Greek, Jewish, Iranian, Christian (in Manicheism also Indian
> and from the Far East). To this extent Gnosis . . . is a product of
> hellenistic syncretism, that is the mingling of Greek and
> Oriental traditions and ideas subsequent to the conquests of
> Alexander the Great. The gnostic expositions gain their thread
> of continuity or their consistence just through the gnostic
> "myth."[24] The individual parts of the "myth" can be called the
> gnostic myths; they confront us throughout as parts of one or
> another gnostic system.[25]

> This syncretism can be described as parasitic, for Gnostic thought "prospers on the soil of host religions."[26]

> To this extent Gnosticism strictly speaking has no tradition of its
> own but only a borrowed one. Its mythology is a tradition con-
> sciously created from alien material, which it has appropriated
> to match its own basic conception. Considered in its own light,
> however, it is for Gnosticism a further confirmation of its truth,
> which it often traces back to a primal revelation, i.e. derives
> from primitive times; the knowledge of it [they would say] was
> only temporarily extinguished or concealed.[27]

The following precis on the Gnostic view of God (its dualism) and the origin of evil should shed light on the matter of Jung's doctrine of "a degraded element of divinity":

Dualism dominates the whole of gnostic cosmology, and particularly in relation to creation and its authors. The form it takes in the individual systems is however very varied, and sometimes even contradictory. This can be seen above all in the conception of the place of evil and of matter in the formation of the world. While in one branch of Gnosis—especially in Mandeism and in Manicheism—there are two basic principles existing from the very beginning, mythologically described as (1) the kingdom of light and the kingdom of darkness, which are brought into contact with one another almost by accident and so set the baleful history of the world into motion, (2) in other systems a graduated decline from the highest deity (the "unknown God") is the cause of the origin of the evil and dark powers. Hans Jonas has described the first type as the "Iranian", since it stands formally very close to the Iranian-Zoroastrian dualism. . . . The other form Jonas called the "Syrian-Egyptian type" because of its geographical distribution. The majority of our [the gnostic] texts, including those from Nag Hammadi, belong to this type. Their common characteristic is the idea of a downward movement, the beginning of which is variously located in the godhead itself as an internal process of self-reproduction, and which finally at the end leads to a breach in the kingdom of light, as a result of which the earthly world and the powers who hold it in subjection come into being. Evil here is not a pre-existent principle, but (according to Jonas) a "darkened level of being," a "degraded element of divinity."[28]

One of the Nag Hamadi texts (Iranian-Zoroastrian), as mentioned in the above, is named after Jung (Codex Jung), because of his his interest in and work with the Gnostic texts.

As I wrote in an earlier book (*The Broken Image*, "Appendix: Listening to Our Dreams"):

The Christian who *uncritically* introduces Jungian thought into Christian counseling and healing does a great disservice to the Body of Christ, for Gnosticism is and always has been the worst enemy of Christianity. That is because, basically and finally, it is an interpretive system of subjective revelation, one that denies the Incarnation, and invariably ends in anthropocentricity and an erroneous view of God. Separated from the truth of the indwelling Christ by the Holy Spirit in man, it can end and often does in a psychic or "soulish" interpretation of unconscious revelation. By just such an interpretation of his own dreams, Jung deemed God to be both good and evil.[29]

Jung, Gnosticism, and the Worship of Baal

The attempt to combine good and evil is surely one of the greatest threats facing not only Christendom but all mankind today. Behind it are powers of darkness that would defy the capacities of most moderns to imagine. At stake in this issue is the freedom and the welfare of us all. The Christian view of God and of man are in our day severely jeopardized by a powerful intellectual thrust toward reconciling good and evil, and with Jung, a powerful imaginative one as well. Beyond this, however, we find in Jung a deliberate insinuation of the obscene into the holy. In true Gnostic fashion, he insists on blaspheming Yahweh.

An example of this we see in the following "scene" which, like his earlier vision, was key in fashioning his worldview and psychological doctrines. This experience started out as part of the demonic oppression to which he was subject, and was in fact a demonic attempt to give him false revelation. He received it; and even though it was obscene, he attributed it to God.

For three days he had a terrible fear. He was "afraid to think a thought to the end," knowing that it was not going to be something good. Before receiving the vision, he reasoned that it was God's intention that he should sin because he, like Adam and Eve before him, "couldn't help it."[30] Obviously in the throes of strong compulsion, he asks:

> Is it possible that God wishes to see whether I am capable of obeying His will even though my faith and my reason raise before me the specters of death and hell? Obviously God also desires me to show courage. . . . If that is so and I go through with it, then He will give me His grace and illumination.[31]

When he opened himself to the "thought," it came as a visual "revelation," one of the sort that could be expected if one has earlier claimed a terrifying phallic image to be a part of God:

> I saw before me the cathedral, the blue sky. God sits on His golden throne, high above the world—and from under the throne an enormous turd falls upon the sparkling new roof, shatters it, and breaks the walls of the cathedral asunder.[32]

He then goes on to call this "Grace" even though depression followed, along with the feeling of being "infinitely depraved," a condition that lasted for years.

There is nothing of the scientist here. When he later speaks objectively of a "chthonic spirit," there should be the recognition of the subjective, compulsive material behind it. Otherwise, one will make the mistake of thinking that for Jung this is an impersonal kind of spirit.

Jung's doctrines, then, from their very inception, are predicated on an actual insinuation of the obscene into the holy, a kind of black mass played out on the plane of his soul. He is not to be blamed for suffering these compulsions in the sense that they were indeed engineered by something other than himself. In this he needed and could have received healing. But he *is* responsible for the deliberate and untenable interpretation he made of the vision. Later, as a psychoanalyst, he surely did not lead his patients to take their compulsive disorders and the symbolic confusion that resulted from them as revelatory of "divine" truth.

I have seen literally hundreds of people suffering a like oppression, and all without exception are able to come out from under it. They never would have, however, had they accepted and interpreted such an experience in the way Jung did.

In this deliberate insinuation of the obscene into the holy, Jung has struck as rebellious and destructive a blow as it is possible to make against the true nature of God and the Christian faith. This is because holiness is not so much an attribute of God as it is the very foundation of His being; it is that out of which all else that He is proceeds. Totally good, and totally other than the world He created, He speaks and says, "I am God and not a man, the Holy One in your midst" (Hosea 11:9, RSV). He imparts His goodness and holiness to us. Holiness is at the heart of the Christian faith.

> To bring sin home, and to bring grace home, we *need that something else should come home which alone gives meaning to both*—the holy. . . . If our gospel be obscure, it is obscure to them in whom the slack God of the period has blinded minds, or a genial God unbraced them, and hidden the Holy One who inhabits eternity. This holiness of God is . . . the ruling interest of the Christian religion. . . .
>
> Neither love, grace, faith, nor sin has any but a passing meaning except as they rest on the holiness of God, except as they arise from it, and return to it, except as they satisfy it, show it forth, set it up, and secure it everywhere and forever. Love is but its outgoing; sin is but its defiance; grace is but its action on sin; the Cross is but its victory; faith is but its worship. . . . What we on earth call righteousness among men, the saints in heaven call holiness in Him.[33]

Within the soul of the Christian who adopts the Jungian interpretative system, to any degree, there will inevitably be the insinuation of the obscene into the holy: an eventual black mass of sorts within the soul itself.

Jung has tapped into the demonic plane of the supernatural world, which is hostile not only to the Judeo-Christian worldview, but to all systems containing objective moral and spiritual value. Within this world the self becomes god. What the self wants is what is finally right or moral.[34] Alien gods are involved in and lend power to this position.

Jung's view of God as a blind, inarticulate Force is what C. S. Lewis refers to as the "inbetween" or "third" view—one that is between naturalism (atheism) and supernaturalism (belief in a God outside of Nature). It is the "Life-Force" view, and in Lewis's novel *Perelandra*, the scientist Weston illustrates this position.[35] Having come out of his atheistic materialism (as seen in *Out of the Silent Planet*) and having despaired of objective truth, Weston finds he is "guided by the Force."

As Weston explains his new religious view of life and his new "Mission" to Ransom, likening them to Ransom's "outmoded" Christian beliefs, Ransom cries out, "I don't know much about what people call the religious view of life. . . . You see, I'm a Christian. And what we mean by the Holy Ghost is not a blind, inarticulate purposiveness."

To this outburst Weston, in a very superior manner, responds that God is a spirit, and, equating this "Spirit" with mind, freedom, and spontaneity, cries out that we are moving toward "Pure Spirit." When Ransom asks if this spirit is in any sense personal or alive, Weston's face contorts and his voice undergoes a change: "Call it a Force. A great, inscrutable Force, pouring up into us from the dark bases of being. A Force that can choose its instruments."

Knowing this "Force" experientially, Weston claims ecstatically, "I'm being guided. I know now that I am the greatest scientist the world has yet produced. I've been made so for a purpose. It is through me that Spirit itself is at this moment pushing on to its goal." To this assertion Ransom replies, "One wants to be careful about this sort of thing. There are spirits and spirits you know." Finding Weston to equate the good with the spiritual, Ransom is quick to point out that to be spirit is not necessarily to be good; after all, "The Devil is a spirit," and Christians worship God not because He is Spirit but because He is wise and good.

But Weston, rejecting the idea of a personal God or a Holy Spirit, thinks that spirit itself is the only good and is superior to conventional ideas of right and wrong. He cannot, or will not, differentiate between good and evil spirits. Inevitably he attempts to reconcile good and evil, and tells Ransom, "Your Devil and your God are both pictures of the same Force." Soon Ransom realizes that Weston not only cannot discern between good and evil powers, but is actually possessed by an evil one. The rest of his (Weston's) story is one of incarnational evil: a supernatural evil force speaking and acting through one who has lost the good of reason and of humanity. Weston has become "the Unman."[36]

Jung freely acknowledges his Gnosticism. His book *Memories,*

Dreams, Reflections, written at the end of his life, contains his religious testament. It is, according to his recorder and editor, Aniela Jaffe, "the only place in his extensive writings in which Jung speaks of God and his personal experience of God."

This book, by Jung's request, was not made part of his collected works. "I have guarded this material all my life, and have never wanted it exposed to the world; for if it is assailed, I shall be affected even more than in the case of my other books."

As far as we Christians are concerned, this is the most important book Jung has written in terms of helping us understand him—his Gnosticism, spiritism, occultism, and dark revelations, some of which I would term demonic oppression, which provide the basis for his psychological doctrines.

Jung's discovery of alchemy was, he said, "decisive":

> Grounded in the natural philosophy of the Middle Ages, alchemy
> formed the bridge on the one hand into the past, to Gnosticism,
> and on the other into the future, to the modern psychology of the
> unconscious.[37]

The historical prefiguration for Jung's inner experience, the contents of his unconscious, he found in the Gnostics.[38] In other words, Jung got into their literature, as well as into the myth and folklore of the world, and he studied the common symbols as they show up in all peoples and in all ages. Because of his hostility to Christ, he chose not Christianity, but Gnosticism as his intellectual and spiritual framework. Thus his interpretation of symbol, as it shows up universally in literature and in the psyche of man (dreams, visions, etc.), always reconciles good and evil. This is why Jungian psychology per se can never be divorced from Gnosticism, even as Christ's teaching cannot be severed from the New Testament.

Many Christians today are at an *enormous* disadvantage with Jung. They've lost the wisdom of Daniel (the Judeo-Christian tradition of understanding the heart's capacity to symbolize, and the head's capacity to be informed by what is in the heart):

> To these four young men God gave knowledge and understand-
> ing of all kinds of literature and learning. And Daniel could
> understand visions and dreams of all kinds. (Daniel 1:17)

Daniel, in studying Babylonian and/or Chaldean literature, ran into all the occult lore of his time. But because he knew, obeyed, and bowed down three times a day before a holy God, he was given wisdom to understand and interpret the symbols aright. "In every matter of wisdom and understanding" about which King Nebuchadnezzar questioned Daniel and the three young men, he found them "ten times better than all the magicians and enchanters in his whole kingdom" (1:20).

It's not that the Babylonians or Chaldeans did not have knowledge of symbols of dreams, for they did (and Jung does—this is his value). But it was imperfect. Their interpretation was based on their systems of belief, unassisted by God. When God was speaking a word, through a dream, vision, or handwriting on the wall, they could never divine it. Also, of course, they would not have the power to discern principalities and powers, the lying, ruling spirits which war against man.

Daniel, studying literature, had full knowledge of what the wise pagans knew. But he had the higher wisdom, the very mind of God on the same matters, as well as on matters they could not divine at all. He therefore interpreted the data of dreams and visions aright (i.e., the symbols of the unconscious).

> "No wise man, enchanter, magician or diviner can explain to the
> king the mystery he has asked about, but there is a God in
> heaven who reveals mysteries" (Daniel 2:27, 28).

The wise men of the Church today are so far from understanding what Daniel did that they would be the first to call Daniel an occultist should he stand up and speak today. They would make the same mistake his captors made when they named him the chief magician, but would then lack the wisdom they had in placing him over the magicians, astrologers, sorcerers, diviners, and so on. I cannot imagine having such a job assignment as he had, but such is the lot of the people of God when in captivity.

Jung's worldview then, intellectually, imaginatively, and symbolically, is basically Gnostic. That is the framework for all his thought, as his writings and his autobiography very clearly reveal. His autobiography, he says, "is my life. . . . The way I am and the way I write are a unity. All my ideas and all my endeavors are myself. Thus the 'autobiography' is merely the dot on the i."[39]

Though his framework was fully conscious, fully thought through, few there be of those influenced by him who can say the same thing. Today we have the spectacle of persons holding to an orthodox Christian creed while at the same time their symbolic and imaginative view of reality is altered. It is not at all unusual to pray with a Christian who, when he publishes his thought in print, is found to be reasonably orthodox in his theology, while at the same time his heart contains an emotional and symbolic view of God which is entirely alien in some way or another to the Scriptural view. What we hold to intellectually and what we believe emotionally can be two different things. We now have the phenomenon of Christians as "victims" of a Jungian resymbolization, a "re-mythologizing" of the heart that leaves them with a view of man—and of God—that widely misses the mark.

Today the largest audience for Jungianism is found among Christians, with Jungian retreat and conference speakers, books and magazine articles being featured regularly and prominently in monasteries, convents, and even seminaries which only a few years ago were centers of prayer and renewal, but are now quite heavily infiltrated by Jungian spirituality.[40] Young Christians, yearning for true spiritual formation, and traveling to these places in hopes of finding healing, are instead treated to something that has the power to loosen, if ever so subtly, their Christian moral and spiritual framework. In failing to discern the underlying assumptions in what they are receiving, their worldview, along with that of their instructors, is seriously altered. Perhaps the sin they had hoped to overcome will gain a respectable psychological name and gain acceptance in their lives. It is in this way that the obscene insinuates itself into our lives and we lose the sense of the holy.

Among the many affected in this way today, surely some will stop to wonder why the joy has departed, why the Healing Presence and gifts of the Holy Spirit have vanished, along with the cutting edge of their ministries. Some will surely wonder why there is so much depression among the leaders, and why sexual falls (due to the influence of phallic spirits in Jungian spirituality) occur where one would least expect them. They may also wonder why it is more and more difficult to love Christ, to speak the name of Jesus. (I have watched this for twenty years, and have seen one leader after another fall, one significant healing ministry after another fail.) The amazing thing is that the persons who come under the deception never seem to come out, never make the connection between first of all getting into Jungian thought and spirituality and then what occurs in their lives and in their ministries after that. I have spoken out on this for years, but few within the movement have ears to hear. One of the very large reasons for this "deafness," I feel, besides the fact of the involvement of a principality and power that would keep the believer blinded, is the need so many Christians have for self-acceptance and healing. So few come out of puberty having been affirmed (a vital developmental step), and when the Church is weak and does not recognize the full soul of man and know how to help it into its full identity in Christ, then Jung's self-actualization and promise of psychological wholeness is a strong drawing card. Many a man, failing to be affirmed by his father, has followed the Christian Jungian pied piper, because he is in need of a secure personal and sexual identity.

From being God-centered, then, these Christians can quickly become man-centered and self-centered, without even knowing it. This is why Dr. Paul Vitz can say of Jungian Christians that Jungian categories have powerfully overshadowed their Christianity.

What Is Right About Jung and Freud

In Karl Stern's book *The Third Revolution: A Study of Psychiatry and Religion*,[41] he is concerned to show how the psychoanalytical method, as founded by Freud and carried on by Jung, can be made philosophically neutral (that is, freed from the materialistic and Gnostic superimpositions of its founders). The great value in what these men did was to move a significant portion of the psychiatric world away from its more mechanistic models: those that viewed psychological illness as exclusively biologically determined, or were otherwise hostile to intuition and to the process of *understanding* as being "unscientific" (as in Pavlov's reflexology or in Watson's behaviorism). A true understanding of the soul, as anyone not entirely cut off from his own heart would know, be he Christian, Jew, or pagan, requires the empathic. And with the advent of psychoanalysis, human empathy with its deep consideration of and commonality with the things of the deep mind of man found its place in psychiatry. Not only that, with its understanding of the symbolic language of the unconscious, it "pushed back the frontiers of empathy."[42]

Jung's discoveries in making meaningful the irrational free-floating thoughts, dreams, and so on in the mentally disturbed in effect "consolidated the foundations of psychoanalytic theory."[43] He learned to read the "meaningless." As Karl Stern says:

> [The] vast dark universe of the "meaningless" which exists outside the world illuminated by logic becomes one meaningful structure once we have introduced certain tentative premises. Before we form concepts, before we think in words, and before we begin to think in logical abstractions we go through an infantile phase in which the universe of our mind consists of sensation and imagery. The connection between that preconceptual rock bottom and the upper layer of logical conceptual thinking is mysterious. But it is not unfathomable.[44]

"This," says Karl Stern, is a tremendous step forward. . . . It is no exaggeration to compare this, in the history of psychology, with the Galilean revolution in the history of physics."[45]

The fact that psychoanalysis is still colored by the philosophies of its founders, and that it reduces the Christian concepts of man's intelligence and will to collections of compulsive acts, unconscious urges, and blind reactions, is what makes it so dangerous.

Freud and Jung, driven by their own need to understand the diseased matter in the unconscious, made valuable discoveries that Christian physicians such as Dr. Karl Stern have put to great and good use. But he did it with his own thoroughly Christian intellectual and symbolic system intact. That makes what he and others like him do with the valid discoveries and insights that come out of secular psychology differ enormously from what has in fact been done by lesser minds who have adopted the Jungian hermeneutic and placed it as a grid over the Scriptures and over the entirely superior Judeo-Christian symbolic understanding of reality. No matter how many valid Christian sermons and valid Christian insights they include, they have resymbolized or nullified them by having adopted, not the creative and valid insights of a Freud or a Jung, but their spirituality. They have reconciled good and evil and are teaching others to do the same. The syntheses of Jungian and Christian teachings that are flooding our Christian retreat houses are light-years away from what Karl Stern could have conceived to be the Christian use of the valid insights of psychoanalysis.

Appropriating the Holy

One of the most incredibly wonderful things that we see in the healing ministry occurs just after we have led the people in repentance and in renunciation of their false gods and idols. The release that takes place at such times can only be described as miraculous and phenomenal. But the highpoint is what comes after, when God sets in the holy. Those who have all their lives felt degraded, unholy, even utterly filthy and obscene, have the Presence of the Holy descend into them in such a way that they are never the same again. Every cell is cleansed. The temple of God is made holy. It is sanctified. As Oswald Chambers rightly says, "Santification is not something Jesus Christ puts into me: it is Himself in me."[46] Christ descends into us, and we cry, "Holy, holy, holy is the Lamb of God. Holy, holy, holy is the Lord of Hosts." We once again "acknowledge the holiness of the Holy One of Jacob" (Isaiah 29:22, 23), and that He and He alone is our God. The sense of the holy is restored. We begin to come out of our twentieth-century stupor with its loss of the sense of the Presence of God, its loss of the sense of the holy.

As a ministry, we come forward like Elijah and ask that the sin question be settled. Like Elijah, we go before the people and say: "How long will you waver between two opinions? If the Lord is God, follow him; but if Baal is God, follow him" (1 Kings 18:21). We pray in the manner that he prayed:

"O Lord, God of Abraham, Isaac and Israel, let it be known today that you are God in Israel and that I am your servant and have done all these things at your command. Answer me, O Lord, answer me, so that these people will know that you, O Lord, are God, and that you are turning their hearts back again." (1 Kings 18:36, 37)

We say with utter confidence, "The God who answers by fire—he is God" (v. 24). Send your lightning, Lord! And that is what happens. The fire of the Lord falls, and the altar to Baal, with its insinuation of the obscene into the mind of one who would serve a holy God, is destroyed. The demons who have served that altar flee. The holy descends. Holiness is set in. That is the birthright of the children of God.

God Is Wholly Good and Wholly Light

No one is good—except God alone. (Mark 10:18)

God is light; in him there is no darkness at all. (1 John 1:5)

Darkness cannot abide absolute goodness, the Light. This horror of the Light consists in the fact that we, as sinners, must die to our old, false, usurping selves, submitting, like Eustace, to Aslan's claws.[47] We are fearful because we know we must have our scaly dragon hides ripped off before we can be thrown into the healing waters, be cleansed, and come up into the Presence. Only then are we prepared for that Presence to enter fully into us so that we might cease to do our works, that Another might take over and live through us.

God is good. But modern man often seems bent on believing otherwise. His motive for doing so is admirably reflected in the confession of Orual in *Till We Have Faces*: "Do you think the mortals will find you gods easier to bear if you're beautiful? . . . We want to be our own." The darkness in the world did not overcome the Light who came incarnate into the world. And it is this Light that enters into all who believe in Him. Of the utter purity of this Light, none who know it will question. We must become

> . . . *as glass*
> *To let the white light without flame, the Father pass*
> *Unstained.*[48]

Before I tried to write on the contrasts between a truly Christian psychology and that which has atheistic and Gnostic-pagan presuppositions, my prayer partners and I were in prayer about it. We were given two powerful images—technicolor visions might be a better description. The first was of a mountain: beautiful, bejeweled, and glittery. It had tremendous attracting power. It was the mountain of materialistic and Gnostic-pagan psychology. But the roots were revealed, and they were black and decayed. The decay, which wasn't visible from the outside, was feeding up into the mountain. It was a shell—very attractive outside, but inside there was disintegration and death.

We were then shown another mountain—the awesome mountain of our God, filled with His solidity, strength, wisdom, and knowledge. There we recognized His Healing Presence, full of grace and truth. All that was needed for us as Christians to come up with a truly knowledgeable psychology, one that would yield the finest of spiritual and psychological insight into our interior movements, whether conscious or unconscious, symbolic or literal, feeling or rational and intelligent, was there, along with His power to heal. There was a mighty figure atop this mountain (Michael the Archangel perhaps), and he cried, "Holy, holy, holy" as he aimed a great javelin that we knew would go to the very roots of the mountain that is Gnostic and atheistic in its view of man and reality. There was an awesome and fearful power here, the very thing that Jung so consciously and deliberately tried to undermine. It was the power that can only emanate from a good that is unmitigated, a Light in which there is no darkness.

This power God has for us as we Christians in the ministerial, theological, psychological, psychiatric, medical, therapeutic, and counseling fields regain, first of all, an incarnational understanding of Christian reality, and then come together in unity, learn from one another, and collaborate with the God who is with us. If and when we get our act together, the world will once again, in regard to the soul of man, have everything to learn from us.

The early Christians had so much love for the pagans surrounding them, and so much respect for them as having been made in the image of God, that they even buried their dead rather than seeing their bodies desecrated and dishonored. They feared no other worldview, but moved powerfully out of theirs—and saw a needy world brought into the Presence. In the closing days of this century, and perhaps even of the final Christian era that will see Christ's return, may we once again love with His love.

Maranatha! Come, Lord Jesus!
Love your world through us.
AMEN!

Notes

CHAPTER 1: Celebrating Our Smallness

1. C. S. Lewis, *Perelandra* (New York: Collier, 1962), p. 197.

CHAPTER 2: Practicing the Presence

1. C. S. Lewis, *Letters to an American Lady*, ed. Clyde S. Kilby (Grand Rapids, MI: Eerdmans, 1967), pp. 36, 37.
2. Oswald Chambers, *My Utmost for His Highest* (New York: Dodd, Mead & Co., n.d.), June 14.
3. *Ibid.*, July 15.
4. *Practicing His Presence: Frank Laubach, Brother Lawrence*, Library of Spiritual Classics, Volume 1 (Portland, ME: Christian Books, 1981), pp. 6, 7.
5. *Ibid.*, p. 26.
6. C. S. Lewis, *Letters to Malcolm: Chiefly on Prayer* (New York: Harcourt, Brace and World, 1963), p. 114.
7. C. S. Lewis, *Mere Christianity* (New York: Macmillan, 1978), p. 167.
8. *Ibid.*, pp. 168, 169.
9. *Ibid.*, p. 76.
10. *Ibid.*, p. 46.
11. *Practicing His Presence*, pp. 41, 42.
12. *Ibid.*, pp. 88, 89.
13. *Ibid.*, p. 92.
14. Henri Nouwen, *The Living Reminder: Service and Prayer in Memory of Jesus Christ* (New York: Seabury Press, 1977), pp. 30, 31.

CHAPTER 3: Spiritual Power and Authority

1. Oswald Chambers, *My Utmost for His Highest* (New York: Dodd, Mead & Co., n.d.), April 12.
2. *Ibid.*, November 25.
3. Dom Gregory Dix, *The Shape of the Liturgy* (London: Dacre Press, A. and C. Black, Ltd., 1978), p. xii.
4. Agnes Sanford, *The Healing Gifts of the Spirit* (Philadelphia/New York: Lippincott, 1966), p. 67.
5. *Ibid.*, pp. 67-70.

CHAPTER 4: Separation from the Presence:
The Fall from God-consciousness into Self-consciousness

1. C. S. Lewis, *The Problem of Pain* (London: Fontana, Collins, 1959), p. 28.
2. Walker Percy, *The Message in the Bottle* (New York: Farrar, Straus and Giroux, 1980), p.8.
3. C. S. Lewis, *The Four Loves* (New York: Harcourt, Brace & Co., 1960), Chapter 1.
4. Oswald Chambers, *My Utmost for His Highest* (New York: Dodd, Mead, & Co., n.d.), December 12.
5. Leanne Payne, *The Broken Image* (Westchester, IL: Crossway Books, 1981), p. 139.
6. Karl Barth, *Church Dogmatics Index Volume with Aids for the Preacher* (Edinburgh: T. & T. Clark, 1977), p. 495.
7. John Gaynor Banks, *The Master and the Disciple* (St. Paul, MN: Macalester, 1954), p. 119.
8. Payne, *The Broken Image*, pp. 102-106.
9. See Lori Thorkelson Rentzel, *Emotional Dependency: A Threat to Close Friendships* (San Rafael, CA: Exodus International, n.d.).
10. See Melody Beattie, *Codependent No More: How to Stop Controlling Others and Start Caring for Yourself* (New York: Harper/Hazelden, 1987).
11. Joseph and Lois Bird, *The Freedom of Sexual Love* (Garden City, NY: Image Books/Doubleday, 1970), p. 46.
12. David and Karen Mains, *Living, Loving, Leading* (Portland: Multnomah, 1988), n.p.
13. *Ibid.*
14. *Ibid.*
15. *Ibid.*
16. C. S. Lewis, *Perelandra* (New York: Collier, 1962), p. 137.
17. *Ibid.*, pp. 183, 139.
18. *Ibid.*, p. 60.
19. *Ibid.*, p. 76.

CHAPTER 5: Creative Power

1. C. S. Lewis, *The Problem of Pain* (New York: Macmillan, 1966), p. 102.
2. Charles Williams, *The Descent of the Dove* (Grand Rapids, MI: Eerdmans, 1968), p. 28.

PART II: Incarnational Reality:
The Presence of God Within Us

1. P. T. Forsythe, *The Creative Theology of P. T. Forsythe*, ed. Samuel J. Mikolaski (Grand Rapids, MI: Eerdmans, 1969), p. 260.

CHAPTER 6: The Presence of God Within Us

1. Fr. John Gaynor Banks, *The Master and the Disciple* (St. Paul, MN: Macalester, 1954), p. 15.

2. In *Witchcraft* (New York/Cleveland: Meridian Books, 1971), p. 310.
3. In *Arthurian Torso* (London: Oxford University Press, 1969), p. 132.
4. *Ibid.*
5. C. S. Lewis, *Perelandra* (New York: Collier, 1962), p. 60.

CHAPTER 7: Incarnational Reality: The Christian Union with God

1. Donald Bloesch, *Is the Bible Sexist?* (Westchester, IL: Crossway Books, 1982), p. 121.
2. Oswald Chambers, *My Utmost for His Highest* (New York: Dodd, Mead, & Co., n.d.), November 14.
3. Charles Williams, *The Descent of the Dove: A Short History of the Holy Spirit in the Church* (Grand Rapids, MI: Eerdmans, 1968), p. 28.
4. *Ibid.*, p. 161
5. "C. S. Lewis Ten Years Later," *Christianity Today*, November 9, 1973.
6. For more on this, see Leanne Payne, *Real Presence* (Westchester, IL: Crossway Books, 1979), Chapter 9 ("The Whole Intellect"), esp. pp. 111-113.
7. William Barrett, *Death of the Soul: From Descartes to the Computer* (Garden City, NY: Doubleday, 1987), p. 14.
8. *Ibid.*, pp. 17-19.
9. John A. Mackay, *Christian Reality and Appearance* (Richmond, VA: John Knox Press, 1969), p.13.
10. Charles Williams, *The Descent of the Dove*, p. 217.
11. Donald G. Bloesch, *The Battle for the Trinity* (Ann Arbor, MI: Servant, 1985), p. 11.
12. From a letter of C. S. Lewis to Dom Bede Griffiths, O.S. B., undated (ca. July-September 1936), Wade Collection, Wheaton College.
13. C. S. Lewis, *Mere Christianity* (New York: Macmillan, 1964), p. 64
14. *Ibid.*, p. 128.
15. *Ibid.*, p. 130.
16. *Ibid.*
17. Dr. Os Guiness speaks on "calling" and "vocation" better than anyone I know, and possibly will soon publish his lectures on the subject. A lecture entitled "Vocation" by him is available through Pastoral Care Ministries, Inc., P. O. Box 17702, Milwaukee, WI 53217.

PART III: Imagery and Symbol

1. A. W. Tozer, *The Knowledge of the Holy* (San Francisco: Harper and Row, 1961), p. 10.
2. *Ibid.*, p. 12.

CHAPTER 8: Perceiving God Aright

1. C. S. Lewis, *Reflections on the Psalms* (New York: Harcourt, Brace and World, 1964), Chapter 6.
2. C. S. Lewis, *Surprised by Joy* (New York: Harcourt, Brace and World, 1966), Chapter 4.

3. *Ibid.*
4. C. S. Lewis, *The Problem of Pain* (New York: Macmillan, 1966), pp. 34, 35.
5. C. S. Lewis, *Mere Christianity* (New York: Macmillan, 1964), pp. 117, 118.
6. "The Poison of Subjectivism," in *Christian Reflections* (Grand Rapids, MI: Eerdmans, 1971).
7. For more on this, read *Real Presence: The Christian Worldview of C. S. Lewis as Incarnational Reality* (Westchester, IL: Crossway Books, 1979), "Appendix: The Great Divorce."
8. For more on the healing of the unaffirmed by God the Father, see Leanne Payne, *Crisis in Masculinity* (Westchester, IL: Crossway Books, 1985).

CHAPTER 9: Imagery and Symbol: "The Imagery Really Matters"

1. All quotations by Tom Howard in this chapter are taken from "The Imagery Really Matters," a lecture he gave at Wheaton College. Used by permission.
2. All Alan Jones quotations used in this chapter are taken from "The Drama of the Spiritual Journey: An Exploration of Dante's *Divine Comedy*," by Alan Jones, Catacomb Cassettes, 1980, a division of Episcopal-Radio-TV Foundation, Atlanta, Georgia.
3. For more on the "cannibal compulsion," see Leanne Payne, *The Broken Image* (Westchester, IL: Crossway Books, 1982), "Matthew's Story," Chapter 3.
4. *Ibid.*, Chapter 4 ("Homosexual and Lesbian Behavior Related to Failure of the Infant to Achieve an Adequate Sense of Being").
5. C. S. Lewis, "Priestesses in the Church?," *God in the Dock*, ed. Walter Hooper (Grand Rapids, MI: Eerdmans, 1970), p. 273.
6. *Ibid.*
7. Mircea Eliade, *The Sacred and the Profane* (New York: Harper and Row, n.d.), p. 141.

CHAPTER 10: The Terrible Schism in the Heart of Man

1. Thomas Molnar, *The Pagan Temptation* (Grand Rapids, MI: Eerdmans, 1987), p. 60.
2. Oswald Chambers, *My Utmost for His Highest* (New York: Dodd, Mead and Co., n.d.), March 19.
3. Thomas Molnar, *The Pagan Temptation*, pp. 61, 62.
4. *New International Version Study Bible*, commentary on Psalm 4:7.
5. Fr. John Gaynor Banks, *The Master and the Disciple* (St. Paul, MN: Macalester, 1954), September 2.

CHAPTER 11: The True Imagination

1. For more on this, see Leanne Payne, *Real Presence* (Westchester, IL: Crossway Books, 1979), Chapters One, Two, and Four, but especially Chapter Four, "Spirit, Soul, and Body."
2. C. S. Lewis, "Membership," *The Weight of Glory* (Grand Rapids, MI: Eerdmans, 1975), p. 411.
3. I believe the division we must make between Nature and Super-Nature is indeed an accident of our limited point of view. See my book *Real Presence*, p. 21 for C. S. Lewis's theory of the reason we do not ordinarily see angels.

4. Oswald Chambers, *My Utmost for His Highest* (New York: Dodd, Mead & Co., n.d.), p. 68.
5. *Ibid.*, February 10.
6. C. S. Lewis, *Letters to Malcolm: Chiefly on Prayer* (New York: Harcourt, Brace and World, 1963), p. 86.

CHAPTER 12: Introspection Versus True Imagination

1. C. S. Lewis, *The Great Divorce* (New York: Macmillan, 1971).
2. C. S. Lewis, *God in the Dock: Essays on Theology and Ethics*, ed. Walter Hooper (Grand Rapids, MI: Eerdmans, 1970), pp. 65, 66.
3. *Ibid.*, p. 65.
4. This and other quotes by Dr. Clyde S. Kilby in this chapter are quoted from a handout sheet he prepared for his students.
5. Leanne Payne, *The Broken Image* (Westchester, IL: Crossway Books, 1981), p. 68.
6. Translated from Spanish and quoted by John A. Mackay, *Christian Reality and Appearance* (Richmond, VA: John Knox Press, 1970), p. 43.
7. For more on this subject, see C. S. Lewis' thesis regarding beloved pets, in "Animal Pain," *The Problem of Pain* (New York: Macmillan, 1966).
8. For more on the fact that "love, in the Christian sense, does not mean an emotion," see C. S. Lewis, *Mere Christianity* (New York: Macmillan, 1964), Chapter Nine ("Charity").

CHAPTER 13: Incarnational Reality: The Key to Carrying the Cross

1. For example, see Louis Bouyer, *Introduction to Spirituality*, trans. Mary Perkins Ryan (Collegeville, MN: Liturgical Press, n.d.), pp. 136-141.
2. F. B. Meyer, *Our Daily Walk* (Grand Rapids, MI: Zondervan, 1982), March 21.
3. *Ibid.*
4. *Ibid.*
5. *Ibid.*, March 22.
6. Agnes Sanford, *Behold Your God* (St. Paul, MN: Macalester, 1972), p. 89.
7. *Ibid.*, p. 71.
8. *Ibid.*, p. 77.
9. C. S. Lewis, *Mere Christianity* (New York: Macmillan, 1964), p. 154.
10. Fr. John Gaynor Banks, *The Master and the Disciple* (St. Paul, MN: Macalester, 1954), September 1.
11. C. S. Lewis, *The Problem of Pain* (New York: Macmillan, 1966), p. 87.
12. *Ibid.*, Chapter 10.
13. William Barclay, *The Letters to the Corinthians*.
14. Alexander Solzhenitsyn, *The Gulag Archipelago*.
15. Louis Bouyer, *Introduction to Spirituality*, p. 137.
16. Agnes Sanford, *Behold Your God*, p. 95.
17. This in turn is rooted in another erroneous doctrine of Charles Williams, one that affirms all images as good. I.e., his doctrine of good and evil reconciles the two. See Leanne Payne, *Real Presence* (Westchester, IL: Crossway Books, 1979), p. 172ff.
18. Charles Williams, *He Came Down from Heaven: And the Forgiveness of Sins* (London: Faber and Faber, 1956), p. 88.
19. Charles Williams, "The Way of Exchange," in *Charles Williams' Selected Writings*, ed. Anne Ridler (London: Oxford University Press, 1961), p. 130.

20. C. S. Lewis, *Essays Presented to Charles Williams*, p. ix.
21. Letter to Dom Bede Griffiths, December 16, 1941, Wade Collection, Wheaton College, Wheaton, Illinois.
22. *Charles Williams' Selected Writings*, "The Cross," p. 135.

CHAPTER 14: Renouncing False Gods and Appropriating the Holy

1. The specific historical data on Baal and Ashtoreth is taken from *Dake's Annotated Reference Bible*, ed. Finis Jennings Dake (Lawrenceville, GA: Dakes Bible Sales, 1963) and accords well with other studies on the subject.
2. Many do not realize how far this "worship" can go as persons become literally fixated on their own genitalia. In homosexuality, for example, it can and often does culminate in bizarre forms of padding and binding, of sado-masochism, and so on.
3. *The Gospel of Matthew*, Volume 1, revised edition, pp. 43-58.
4. *Ibid.*
5. *Ibid.*
6. C. S. Lewis, *Till We Have Faces* (Grand Rapids, MI: Eerdmans, 1964), p. 279.
7. *Old Testament History* (Eerdman), from a footnote on section 6, page 16.
8. *Ibid.*, section 6, page 17, italics mine.
9. Jung's quotes in this section are taken from his autobiography, *Memories, Dreams, Reflections*, recorded and edited by Aniela Jaffe, translated from the German by Richard and Clara Winston (New York: Vintage Books, division of Random House, 1961).
10. *Ibid.*, pp. 49, 50.
11. *Ibid.*, p. 12.
12. *Ibid.*, p. 13.
13. *Ibid.*
14. Ibid, p. 15, italics mine.
15. *Ibid.*, p. 168.
16. *Ibid.*, p. 150.
17. *Ibid.*
18. *Ibid.*, p. 152.
19. P. 52.
20. Pp. 53,54, italics mine.
21. See "The Unconscious Confusions of Christian Jungianism (Part 2)", by Kevin Perotta and Leanne Payne, *Pastoral Renewal*, May 1988, Volume 12, Number 10.
22. Kurt Rudolph, *Gnosis* (New York: Harper and Row, 1982), p.54.
23. For a scholarly consideration of this, see James Olney's book *The Rhizome and the Flower*.
24. See Kurt Rudolph's book *Gnosis* for a full exposition of this myth.
25. *Ibid.*, p. 54.
26. *Ibid,. p. 55.*
27. *Ibid.*
28. See *ibid.*, pp 65, 66.
29. P. 179.
30. *Memories*, p. 38.
31. *Ibid.*, p. 39.
32. *Ibid.*
33. P. T. Forsythe, *The Creative Theology of P. T. Forsythe*, ed. Samuel J. Mikolaski (Grand Rapids, MI: Eerdmans, 1969), pp. 55, 56.

34. This, the Luciferian stance, was demonstrated in Jung's life when, for example, he forced his wife to accept his mistress at the same table with herself and their children, and even in the final treatment of that mistress. See Paul J. Stern, *C. G. Jung, The Haunted Prophet* (New York: George Braziller, 1976), Chapter 9.

35. See *Real Presence*, "The Whole Intellect," especially pp. 119-126, for the worldview Jung has opted for. It can be seen in the character of Weston as developed in C. S. Lewis's adult trilogy, beginning with *Out of the Silent Planet*, then *Perelandra*, and finally *That Hideous Strength*.

36. The above four paragraphs are adapted from *Real Presence*, pp 121, 122.

37. *Memories*, p. 201.

38. *Ibid.*, p 200.

39. *Memories,* p. xii.

40. For more on this, see "The Unconscious Confusions of Christian Jungianism," Parts 1 and 2, by Kevin Perotta and Leanne Payne, *Pastoral Renewal*, April and May 1988.

41. (Garden City, NY: Image Books, division of Doubleday, 1961). This book, like his *The Flight From Woman*, is classic. Dr. Stern, noted as a Catholic psychiatrist, was by birth Jewish. Scholarly and erudite, intuitive and empathic as psychiatrist, fervent and strong in Christian faith, he is the ideal one to write on what is right as well as what is wrong in the field of psychoanalysis.

42. *Ibid.*,p. 30.

43. *Ibid.*, 69.

44. *Ibid.*, pp 70, 71.

45. *Ibid.*, p. 71.

46. *My Utmost for His Highest*, July 22.

47. See C. S. Lewis's novel *The Voyage of the Dawn Treader*.

48. From C. S. Lewis, *Pilgrim's Regress*.

Index